Keats and Neg.

Keats and Negative Capability

Li Ou

continuum

Continuum International Publishing Group

The Tower Building   80 Maiden Lane
11 York Road   Suite 704
London SE1 7NX   New York, NY 10038

www.continuumbooks.com

British Library Cataloguing-in-Publication Data
A catalogue record for this book is available from the British Library.

ISBN: PB: 978-1-4411-8790-1

Library of Congress Cataloging-in-Publication Data
A catalog record for this book is available from the Library of Congress.

Typeset by Newgen Imaging Systems Pvt Ltd, Chennai, India
Printed and bound in Great Britain by the MPG Books Group

To
My Parents

Contents

Preface

The term negative capability, used by Keats once only in his letter to his brothers, has become the best known and the most widely adopted phrase of Keats's not only in literary study but in diverse fields quite foreign to literature. For all its popularity and the numerous discussions of it by almost all the major Keatsians since the beginning of the last century, the only book-length study of the idea itself until today is Walter Jackson Bate's 1939 monograph published from his Harvard honours thesis. As the most important of Keats's aesthetic ideas, it received most attention in the 1950s and 1960s in accordance with the general trends of literary criticism, after which it became a relatively settled, and thus untended, issue in Keats scholarship. This, however, does not mean that the study of the idea has been exhausted and the state of knowledge has achieved a fully developed level. The annotation to the term provided by *The Norton Anthology of English Literature*, for instance, was seriously inaccurate, but remained unchanged from the 1962 first edition to the seventh edition published in 2000. Now that about half a century has passed since its heyday in criticism and almost two centuries since it came into existence, the idea calls for a more precise and thorough treatment from a longer historical perspective.

Negative capability is such an essential idea of Keats's that any criticism of him has to deal with it at least in passing. Critics have treated it at various lengths, with different degrees of interest and from diverse perspectives. Yet more often than not, it is discussed as a key issue in the critics' overall projects in a bigger framework, be it aesthetic, intellectual, philosophical, stylistic, biographical, ethical, moral, psychological, religious, historical, socio-political, or feminist, while the idea *per se* rarely constitutes the project itself. Some of these critics have examined the idea at a microscopic level, exploring its meaning, analysing its different aspects, pursuing its convergence with or divergence from other passages in Keats's letters, drawing attention to its inherent complexity, but their study of the idea is still a means serving another end. When the idea does take up the central place in criticism, it is usually found in shorter pieces, which, due to their length, tend to take a rather limited perspective. In consequence, the present state of knowledge concerning negative capability ends up approximately like Lincoln's famous saying, with my adaptation: you can find something about the idea in all of the criticisms, and all about the idea in some of the criticisms, but you cannot find all about the idea in all of the criticisms. The broader discussions tend to be cursory, and the closer ones, narrow. This book, therefore, intends to make the idea the end itself, the richness of which argues for its becoming an independent critical field in Keats studies.

Given the nature of this field of knowledge, what I propose is not to open new frontiers, but rather, to till this fertile piece of land which has not yet been thoroughly ploughed. To start with, I shall offer a story of how the phrase was salvaged from obscurity and became known and gradually gained currency, for although the critical heritage of Keats's poetry and prose can be found, we still need a critical heritage of the term itself. The idea itself, like a constellation of several stars, holds together many intricately interrelated components. Again, all these components have been commented upon in various works, but the commentaries are spread out diversely and unevenly, so that all of them become partial views, while the idea is still in want of an overall picture that at the same time does not ignore any of its component parts. To understand the complex structure of this organic idea, we need to analyse how its interlocking ramifications connect with one another and how they compose a whole by all being tied up to a central core. Only by unravelling the key threads of this idea, can we clearly see how its 'beautiful circuiting' weaves into 'a tapestry empyrean' (*KL* I:232). Similarly, though negative capability has been treated as a key intellectual or aesthetic idea in Keats's poetic evolution, the task of showing whether and, if so, how his poetry embodies and demonstrates the idea has never been taken up as a critical enterprise, which is rather incongruent with the significance critics commonly attach to the idea itself. So is it with the history of the idea. Just as the idea itself holds together many components, negative capability is also part of a cluster of ideas with complex antecedents and successors. Its sources have been either explored or briefly suggested, and many critics, including Shakespeare scholars, have noticed the special importance of *King Lear* to Keats. What in *King Lear* gave rise to Keats's thought on negative capability, how *King Lear* exemplifies this idea and in turn illuminates it, however, have never been given close attention. As for the cultural legacy of the idea, pointing out the link between negative capability and modernist impersonality is no longer a novel idea, but how exactly modernist poetry manifests the heritage of Keats's notion has not been pursued.

All these gaps need to be filled; all the fragments picked up and left randomly need to be assembled meaningfully, so that we can have a full and clear view of the overall pattern of negative capability. This book will, therefore, take a holistic view of the idea by a close study of its history, and by doing so, make the case that negative capability reveals a prominent non-egotistical tradition in English poetry, which can be traced back to Shakespeare and was taken over by Keats, and through Keats, carried on to the modernist poets. As the modernists show, this poetic tradition is itself embedded in a much deeper and wider human tradition, involving not only poetry and aesthetics but also philosophy and religion, one that transcends cultural borders.

Acknowledgements

Two persons have had tremendous influence on me in my relatively long study and comparatively shorter academic career. They are Professor David Parker at the Chinese University of Hong Kong and Professor William Moss at Wake Forest University. Without them, it would be unlikely for me to develop my interest in literature in any constructive way, and even if I would still be doing what I am doing now, I would have experienced much more struggles and doubts in a much slower process of growth. I do not really know how to thank them, or how to describe the warm weight of feelings I have for them, but I do know that the feelings will remain with me throughout my life. The publication of this book is certainly a significant event for me. While it clearly showed what a long way I still need to go in the field of literary studies, it also finally made manifest, though only on a very small scale, what I have owed to them.

Dr. Peter Crisp at CUHK and Professor Simon Haines at the Australia National University probably do not know how much they have helped and inspired me with the range and depth of their learning and professionalism. They showed me by their own examples what a scholar of humanities should be like. It is an honour for me to know them and to learn from them.

This book is developed from the PhD thesis I did at CUHK in 2007. Among many colleagues and students at CUHK who have given me invaluable suggestions and assistance, I wish to thank Professors Jason Gleckman, David Huddart, and Mr. Mao Yuanbo especially.

It was Peking University where I taught for four years that gave me the opportunity to start this research, without which this book would not have existed. I must mention Professors Ding Hongwei and Cheng Zhaoxiang in particular, who were the most supportive and generous colleagues I ever knew.

Continuum made it possible for me to publish this research project, and the benefit it is to bring me will be long and profound. The editor of this book, Ms. Colleen Coalter, whom I have never met in person, has made her presence warm and close by her patience and efficiency.

I would also like to thank the London Metropolitan Archives and the National Library of Scotland for their kind assistance for my research conducted there.

I cannot possibly list all the names of those who have given me help and support, but I will be ever grateful to them.

Li Ou
Hong Kong
December 2008

List of Illustrations

List of Abbreviations

EI	*Essays and Introductions*, W. B. Yeats
EL	*The Letters of T. S. Eliot*, Vol. I
KC	*The Keats Circle*
KL	*The Letters of John Keats, 1814–1821*
KPA	*The Poems of John Keats*, Ed. Miriam Allott
KPB	*John Keats: The Complete Poems*, Ed. John Barnard
KPS	*The Poems of John Keats*, Ed. Jack Stillinger
MV	*The John Keats Memorial Volume*
OBMV	*The Oxford Book of Modern Verse*
PP	*On Poetry and Poets*
SE	*Selected Essays*, T. S. Eliot
SP	*Selected Prose of T. S. Eliot*
SW	*The Sacred Wood*
UP	*The Use of Poetry and the Use of Criticism*
YL	*The Letters of W. B. Yeats*

Introduction

Anatomy of Negative Capability

I shall first give an anatomy of the idea itself before tracing its trajectory, showing how it entered literary critical discourse and gradually became a widely used, and sometimes misused, popular phrase. In the process, I will also review the various interpretations of it that accumulated for about a century as well as the increasingly freer usages from the mid-twentieth century to the present age of the internet.

Anatomy of the Negative Capability

At the outset, the idea itself, for all its familiarity, must be quoted again as the basic reference point of the ensuing discussion:

> I had not a dispute but a disquisition with Dilke, on various subjects; several things dovetailed in my mind, & at once it struck me, what quality went to form a Man of Achievement especially in Literature & which Shakespeare posessed so enormously – I mean *Negative Capability*, that is when man is capable of being in uncertainties, Mysteries, doubts, without any irritable reaching after fact & reason – Coleridge, for instance, would let go by a fine isolated verisimilitude caught from the Penetralium of mystery, from being incapable of remaining content with half knowledge. This pursued through Volumes would perhaps take us no further than this, that with a great poet the sense of Beauty overcomes every other consideration, or rather obliterates all consideration. (*KL* I:193–4)[1]

But it is important to bear in mind that even this reference point needs to be given some benefit of the doubt, for the letter exists only in the 'very puzzling' transcript of John Jeffery (*KL* I:191n, 23), who possessed it together with some other letters from Keats to his brother George by his marriage to George's widow Georgiana. Jeffery is not a reliable transcriber. He made changes and omissions according to his own liking when copying the letters for Keats's first biographer R. M. Milnes in 1845, and what he did with this important letter is no different. As Hyder Edward Rollins, the editor of today's standard edition of Keats's letters, notes, he 'omitted some words (possibly even a page or two) after the first sentence' of the letter, and J. G. Speed, George's grandson, when 'editing the letters in 1883 . . . made the identical omission' (*KL* I:191n). Jeffery dated the letter 'Sunday, December 22, 1818', but Rollins suggests that 'the year should be 1817, while Sunday was December 21', and since the latter half of the letter where negative capability is mentioned was written after Christmas and before the 28th, Rollins gives the letter conjectural dates of '21, 27 (?) December 1817' (*KL* I:191n,193n).

This, however, does not necessarily mean that all the criticism including the present book on negative capability is built on a shaky ground. However elusive the phrase itself sounds, it reveals a quite perceptible conceptual core, though many elements branch out from this core. At the centre is a great poet's capability of remaining 'negative', in the sense of being able to resist the instinctive clinging to certitude, resolution and closure in the firm belief that great poetry is marked by its allowance for a full-scale human experience that is too copious and diverse to be reduced to a neatly unified or conceptualized system. To be negatively capable is to be open to the actual vastness and complexity of experience, and one cannot possess this openness unless one can abandon the comfortable enclosure of doctrinaire knowledge, safely guarding the self's identity, for a more truthful view of the world which is necessarily more disturbing or even agonizing for the self. This central idea was consistently developed by Keats throughout his poetic career, and, by looking at its various expressions in many other letters of Keats's, we may also see how negative capability, being itself an organic conception, grows increasingly richer over a very short period.

In what critics usually regard as Keats's first important letter, the almost equally famous one addressed to Benjamin Bailey written about a month before the negative capability letter, Keats had already expressed his refusal to commit to any single opinion:

> I am certain of nothing but of the holiness of the Heart's affections and the truth of Imagination – What the imagination seizes as Beauty must be truth. . . . The Imagination may be compared to Adam's dream – he awoke and found it truth. I am the more zealous in this affair, because I have never yet been able to perceive how any thing can be known for truth by consequitive reasoning. (*KL* I:184–5)

Emotion and imagination are posed against 'consequitive' reasoning, as the sense of Beauty 'overcomes' or 'obliterates' every other 'consideration'. The parallel here associates negative capability with the primacy of feeling and imagination, which, with their intensity, compose the poetic truth that cannot be achieved by fact and reason. An emotionally and imaginatively intense experience of life, therefore, is pivotal to negative capability, and intensity does not only apply to life experience but to aesthetic experience, as Keats expresses succinctly when commenting on Benjamin West's painting, *Death on the Pale Horse,* just before talking about negative capability:

> [T]he excellence of every Art is its intensity, capable of making all disagree-ables evaporate, from their being in close relationship with Beauty & Truth – Examine King Lear & you will find this examplified throughout; but in this picture we have unpleasantness without any momentous depth of specula-tion excited, in which to bury its repulsiveness. (*KL* I:192)

As illustrated here, Keats often uses 'beauty' or 'truth' loosely as synonyms of the ideal, without quite conforming to the normal denotations of the two words. They are now closely associated with their opposites, 'disagreeables', which will 'evaporate' in the execution of artistic intensity. With this reference, it becomes clear that negative capability, with its overpowering sense of beauty dispelling the 'consequitive' 'consideration', does not imply sensuousness, but an intense aesthetic experience that embodies the actual human life that is full of 'disagreeables', and by its intensity, transforms it into artistic beauty and poetic truth.

Negative capability is expressed with a pair of antithetical figures of the flower and the bee for the 'receiver' and the 'giver' in his letter to J. H. Reynolds dated 19 February 1818:

> [L]et us not therefore go hurrying about and collecting honey-bee like, buzz-ing here and there impatiently from a knowledge of what is to be arrived at: but let us open our leaves like a flower and be passive and receptive – bud-ding patiently under the eye of Apollo and taking hints from evey noble insect that favors us with a visit – (*KL* I:232)

The 'flower' figure is more strongly reminiscent than the negative capability passage itself of Wordsworth's 'wise passiveness', which, with its contrast with the 'honey-bee', symbolizes a receptive openness in its passivity. On 13 March 1818, Keats again wrote to Benjamin Bailey on the same idea:

> [I]t is an old maxim of mine and of course must be well known that evey point of thought is the centre of an intellectual world – the two uppermost thoughts in a Man's mind are the two poles of his World he revolves on them and every thing is southward or northward to him through their means – We take but three steps from feathers to iron. Now my dear fellow I must once for all tell you I have not one Idea of the truth of any of my speculations – I shall never be a Reasoner because I care not to be in the right, when retired from bickering and in a proper philosophical temper – (*KL* I:243)

Here not having any single idea of the truth is being capable of staying in uncertainties, mysteries and doubts, while not caring to be in the right is to 'remain content with half knowledge'. At the same time, the figure for the human mind as a complex entity composed of two poles that are distinct and antithetical is particularly revealing, for it involves another key element of negative capability, the ability to be neutral and to contain completely contrary ideas.

A similar thought is found again in his letter to James Rice written about ten days later (24 March 1818):

> What a happy thing it would be if we could settle our thoughts, make our minds up on any matter in five Minutes and remain content – that is to build a sort of mental Cottage of feelings quiet and pleasant – to have a sort of Philosophical Back Garden, and cheerful holiday-keeping front one – but Alas! this never can be: <the> for as the material Cottager knows there are such places as france and Italy and the Andes and the Burning Mountains – so the spiritual Cottager has knowledge of the terra semi incognita of things unearthly; and cannot for his Life, keep in the check rein – Or I should stop here quiet and comfortable in my theory of Nettles. (*KL* I:254–5)

While reiterating the negative capability passage with an opposite case, this letter also elaborates on the unsettledness of the mind as closer to the actual truth, yet more trying, while the irritable reaching after fact and reason is self-deceptive, but more comfortable. The thought is further developed when he wrote to George and Georgiana on 31 December 1818:

> The more we know the more inadequacy we discover in the world to satisfy us – this is an old observation; but I have made up my Mind never to take any thing for granted – but even to examine the truth of the commonest proverbs. . . . I never can feel certain of any truth but from a clear perception of its Beauty – and I find myself very young minded even in that perceptive power – (*KL* II:18–9)

The connection of negative capability with a sober, unflinching look at the world as it is, instead of tailor-making it to one's own need, is only implied when the phrase itself is enunciated. This truthful view of the world, though not contradictory, does not quite conform to 'the authenticity of imagination' he pledged faith in back in November 1817. As with his poetry, so is the idea of negative capability constantly ripening, the very openness within itself nourishing its constant growth. This openness derives from the insistence on examining 'the truth of the commonest proverbs' by actual experience, which reveals the deep faith in experience to entertain its disturbing uncertainties, mysteries, doubts and the objection to facile, proverbial fact and reason that reduce experience into abstract truths. Negative capability is fundamentally experiential, aiming to encompass and convey the concreteness and complexity of experience, as opposed to an idealist stance, which seeks to abstract ideas or doctrines from experience.

The passage on negative capability itself is provoked by the 'disquisition with Dilke', on whose character the poet later comments in his letter to George and Georgiana written on 24 September 1819:

> Dilke was a Man who cannot feel he has a personal identity unless he has made up his Mind about every thing. The only means of strengthening one's intellect is to make up ones mind about nothing – to let the mind be a thoroughfare for all thoughts. . . . Dilke will never come at a truth as long as he lives; because he is always trying at it. He is a Godwin-methodist. (*KL* II:213)

Keats's comment on Dilke as a 'Godwin-methodist' here can be glossed by another reference he has made to Dilke in his letters, 'a Godwin perfectibil[it]y Man' (*KL* I:397). With his urge to look at the world as it truthfully is, Keats refuses to believe in 'this sort of perfectibility', for 'the nature of the world will not admit of it' (*KL* II:101). Further, the Godwinian association makes Dilke, like Coleridge who reaches after fact and reason irritably, an example of something opposite to negative capability in his 'consequitive' and dogmatic approach to experience. On the other hand, the mind being 'a thoroughfare for all thoughts' becomes the latest figure for negative capability, and the date of the letter suggests that negative capability was a central idea of Keats's till he was almost at the end of his creative time. As shown above, the idea, with its core of receptive openness, is composed of many other elements: the primacy of feeling and imagination, the mind's ability to contain discordant or even contradictory ideas, and the embrace of the experiential life and artistic intensity. Here, still another component of negative capability is revealed by Dilke's lack of it, which was tied up with his fast hold on his 'personal identity', which, as other letters have indicated, can only become a barricade to the open thoroughfare of the mind.

At the other extreme, Shakespeare is the exemplar who possesses negative capability 'so enormously' as 'a Man of Achievement', the wording of which is reminiscent of another part of the letter to Bailey written on 22 November 1817:

> I must say of one thing that has pressed upon me lately and encreased my Humility and capability of submission and that is this truth – Men of Genius are great as certain ethereal Chemicals operating on the Mass of neutral intellect – by[2] they have not any individuality, any determined Character. I would call the top and head of those who have a proper self Men of Power – (*KL* I:184)

The passage brings together two key elements of negative capability, the submission of the proper self and the mind's magnanimity so as to contain both poles of the intellectual world, be it 'feathers' or 'iron'. Another famous letter of Keats's expresses this more elaborately, written on 27 October 1818:

> As to the poetical Character itself, (I mean that sort of which, if I am any thing, I am a Member; that sort distinguished from the wordsworthian or egotistical sublime; which is a thing per se and stands alone) it is not itself – it has no self – it is every thing and nothing – It has no character – it enjoys light and shade; it lives in gusto, be it foul or fair, high or low, rich or poor, mean or elevated – It has as much delight in conceiving an Iago as an Imogen. What shocks the virtuous philosop[h]er, delights the camelion Poet. It does no harm from its relish of the dark side of things any more than from its taste for the bright one; because they both end in speculation. A Poet is the most unpoetical of any thing in existence; because he has no Identity – he is continually in for – and filling some other Body – (*KL* I:386–7)

A Man of Achievement with negative capability is a camelion poet with no proper self but metamorphic identities, which furnish him with constant sympathetic identifications with nature or human beings alike, and a disinterested embrace of disparate or completely opposite aspects of life. In this sense, the passage reveals the essential difference between a dramatic poet and a lyrical one. No wonder Shakespeare is again indicated as the exemplary camelion poet, while Wordsworth, like Coleridge formerly, is set on the opposite side. The juxtaposition had been more fully expressed in his letter written on 3 February of the same year:

> It may be said that we ought to read our Contemporaries. that Wordsworth &c should have their due from us. but for the sake of a few fine imaginative or domestic passages, are we to be bullied into a certain Philosophy engendered in the whims of an Egotist – Every man has his speculations, but every man does not brood and peacock over them till he makes a false coinage and deceives himself – Many a man can travel to the very bourne of Heaven, and yet want confidence to put down his halfseeing. Sancho will invent a Journey heavenward as well as any body. We hate poetry that has a palpable design upon us – and if we do not agree, seems to put its hand in its breeches pocket. Poetry should be great & unobtrusive, a thing which enters into one's soul, and does not startle it or amaze it with itself but with its subject. – How beautiful are the retired flowers! how would they lose their beauty were they to throng into the highway crying out, 'admire me I am a violet! dote upon me I am a primrose! Modern poets differ from the Elizabethans in this. Each of the moderns like an Elector of Hanover governs his petty state, & knows how

many straws are swept daily from the Causeways in all his dominions & has a continual itching that all the Housewives should have their coppers well scoured: the ancients were <Emperors of large> Emperors of vast Provinces, they had only heard of the remote ones and scarcely cared to visit them. (*KL* I:223–4)

By illustrating the weakness of his contemporaries in comparison with the Elizabethans, Shakespeare in particular, Keats has also demonstrated the ways in which they lack negative capability. With their fixed palpable design, his contemporary poets become the 'virtuous philosopher', whose philosophy 'bullies' not only the readers but themselves, leading them to let go by the fine isolated verisimilitude caught from the Penetralium of mystery from being incapable of remaining content with 'halfseeing'. Such a bullying philosophy is engendered from egotism, which confines the domain of their poetry to petty self-expression. A great poet of negative capability, like the retired flowers 'budding patiently' and absorbing from 'every noble insect', by disregarding the self-interest of giving or taking and directing the sole attention to the object, opens his poetry to a much vaster realm than the self. Magnanimity derives from disinterestedness.

Disinterestedness has run under the current of negative capability all the way through. But in the spring of 1819, Keats's thought seemed to take an apparently different path, reflecting that '[v]ery few men have ever arrived at a complete disinterestedness of Mind' (*KL* II:79) and not long after writing the well-known passage on the making of the soul, which he emphasizes derives from the acquisition of self-identity. Some critics regard this as a repudiation of negative capability, but it is only a maturation of it, rendered in his letter to George and Georgiana dated 21 April 1819 as:

Call the world if you Please 'The vale of Soul-making' Then you will find out the use of the world . . . . I say '*Soul-making*' Soul as distinguished from an Intelligence – There may be intelligences or sparks of the divinity in millions – but they are not Souls <the> till they acquire identities, till each one is personally itself. I[n]telligences are atoms of perception – they know and they see and they are pure, in short they are God – how then are Souls to be made? How then are these sparks which are God to have identity given them – so as ever to possess a bliss peculiar to each ones individual existence? How, but by the medium of a world like this? . . . Do you not see how necessary a World of Pains and troubles is to school an Intelligence and make it a soul? A Place where the heart must feel and suffer in a thousand diverse ways! (*KL* II:102)

This is a truthful view of the world that gives the poet the tragic vision of a world of pains and troubles that should be not only accepted but welcomed for its power to shape the unformed heart and mind into a soul with a distinctive identity. The emphasis on the possession of personal identity does not make it an expression of egotism, just as the tragic vision is not meant to be a resolution or closure. No doubt, the poet's mind had taken strides since the winter of 1817–1818, but the transformation lies in a clearer insight into the tragic nature of human experience, while the belief in the full exposure to this tragic experience remains unwavering. Nor has he been converted from his faith in the 'holiness' of the heart: only its 'affections' have become the thousand diverse ways in which the heart must feel and suffer. A negatively capable poet is not a poet without a self, but one with a self that embraces human experience to the point of eliciting the paradoxical soul-making power from pains and troubles, and by so doing, transcends the 'egotistical sublime' of one's own suffering. As ever, Shakespeare is regarded as an exemplar of this, as Keats wrote not long after in his letter: 'One of the great reasons that the english have produced the finest writers in the world; is, that the English world has ill-treated them during their lives and foster'd them after their deaths'. Therefore, Keats continues, the Italian Boiardo 'was a noble Poet of Romance; not a miserable and mighty Poet of the human Heart' as Shakespeare, '[t]he middle age of [whom] was all couded over; his days were not more happy than Hamlet's who is perhaps more like Shakspeare himself in his common every day Life than any other of his Characters' (*KL* II:115–6).

Negative capability, therefore, with its development over time, has evolved into a more mature and pregnant conception without contradicting its original central idea of opening the self to the multifarious otherness of the world and human beings. The composite key elements of negative capability may include imaginativeness, experiential and artistic intensity, submission of the self, sympathetic identification, the dramatic quality of the poet, disinterestedness, a neutral intellect tolerating diversity and contradiction, and a tragic vision of human experience, all of which are intricately related to one another. It is only pitifully ironic that by the end of his life, in his last known letter, Keats writes to Charles Brown that now 'the knowledge of contrast, feeling for light and shade, all that information (primitive sense) necessary for a poem are great enemies' (*KL* II:360) to his life, which was soon to be cut short.

The Critical Heritage of Negative Capability

Negative capability enjoyed a rather dramatic after life. In silence and slow time, it was gradually resurrected and became a foster child later generations adopted with their various understandings of its nature. As is the common practice, the starting point has to be traced to the first publication of Keats's letters in 1848 by R. M. Milnes in *Life, Letters, and Literary Remains*, 'the dividing-line between Keats's obscurity and his fame' (Matthews 1971: 31). In 1867 it became a new edition without 'literary remains', which was later reprinted in cheaper editions of the New Universal Library, Everyman's Library, and the Oxford World Classics, and remained the standard biography until the 1920s (Stillinger 1985: 669, 671). Milnes, or Lord Houghton, was himself a poet, whose interest in Keats started from his Cambridge days, when he, together with Tennyson and Hallam, re-published Shelley's *Adonais*. In his low-keyed, objective style, Milnes includes the complete negative capability letter without any comment, so it is impossible to tell how many readers of the book noticed the term. When H. Buxton Forman enlarged the number of letters from about eighty in Milnes's edition to nearly two hundred in 1883, the letter is naturally found there. When his son, M. B. Forman, further expanded the number of the letters in successive Oxford editions from 1931 to 1952 (Stillinger 1985: 669), negative capability became significant enough to be listed in the index.

Milnes's biography was reviewed in the *Edinburgh Review* in October 1849 by the Irish poet Aubrey Thomas de Vere (1814–1902), who already noted the phrase and assigned the quality to Keats himself, becoming the first critic making this connection:

> His mind had itself much of that 'negative capability' which he remarked on as a large part of Shakspeare's greatness, and which he described as a power 'of being in uncertainties, mysteries, doubts, without any irritable reaching after fact and reason'. There is assuredly such a thing as philosophical doubt, as well as of philosophical belief: it is the doubt which belongs to the mind, not to the will; to which we are not drawn by love of singularity, and from which we are not scared by nervous tremours; the doubt which is not the denial of any thing, so much as the proving of all things; the doubt of one who would rather walk in mystery than in false lights, who waits that he may win, and who prefers the broken fragments of truth to the imposing completeness of a delusion. (Matthews 1971:345)

Presumably, there would have been a bigger population reading the *Edinburgh Review* than Milnes's book. With the circulation of the journal and the status of the poet taken into account, the review might be the first occasion for the term to be introduced to the literary public. A decade later, David Masson wrote an article entitled 'The Life and Poetry of Keats' in *Macmillan's Magazine* (November 1860) which also cites the phrase, and paraphrases it as,

> [A] power of remaining, and, as it were, luxuriously lolling, in doubts, mysteries, and half-solutions, toying with them, and tossing them, in all their complexity, into forms of beauty, instead of piercing on narrowly and in pain after Truth absolute and inaccessible. (Matthews 1971: 374)

It is hard to estimate the influence of the article, though Matthews's *Critical Heritage* records it as 'the work of an English don discussing an established classic author, and marks the beginning of modern Keats criticism' (5), showing 'greater maturity of understanding than anything else written on Keats up to 1860' (368). This comment on negative capability, however, is obviously coloured by the Victorian impression of Keats, making it closer to an indulgence of the senses.

The first really influential critic of Keats is Matthew Arnold, whose essay on Keats was first published as 'an introduction to the Keats selections in T. H. Ward's *The English Poets*, vol.4' (Stillinger 1985: 677) in 1880 and later reprinted in *Essays in Criticism: Second Series* in 1888. At the end of the essay, Arnold sums up by saying that he has 'chiefly spoken . . . of the man, and of the elements in him which explain the production of such work', with disinterestedness at the centre of them. Then follows the famous 'he is with Shakespeare', and that 'Shakespearian work it is; not imitative, indeed, of Shakespeare, but Shakespearian' (291). Nonetheless, the term itself has not appeared in the essay, though the concluding sentence of the negative capability paragraph is quoted right at the opening of the essay: 'with a great Poet the sense of Beauty overcomes every other consideration, or rather obliterates all consideration' (282).

After Matthew Arnold, William Michael Rossetti and Robert Bridges are the late nineteenth-century men of letters who became respectively important Keats biographer and critic. The former published his *Life of John Keats* in 1887, while the latter's long essay on Keats came out first in 1895 and was then included as an introduction to Keats's *Poems* in 1896, and later reprinted as Volume 4 of Bridges's *Collected Essays, Papers, etc.* (1929) (Stillinger 1985; 677). Rossetti quotes the parts of the letter on *King Lear* and negative capability without dwelling much on the concept, but in order to demonstrate that 'Keats had a mind both active and capacious' (150). Robert Bridges focuses on Keats's poetic achievement by covering all categories of Keats's poems, including the two dramas, but he assumes 'some acquaintance with [Keats's] letters' on the part of his readers, and 'since these make of themselves a most charming book', he decides, 'this view of the subject will here be disregarded' (79). The only place he comes close to negative capability is when he summarizes Keats's intellectual element by '[Keats's] reiterated impatience for more knowledge' (166).[3] One wonders whether he has chiefly 'O for a Life of Sensations rather than of Thoughts!' (*KL* I:185) in mind, which is often quoted with a disregard for its context and its early date in the complex process of Keats's intellectual evolution. Sidney Colvin's biography *Keats* published earlier in the same year as Rossetti's does not mention negative capability either, only recounting the activities Keats records in the letter preceding the discussion of negative capability (81).

A. C. Bradley is the first important twentieth-century critic of Keats. One of his *Oxford Lectures on Poetry* focuses particularly on 'The Letters of Keats', where he quotes extensively from Keats's letters but only paraphrases the term without directly citing it:

[H]e had . . . a strong feeling that a man, and especially a poet, must not be in a hurry to arrive at results, and must not shut up his mind in the box of his supposed results, but must be content with half-knowledge, and capable of 'living in uncertainties, mysteries, doubts, without any irritable reaching after fact and reason'. (235)

Though not repeating the term, Bradley is the first critic to give the full attention to Keats's intellectual power that it deserves. He has touched upon the essence of negative capability, noting Keats's 'instinctive feeling' 'that it is essential to the growth of the poetic mind to preserve its natural receptiveness and to welcome all the influences that stream in upon it' (220), and linking it with Wordsworth's 'wise passiveness' (221). The Shakespearean critic has also commented on Keats's particular attachment to *King Lear* and his notion of intensity:

[Keats] would not have said that the *Midsummer Night's Dream* is superior to *King Lear* in beauty, but inferior to it in some other respect; it is inferior in *beauty* to *King Lear*. Let art only be 'intense' enough, let the poet only look hard enough and feel with force enough, so that the pain in his object is seen truly as the vesture of great passion and action, and all 'disagreeables' will 'evaporate', and nothing will remain but beauty. (233)

Further, he has also discussed Keats's Shakespearean sympathetic identificat-ion, and following Bridges,[4] he is one of the earliest critics who believe that Keats's 'hope of ultimate success in dramatic poetry was well founded' (219). Delivered in 1905, the rather thorough approach of Bradley's lecture makes it an important achievement in introducing to the public Keats's letters as reveal-ing a remarkably rich and active mind. Together with Arnold, Bradley has made Keats's association with Shakespeare unbreakable: 'he was of Shakespeare's tribe', which is explicitly distinguished from 'the sublime egotism of Milton and Wordsworth' (211).

With A. C. Bradley starting the twentieth-century enthusiasm for Keats, Amy Lowell's bulky biography appeared in 1924. The negative capability letter is quoted as an 'interesting bow-shot at a truth', to demonstrate that 'Keats was content to leave ultimate purpose unsolved' (I:506) in the process of poetic creation, but no further comment is made. Not long after, Amy Lowell's biog-raphy was severely attacked by the biographer on the other side of the ocean, H. W. Garrod, who published his *Keats* in 1926 from his lectures at Oxford in the previous year, in which Garrod quotes the negative capability letter, and inserts a parenthetical remark on the term: 'a quality not essentially different, I fancy, from what Wordsworth calls "wise passivity"' (40). The easy dismissal is consistent with his assertion made in the Preface written in 1939, 'I still think [Keats] the great poet he is only when the senses capture him, when he finds truth in beauty, that is to say, when he does not trouble to find truth at all'.

In the crossfire, John Middleton Murry published his influential *Keats and Shakespeare* in 1925, which, though apparently an elaboration of Arnold and Bradley, is the first book-length discussion of Keats's Shakespearean quality, and not only is the negative capability letter quoted in full, but treated as the most important sign of Keats's Shakespearean quality, as Murry remarks: 'if any single piece of evidence can make palpable the intimate nature of the relation by now established between Keats and Shakespeare, it is this letter' (41). Murry analyses the letter closely, arguing:

> [T]his Negative Capability is in fact a very positive capability, and further that in Keats's eyes it is the highest of all capabilities. The mere fact that 'Shakespeare possessed it so enormously' is proof enough of this. . . . For this supreme quality there is no familiar name . . . . For the moral quality we can find a word; it is more than tolerance, it is forgiveness. It is that quality which Christ pre-eminently possessed. But for this other kind of forgiveness, a forgiveness which forgives not only men, but life itself . . . we have no word . . . . Let it be called, though the word cannot fail to be misunderstood, Acceptance. (48)

Though Murry's emotional and moral overtones date his criticism to another era, he is still the first book-length author on Keats to bring negative capability into the centre of critical discourse. When M. R. Ridley published his pioneer work, *Keats' Craftsmanship* in 1933, he was already able to call the term 'odd and famous' (6). In the same year, T. S. Eliot's essay 'Shelley and Keats' fully established the status of Keats's letters, claiming them to be 'the most notable and the most important ever written by any English poet' (*UP* 100). Though Eliot does not quote the term, one would assume his familiarity with it. The conclusion of his essay, that, unlike Wordsworth and Shelley, Keats 'had no theories, yet in the sense appropriate to the poet, in the same sense, though to a lesser degree than Shakespeare, he had a "philosophic" mind' (102), captures the very essence of negative capability.

Claude Lee Finney's two-volume study of Keats's poetry, which 'treats virtually every poem that Keats wrote' (Stillinger 1985: 678) and came out in 1936, talks about negative capability as a serious philosophical concept that Keats has discovered, and discusses it throughout the evolutionary process of Keats's poetic creation, though somewhat pedantically. At the end of his 'impressive compilation' (Stillinger 1985: 678), it is with our key term that Finney summarizes the evolution of Keats's intellect: 'He had a negative capability of mind, a suspension of judgment, which enabled him to see both sides of every question and to seek truth without egotistic bias, and an imaginative and objective insight into the minds of other men' (II:740). This intellectual evolution is then divided with rather rigid chronological boundaries:

In the fall of 1817 he began to understand the philosophy of negative cap-
ability which he developed out of Shakespeare's plays; but in 1818 he was
drawn away from this philosophy by the windy humanitarianism which he
developed . . . out of Wordsworth's *Excursion*. In the fall of 1818 he resumed
his philosophy of negative capability, and, in the spring of 1819, he estab-
lished it upon a sound empirical basis. (II:741)

All the sources Finney has mentioned are extremely useful, but it was not in
the nature of Keats's negatively capable mind to fix on definite philosophical
doctrines, even if adopted one at a time. Negative capability is treated as a dog-
matic principle when it is rather an organic conception that is itself growing all
the time.

After Murry's and Finney's frequent references, negative capability has
gradually become a widely acknowledged term in Keats criticism. Three years
later, W. J. Bate, 'the leading expounder' of negative capability 'for several
decades' (Stillinger 1985: 694), published his Harvard undergraduate honours
thesis, *Negative Capability: The Intuitive Approach in Keats* (1939), which seems
to be the first piece of Keats criticism including the term in its title.

According to Bate, negative capability is 'the quality which characterizes
both the poet and his approach', and he sets out to state his purpose, to 'clarify
and describe' 'the critical articulation of the philosophy of *Negative Capability*,
Keats's own abidance by it, and the peculiar bent of mind which gave rise to it'
(9–10). By the end of the thesis, he concludes that 'Keats's own accomplish-
ment in verse is by no means that of a poet who possesses perfectly the quality
of *Negative Capability*', but it is his 'character of mind that gave rise to his critical
philosophy' (65–6). The concept, therefore, needs 'a narrowing down . . . to its
actual meaning' (66). It is 'not objectivity nor yet Wordsworth's "wise passive-
ness"', Bate asserts, 'neither is it an implicit trust in the Imagination nor, even,
the Shakespearean quality of annihilating one's own identity'. Instead, '[t]hese
qualities are rather accompaniments and outgrowths of something more pri-
mary which underlies them', which is, and here Bate adopts Murry's term,

[A]n acceptance . . . of the particular, a love of it and a trust in it; and an
acceptance . . . with all its 'half-knowledge', of the 'sense of Beauty', of force,
of intensity, that lies within that particular and is indeed its identity and its
truth. (66)

His clearing of the ground helps him dig out the empirical root of negative
capability, but all those 'accompaniments and outgrowths' are also parts of the
entity, for, as in Yeats's figure of the chestnut tree, is the 'great rooted blos-
somer' 'the leaf, the blossom or the bole'? In fact, these points would be modi-
fied by Bate himself after about two decades. By the end of the 1930s, however,

negative capability was well on its way to not only familiarity but popularity amongst the literary public. This continued on into the 1950s and 1960s when it became an almost unavoidable issue in Keats scholarship, extensively covered in general studies or biographical criticism and discussed in essays.

Lionel Trilling's introduction to his *Selected Letters of John Keats* (1951) is the first influential post-war study of Keats's letters, which, as the reprinted title 'The Poet as Hero' in *The Opposing Self* (1955) indicates, holds that Keats the correspondent is not only a great poet, but a heroic figure too:

> [B]ecause of the letters it is impossible to think of Keats only as a poet – inevitably we think of him as something even more interesting than a poet, we think of him as a man, and as a certain kind of man, a hero. (1)

More importantly, Trilling puts negative capability right at the core of Keats's heroism:

> No one reading the letters of Keats can come on the phrase and its definition without feeling that among the many impressive utterances of the letters this one is especially momentous. It is, indeed, not too much to say that the power and quality of Keats's mind concentrate in this phrase, as does the energy of his heroism, for the conception of Negative Capability leads us to Keats's transactions with the problem of evil, and if we are to understand the high temper of his mind, we must follow where it leads. (25)

Which is what Trilling does in one section of his introductory essay, where he illustrates the connection of 'the problem of evil' with Keats's tragic heroism, which makes negative capability 'anything but a "negative" capability – it is the most *positive* capability[5] imaginable' (29). Significantly, Trilling notes the paradox that negative capability 'is the sign of personal identity', for '[o]nly the self that is certain of its existence, of its identity, can do without the armor of systematic certainties' (30). He also observes that contradiction lies at the heart of negative capability: 'To remain content with half-knowledge is to remain content with contradictory knowledges' (30). These understandings lead Trilling to see the vale of soul-making as not inconsistent with negative capability: 'the idea of soul-making, of souls creating themselves in their confrontation of circumstance, is available to Keats's conception only because he has remained with half-knowledge, with the double knowledge of the self and of the world's evil' (37). By recognizing its complexity of holding apparently contradictory ideas, Trilling has made a significant contribution to the scholarship of negative capability. Interestingly enough, his own critic Robert Boyers associates him with the quality too, commenting that both Trilling and Henry James 'had a very large endowment of negative capability' (44) in a book entitled *Lionel Trilling: Negative Capability and the Wisdom of Avoidance* (1977). One year after Trilling's essay, Jacob D. Wigod published an essay, 'Negative Capability and

Wise Passiveness' (1952), with the purpose of distinguishing the two terms after Garrod had put them together (he does not mention that Bradley did the same), arguing: 'Whereas Keats gladly followed Wordsworth in the principle of wise passiveness, Wordsworth's individualistic poetic strength precluded his assuming a Shakespearean role of negative capability' (390). Both essays make important contributions to the study of the idea, but within the space of an essay, Wigod's presents a close-up view of only some facets of the idea while Trilling's, perspicacious as it is, can only focus on Keats the correspondent and discuss the poet briefly.

Bernice Slote's *Keats and the Dramatic Principle* (1958) may not be as widely read as Trilling's essay, but it is the first book-length discussion of Keats's dramatic quality, an enterprise dealing with a key component, but nevertheless only one component, of negative capability. She looks at this capability of Keats from a dramatic perspective:

[T]he man of negative capability has the fullness, the genesis of life in the incomparable present, in the full tide of his own aliveness which may in that very fact reach to the heart of the mystery. That Keats did accept and use his own contradictory half-knowledge is the key to his poetical character, and to his dramatic view of the world. (22–3)

All of these critical efforts of the 1950s initiated the 1960s' advance in both the criticism of negative capability and in general Keats study, represented above all by W. J. Bate's 1964 biography which takes up the central place in both fields.

Bate's chapter X has the term as its title, narrating the poet's life to the point of just finishing *Endymion*, and using negative capability to analyse what makes it 'another beginning', the title of the following chapter. Calling it 'the curious phrase' in 'one of the most quoted, yet one of the most puzzling, of all his letters' (236–7), Bate approaches it by gathering clues from the chief influences Keats received around the time. Hazlitt is given much attention, whose philosophical and aesthetic ideas are carefully combed and summed up. Bate then discusses what Keats chiefly finds empathetic in Hazlitt: disinterestedness as expressed in *Essay on the Principles of Human Action*, the idea of 'gusto' which finds its way into Keats's 'empathic imagery' (253), Keats's idea of 'intensity' that is particularly inspired by *King Lear*, the play itself as well as Hazlitt's commentary, and *Lectures on the English Poets*, especially the one 'On Shakespeare and Milton' where Hazlitt discusses Shakespeare's impersonality. Other key influences include Keats's frequent visits to the Elgin Marbles and his reading of Shakespeare (247). With all these interwoven clues, Bate comes back to the letter itself:

Using what we know of the background, we could paraphrase these famous sentences as follows. In our life of uncertainties, where no one system or formula can explain everything . . . what is needed is an imaginative openness of mind and heightened receptivity to reality in its full and diverse concreteness. This, however, involves negating one's own ego. . . . To be dissatisfied with such insights as one may attain through this openness, to reject them unless they can be wrenched into a part of a systematic structure of one's own making, is an egoistic assertion of one's own identity. (249)

Here we find that Bate no longer insists on the 'intuitive approach' taken in his youth. By disentangling the key elements of negative capability in the interrelated aspects of disinterestedness, sympathy, impersonality and dramatic poetry, Bate, after Trilling, has established the standard understanding of negative capability that has continued to today. What Bate has chiefly contributed to the knowledge of the term is his exploration of the genealogy of the idea, especially his in-depth treatment of Hazlitt, and his weaving of it into Keats's biography and stylistic development. It is this scope that makes his chapter the canonical reference of the term, just as the book is a standard Keats biography. On the other hand, however, the biographical framework also makes it impossible for the discussion to be thematically independent from the general pattern of narrative. The significance of *King Lear*, for example, is mentioned but not explored.

This is not the only contribution Bate has made to the study of negative capability. In *Criticism: The Major Texts* that he edited in 1970, he includes Keats's negative capability letter and writes an introduction for it, further establishing the canonical status of his interpretation. In the introduction he defines the term more succinctly: 'the ability to negate or lose one's identity in something larger than oneself – a sympathetic openness to the concrete reality without, an imaginative identification, a relishing and understanding of it'. He also emphasizes that the concept is closely knit with the difference between Keats's contemporaries and Shakespeare: 'It is this capacity which "Shakespeare possessed so enormously," and which Keats, like Hazlitt, felt was lacking in much of the poetry of his own day' (347). In 1972, *The Burden of the Past and the English Poet* was published, in which he advocates more fully the influence theory embedded in his biography.

Bate's biography came out a few weeks later than that of Aileen Ward, the former winning the 1964 Pulitzer, the latter, the 1964 National Book Award. Ward's biography, like Bate's, incorporates negative capability into the narrative of the winter of 1817–1818, but her discussion of the idea is quite brief. She rephrases it as 'what today is called "tolerance for ambiguity"', which 'was, as Keats saw it, essential to the poet insofar as he above all men explores the frontiers of human experience and struggles with its endless diversity and contradictions' (161). Like Trilling, she draws attention to the paradoxical relationship between self identity and the negative capability of the artist: 'this capacity for suspending judgment in order to report faithfully on experience also involves . . . the capacity for "annulling self" and thereby entering into other identities'. On the other hand, Ward adds, 'the ability to "annul self" depended on a very firm sense of self' (161).

Harold Bloom then came on the scene, who, more than Bate, interprets negative capability chiefly in the light of influence theory, thus making it a vehicle of his theoretical framework. In his essay 'Keats and the Embarrassments of Poetic Tradition' published in 1965, Keats is regarded as the Romantic who felt 'this embarrassment' of poetic history 'with a particular intensity' (513), in contrast to his predecessor Milton who has a 'positive capability for converting the splendor of the past into a private expressiveness' (517). The latter point is taken up again in his famous *The Anxiety of Influence* (1973), in which he attributes the source of negative capability to Hazlitt's lecture 'On Shakespeare and Milton', where Hazlitt 'remarked upon Milton's positive capability for ingesting his precursors' (34). The relevant part of Hazlitt's lecture is then cited: 'In reading [Milton's] works, we feel ourselves under the influence of a mighty intellect, that the nearer it approaches to others, becomes more distinct to them' (V:58). In his 1976 *Poetry and Repression*, Bloom develops his point further, seeing Keats's preoccupations with the self as 'evidences of a remarkable repression of anxiety' (136) of influence.

Also in 1965, Richard Ellmann and Charles Feidelson Jr. compiled an anthology under title *The Modern Tradition: Backgrounds of Modern Literature*, in which Keats's negative capability letter is listed in the section named 'The State of Doubt' together with a selection from *Conversations of Goethe* (1836) and Flaubert's letter to Mlle. Leroyer de Chantepie (1857), which opens new and vaster realms of exploration for the term. Both Goethe and Flaubert in the excerpts express thoughts congenial to negative capability. Commenting on his countrymen's clinging to abstract ideas, Goethe claims:

> It was . . . not in my line, as a poet, to strive to embody anything *abstract*. I received in my mind impressions, and those of a sensual, animated, charming, varied, hundredfold kind, just as a lively imagination presented them; and I had, as a poet, nothing more to do than artistically to round off and elaborate such views and impressions, and by means of a lively representation so to bring them forward that others might receive the same impression in hearing or reading my representation of them. (69)

Flaubert's letter comes even closer to Keats: 'In order to survive, one must give up having clear-cut opinions about anything at all' (71). Flaubert encourages his addressee to do so: 'you will be amazed to find yourself changing your ideas like a shirt, every day. No matter. There will be nothing bitter about your scepticism'. Then he continues:

> No great genius has come to final conclusions; no great book ever does so, because humanity itself is forever on the march and can arrive at no goal.

Homer comes to no conclusions, nor does Shakespeare, nor Goethe, nor even the Bible. That is why I am so deeply revolted by that fashionable term, the *Social Problem*. The day on which the answer is found will be this planet's last. Life is an eternal problem; so is history and everything else. (72)

Meanwhile, Flaubert emphasizes the significance of sympathy for this inconclusiveness: '*Think less about yourself*', he admonishes, 'you will feel your heart and your mind expanding together till every phantom and every being is enveloped in the cloak of a deep and boundless sympathy,' so, yet again, '*Do try to cease living subjectively*' (72).

By the end of the 1960s, then, negative capability has become not only a theme in Keats study, but an important issue in general literary and intellectual history. The 1962 first edition of *The Norton Anthology of English Literature* provides perhaps the first textbook definition, which first informs the readers that '[t]his famous and elusive phrase has accumulated a heavy body of commentary', and then offers two points in its own annotation:

(1) Keats is concerned with a central aesthetic question of his day: to distinguish between what was called the 'objective' poet, who simply and impersonally presents material, and the 'subjective' or 'sentimental' poet, who presents material as it appears when viewed through the writer's personal interests, beliefs, and feelings. The poet of 'negative capability' is the objective poet . . . . (2) Keats goes on to propose that, within a poem, the presentation of subject matter in an artistic form that appeals to our 'sense of Beauty' is enough, independently of its truth or falsity when considered outside the poem. (*Norton* 1962: 1275; *Norton* 2000, II:889)

The distinction made in the first point is essential to the concept, but the terms 'objective' and 'subjective', though probably intended to be more intelligible to students, are not exactly the same as 'disinterested' and 'egotistical' in Keats's vocabulary. Neither does the former kind of poet 'simply . . . [present] material', without the active participation of imagination. As for the second point, Keats is not emphasizing autonomous beauty within any single poem, but rather making the distinction between an intense experience and a rational process of abstraction. Despite this unsatisfactory definition, being anthologized by *Norton* marks the canonical status of negative capability, though the textbook reference could have been made more helpful even back in the 1960s.[6]

The story after the 1960s is not as exciting. Stuart M. Sperry's *Keats the Poet* (1973) is perhaps the most important criticism on Keats in the 1970s. Sperry lists the 'rich concreteness and immediacy, the fullness of its range of sympathies, its abhorrence of the merely doctrinaire and openness to various points of view' in Keats's poetry as 'qualities that organize themselves generally around' negative capability (10), and he also translates negative capability with the modern term, 'a state of perpetual *indeterminacy*' (245). His arguments are incisive and revealing, but the focus of the book is on the entire body of Keats's aesthetic ideas rather than on negative capability itself. After Sperry, Christopher Ricks's *Keats and Embarrassment* (1974) came out, described in the bibliographical guides as 'the most original' of modern Keats criticism, though 'the originality is frequently merely a kind of perverse eccentricity' (Stillinger 1985: 684), and as 'brilliant if sometimes eccentric' (Kucich 1998: 148). Ricks argues that Keats 'was especially audacious in believing that the healthy strength of a sense of identity depends paradoxically upon the risk and openness and not upon self-protection' (25), for which the negative capability passage is cited as evidence, employed only to pursue his 'original' psychological theory.

Whatever we make of Ricks's study, by the end of the 1970s there is no question about the popularity of the term, which at least can be ascertained by Woody Allen's 1979 *Manhattan* in which Diane Keaton uses negative capability to describe a sculpture at the Guggenheim. This may be the beginning of the adoption of the term in realms other than literature. Similarly, within the field of literary study, it has become such a commonplace phrase that it has begun to be freely associated with many other writers. For instance, in 1980, an essay by William V. Spanos is on 'Charles Olson and Negative Capability'.

By now, negative capability has become part of the general education of literature, beginning to enjoy a more or less established status. When Wolf Z. Hirst's introductory book on Keats of the Twayne English Author series came out in 1981, negative capability is one of the key ideas in the chapter on Keats's letters, the previous study summed up by Hirst as 'that tolerant, self-effacing, sympathetic, and imaginative attitude – that denial of the ego which modern criticism associates with "negative capability"' (40). Hirst also rightly reminds us of 'the irony and paradox involved in [Keats's] negatively capable attitude', for example, 'his skepticism about skepticism' (45).

It is listed as an entry in Jean-Claude Sallé's *A Handbook to English Romanticism* (1992): 'rather than a permanent credo . . . Negative Capability should be viewed as a stage in the evolution of Keats's thinking, as the definition of an aesthetic quietism which his growing scepticism eventually led him to qualify and relinquish' (189). The word 'quietism' fails to capture the receptive passiveness of negative capability but conveys a sense of resignation which diverges from Keats's conception. Further, just as negative capability is not a 'credo', it should not be seen as being 'relinquished' as one either. The end of his definition deals with the sources of the concept, where though Hazlitt is included, he also adds, 'the roots . . . are to be found in Keats's agnosticism' (189), which does not sound convincing.

In the following year, *The New Princeton Encyclopedia of Poetry and Poetics* gives its 'authoritative' definition: 'Keats's phrase for a power of sympathy and a freedom from self-consciousness which peculiarly characterize the artist. It occurs in a letter of 22 December 1818' (824–5). One wonders why it has to follow the date given by the unreliable transcriber after Rollins has already shown it with clear evidence to be wrong. In addition to the letter itself, it also quotes the camelion poet letter. For the history of the idea, it puts Hazlitt as the key source, and suggests that '[t]he modernist precept in favor of "impersonality" . . . carries a trace of its origin in the idea of n.c.' (825), of which T. S. Eliot is cited as the major inheritor. At the end of the entry, the related item 'empathy and sympathy' is what the encyclopaedia directs its readers to, and this cross reference finds its way into the *OED*: '**negative capability**, (Keats's term for) the ability to accept mystery and uncertainty rather than trying to rationalize it, regarded as a quality of a creative artist; (now also, more generally) empathy'. The *Princeton Encyclopedia* certainly gives a panoramic view of the history of the idea, but equal weight could have been given to other elements of negative capability than just identity alone, for the term, after all, is not simply a synonym of empathy or sympathy.[7]

Studies on Keats in the 1980s and 1990s are marked by the new trends of historicism and feminism, and so the criticism of negative capability becomes a means to serve these theoretical ends. While Anne K. Mellor in her *Romanticism and Gender* (1993) associates negative capability with 'feminine empathy' (24), Margaret Homans in her essay 'Keats Reading Women: Women Reading Keats' (1990) sees it as manifesting Keats's ambivalent attitude to women, the congeniality of which to feminine receptiveness is only apparent. Similarly, Nicholas Roe in his essay 'Keats's Commonwealth' (1995) regards it as a disguise of Keats's political attitude, arguing that 'the liberalism of the 1820 volume may have been expressed in *To Autumn* as a covert mischief, the more potent for working under the sign of disinterested imagination, or "negative capability"' (197). The historicist criticism certainly has its value in presenting a more truthful Keats than the escapist figure drawn by the Victorians, but one needs to be on guard against the tendency to simplify all texts into sole products of their socio-historical contexts. Uncovering the complex circumstances of Keats's ideas ought to give us a fuller understanding of Keats, not a narrower one. Similarly, negative capability, though definitely conceived in a particular historical time, should not be explained only by its socio-political framework. Negative capability is a valid aesthetic and intellectual idea in its own right, not circumscribed by its context, and this is precisely the value of studying it today.

Meanwhile, the term itself has taken on a life of its own, embraced by scholars and non-scholars alike. Its classical association is with Shakespeare, as Keats originally meant it to be, and it is quoted in *Encyclopaedia Britannica* to illustrate Shakespeare's 'capacity for assimilation', the Shakespearean feature of being 'comprehensively accommodating'. An essay in 1960 by Clifford Leech is entitled 'The Capability of Shakespeare', quoting Keats's negative capability to comment on Shakespeare's 'readiness to debate' (132). Harold Bloom in his 1998 work, *Shakespeare: The Invention of the Human*, uses the term not just for

Shakespeare himself but also for Hamlet: 'Hamlet's final stance personifies Shakespeare's Negative Capability, as John Keats termed it' (12).

But there are other not altogether expected associations. The online encyclopaedia, Wikipedia, associates the term with Martin Heidegger's concept of Gelassenheit, 'the spirit of disponibilité before What-Is which permits us simply to let things be in whatever may be their uncertainty and their mystery'. The homepage of 'Jung Circle' claims that 'Jung seems the essence of Negative Capability'. An essay in 2005 by Galway Kinnell is titled 'Walt Whitman and Negative Capability'. The 2006 issue of *Keats–Shelley Journal* has Beth Lau's essay discussing Jane Austen's negative capability. Eloise Knapp Hay connects negative capability with *via negativa* in discussing T. S. Eliot.[8] Dan Simmons, an American author, relates negative capability to 'the writer's curse', introducing the concept by F. Scott Fitzgerald's interpretation of it in his autobiographical piece, 'The Crack-Up': 'the test of a first-rate intelligence is the ability to hold two opposing ideas in the mind at the same time, and still retain the ability to function' (Fitzgerald 39). Allen Ginsberg writes an essay named 'Negative Capability: Kerouac's Buddhist Ethic' in 1992. J. M. Coetzee uses the term in his 2003 book *Elizabeth Costello: Eight Lessons,* in which Elizabeth explains her 'belief' to a judge: 'When I claim to be a secretary clean of belief I refer to my ideal self, a self capable of holding opinions and prejudices at bay while the word which it is her function to conduct passes through her"; to which the judge rejoins: 'Negative capability . . . . Is negative capability what you have in mind, what you claim to possess?' (200).

With the aid of Google which yields 68,000 results out of the search on 'negative capability', we may see what wild directions the term may take. It is chosen as the name of an American verse periodical in Alabama that started publication in 1981, and of a collection of contemporary American poetry published by University of Michigan Press in 2001. It has been adopted in religious contexts. Clifton Unitarian Church says that Keats's idea is 'reminiscent of the Buddhist notion of *no mind*', while the award-winning poet Kathleen Norris has written an essay 'Exile, Homeland, and Negative Capability', which sees Keats's term as analogous to the process of understanding religious faith. It is also employed in the realm of education. Dan Simmons writes on the importance of 'nurturing' negative capability in readings at colleges and universities, while at Cornell University in 2003, Jeffery S. Lehman, the 11th President, spoke to the students in the Convocation Address that cultivating negative capability should be their main aim. John Tatum, an EFL teacher, makes the further contribution by regarding it as 'a successful indicator of second language learner aptitude'. It is widely adopted in psychotherapy, believed to be useful for both therapists and patients, and it is also cited as a key term in the field of psychoanalysis. Gavriel Reisner in one chapter of his *The Death-Ego and the Vital Self* (2003) makes a comparative study of the Keatsian term with Freud's negation, purporting to make connections between the fields of literature and psychoanalysis. Politics is rather an unexpected field to take an interest in the term, though the adoption of it by the column of political satire in *Harpers* magazine is less surprising, grouping a list of negatives in George W. Bush's public statements under the title of 'Disavowal: Negative Capability', including 'I'm not a poet', 'I'm not an Iraqi citizen' and 'I'm not a tree, I'm a bush'.

It is given a place on the BBC website, used as the name of a press, of a law school paper, of an album of a rock band, as well as the title of a popular zine, of homepages and blogs, some on alternative media, and one on UFOs. A website called 'Everything' comments on the popularity of the term on the internet:

> [A] far greater proportion of the population have become (loosely speaking) 'artists', due to the commonplace availability of the internet and Web . . . and thus are faced with the issues of identity, self and selflessness about which Keats' notions have prompted speculation and debate.

The virtually dazzling diverse usage of the term may be a bit too far from what Keats meant almost two hundred years ago, but it demonstrates its vigorous life and currency.

Coming back from these contemporary metamorphoses of the term, the book will explore the idea of what Keats meant in 1817 and how its meaning evolved within the realm of literature. It is appropriate in both Keats's case and for the purpose of this book to follow the time line, so Chapter 1 will explore the genealogy of negative capability, with Hazlitt and Shakespeare as the key sources of inspiration for Keats's conception of the idea. Chapter 2 focuses on the most important play of Shakespeare that exerts its influence on Keats and negative capability, *King Lear*, which will be given a close reading in the light of negative capability. Chapter 3 studies the idea in relation to Keats's poetry, the evolution of which is narrated from the perspective of negative capability. Chapter 4 goes forward in time, evaluating the inheritance of the idea by the modernists, Yeats and Eliot being the two poets to be considered. Finally, in the conclusion, I shall argue that the idea embodies a prominent dramatic tradition in English poetry, and that the idea is not confined to formalistic aesthetics but deeply embedded in human traditions of literature, art, religion and philosophy. Ultimately, negative capability is a way of being, conveying an attitude towards human experience.

Chapter 1

Genealogy of Negative Capability

'I am very near Agreeing with Hazlit that Shakspeare is enough for us' (*KL* I:143), Keats writes in his letter dated 11 May 1817. The statement names the two most important figures in the process of Keats's conceiving of the idea of negative capability, the former contemporary yet reflecting on the spirit of his age critically, the latter historical but enjoying a revival in Keats's time to which the former made a significant contribution.

'Hazlitt's Depth of Taste'

Many critics have either glanced over or focused on Keats's connection with Hazlitt, giving similar accounts with more or less the same evidence. Clarence D. Thorpe's 'Keats and Hazlitt: A Record of Personal Relationship and Critical Estimate' (1947), one of the earliest essays in this area, focuses on their personal relationship and gives it a fairly full coverage, concluding that it was 'one of mutual respect and friendship' (502). Kenneth Muir's essay in 1951 and Bate's 'Negative Capability' chapter in his 1964 biography study Hazlitt's intellectual influence on Keats.[1] Muir observes that Keats has derived from Hazlitt 'the ideas . . . on the poetical character, on the nature of Shakespeare's genius, and on the relative deficiencies of Wordsworth and Coleridge' (1958: 158), while Bate, more thoroughly than Muir, discusses Hazlitt's influence on Keats in the aspects of 'the sympathetic character of imagination', his view of drama as 'the highest form of poetry', and '[h]is harsher criticism of his own contemporaries' for their egotism (259). R. S. White gives one chapter of his book, *Keats as a Reader of Shakespeare* (1987), to Hazlitt's impact on Keats in his reading of Shakespeare. Though he does not claim direct relevance to the topic,[2] many connections he makes are also relevant to negative capability, expressed in his subheadings such as, 'a philosophy of particularity', 'the primacy of feeling', 'the pictorial', 'contrast' and 'movement and impression'.

What these critics have more or less agreed on has been challenged by a more recent essay by Uttara Natarajan in 1996, who argues:

[B]y drawing exclusively on Hazlitt's account of Shakespeare in the formulation of his own views on poetic composition, Keats bases his poetic theory on exactly those characteristics of poetic composition that Hazlitt deprecates in almost every other case *but* [emphasis his] Shakespeare's. (66)

The tide-turning conclusion is rather questionable, for Keats's reading and absorption of Hazlitt, as I shall show, are not limited to Hazlitt's commentaries on Shakespeare. Nor is Hazlitt's view on Shakespeare exceptional to his general theory; it is quite consistent with his overall values. Natarajan's arguments, based on some passages of Hazlitt she selects and reads with particular emphases on certain elements, are a bit precarious for such a prolific and wide-ranging writer as Hazlitt. My following arguments, therefore, are closer to those of the earlier critics, but I shall also stress Keats's divergence from Hazlitt in the very aspects he has derived from Hazlitt. The most important ideas Keats has absorbed from Hazlitt are also the most characteristic Hazlittean ones, those of gusto and disinterestedness, which were transformed into the Keatsian terms of intensity, non-egotism and sympathetic imagination to become strands of his idea of negative capability. More specifically with respect to poetry, Hazlitt's high regard for dramatic poetry as against lyrical, and consequently his esteem for Shakespeare and disapproval of contemporary poets, have become important poetic criteria of Keats's own, making him visualize a further horizon than his contemporaries had reached and in turn orienting his own poetry in a more dramatic direction. This aspect of Hazlitt's influence on Keats has been given attention by both John Kinnaird in his 1977 essay and David Bromwich in his chapter on Keats in his 1983 book on Hazlitt. Kinnaird points out that 'Hazlitt's challenge to Wordsworth had the effect of forcing, or encouraging, the second Romantic generation of poets' (14), Keats in particular, who 'healed' the 'breach of imagination' between Wordsworth and Shakespeare by his odes, 'which come as close as any in the language to . . . a genuinely dramatic . . . lyricism of intersubjectivity' (15).[3] Bromwich makes the assertion in a bolder manner: 'by helping Keats to revise his own idea of the imagination, Hazlitt altered the course of modern poetry'. He continues with more vehemence:

All along Hazlitt had been moving him in the direction of Shakespeare, and if one looks in romantic poetry for a Shakespearean fullness, and a Shakespearean gusto in dialogue, the place to find them is nowhere in the poetic drama of the period, but in Keats's odes.

He also carries the point further to extend the lineage to the modernists, remarking, 'Keats's aims in poetry and Hazlitt's in criticism place both in accord with a concern for dramatic form that modern poets have been unwilling to disclaim' (401). In both Kinnaird and Bromwich, however, Hazlitt is the focus while Keats serves as a foil, so their arguments need to be further explored from Keats's point of view.

These ideas of Hazlitt's, as Bromwich rightly stresses, may not be so much an 'influence' (369) on as a communication to Keats, for 'Keats understood

Hazlitt's ideas till they became second nature to him' (370). The affinity, however, did not manifest itself in their actual relationship, which was never really close.

The first link between Keats and Hazlitt was made by Leigh Hunt, who showed some of Keats's early verse to a group including Hazlitt, the Shelleys and Godwin (*KL* I:33), but there is no record of Hazlitt's reaction, though Hunt reported an overall approval. The two met in the winter of 1816–1817 (Muir 139),[4] and became gradually acquainted because of their overlapping circles, but the relationship never turned intimate. Nevertheless, Keats had a deep faith and trust in his older contemporary, thinking of seeking his guidance at two quite critical points in his life. The first was April 1818, not long after he wrote the 'Epistle to J. H. Reynolds', which reveals the crisis he was experiencing at that time. It was also around then that thoughts on 'knowledge' and 'philosophy' frequented Keats's letters, in one of which he tells Reynolds that he will 'prepare [himself] to ask Hazlitt in about a years time the best metaphysical road [he] can take' (*KL* I:274). The other occasion was September 1819, when Keats was caught in financial difficulty and considered making a living by entering journalism, and his first thought was to 'enquire of Hazlitt' (*KL* II:174, 177) about the prospect. What might have brought them closer were the venomous reviewers they shared. *Blackwood's* attacked not only the poetry of Keats and the Cockney School but also the prose of Hazlitt, who was so incensed as to plan to bring suit for libel against it. Keats records this in his letter to Dilke on 20 September 1818: 'I suppose you will have heard that Hazlitt has on foot a prosecution against Blackwood – I dined with him a few days sinc[e] at Hessey's – there was not a word said about [it], though I understand he is excessively vexed' (*KL* I:368). The silence may indicate tacit understanding, but it also suggests a distance in the relationship. When Hazlitt wrote the biting 'Letter to Gifford', editor of the *Quarterly Review* and their common foe again, in March 1819, Keats reported the news to George in exhilaration, and copied for him excerpts from it running as long as about five pages. Ironically, this association also became the way in which Hazlitt chiefly remembered 'poor Keats'[5] after his death, thus joining Shelley and Byron in spreading the myth that Keats was 'killed off' by the malicious reviewers. The last recorded meeting of the two took place at Haydon's exhibition on 25 March 1820, reported by Haydon: 'The room was full. Keats and Hazlitt were up in a corner, really rejoicing' (*KL* II:284n). Some critics tend to read too much into the scene, regarding it as a reassuring sign of a warm friendship between two great men, which, even granted, should not be identified with Hazlitt the critic's estimation of Keats the poet, which can only be described as endorsement with reservation.

Hazlitt's criticism of Keats is most fully expressed in his essay 'Effeminacy of Character' in *Table-Talk* (1821–1822), where he writes:

> I cannot help thinking that the fault of Mr. Keats's poems was a deficiency in masculine energy of style. He had beauty, tenderness, delicacy, in an

uncommon degree, but there was a want of strength and substance. . . . There is a want of action, of character, and so far, of imagination, but there is exquisite fancy. All is soft and fleshy, without bone or muscle. We see in him the youth, without the manhood of poetry. (VIII:254–5)

This view, chiefly based on *Endymion*, was partly altered after Hazlitt read Keats's later poems, but never completely abandoned. In 'On Reading Old Books', written in 1826, Hazlitt remarks: 'the reading of Mr. Keats's Eve of Saint Agnes lately made me regret that I was not young again' (XII:225), which, apparently complimentary, only reminds one of his former criticism. In a 'Critical List of Authors' included in *Select British Poets* Hazlitt compiled in 1824, Hazlitt writes on Keats in a particularly warm tone rarely found in his commentaries on his contemporaries, evaluating Keats as the one who 'gave the greatest promise of genius of any poet of his day' (IX:244), but when he continues, the old reservation comes back:

He displayed extreme tenderness, beauty, originality, and delicacy of fancy; all he wanted was manly strength and fortitude to reject the temptations of singularity in sentiment and expression. Some of his shorter and later pieces are, however, as free from faults as they are full of beauties. (IX:244–5)

The pieces Hazlitt has in mind are represented by his selections: three excerpts from *Endymion*, including the procession part at the beginning, the hymn to Pan, and the song to Sorrow, and one passage from *Hyperion*, as well as 'Ode to a Nightingale', 'Fancy' and 'Robin Hood' (Bromwich 369). Despite his mixed critical attitude to Keats, Hazlitt did become in effect 'Keats's first anthologist' (Bromwich 369).

There is no question, on the other hand, about Keats's admiration for Hazlitt, most explicitly expressed in his often quoted statement made to Haydon in the letter dated 10 January 1818, that together with Wordsworth's *Excursion* and Haydon's paintings, 'Hazlitt's depth of Taste' are the 'three things to rejoice at in this Age' (*KL* I:203). Still earlier, on 21 September 1817, when relating to Reynolds that he was reading Hazlitt's *Round Table*, Keats has already expressed his esteem for Hazlitt warmly, 'I know he thinks himself not estimated by ten People in the world – I wishe he knew he is' (*KL* I:166). Keats might have read the essays in *The Round Table* before, which were collected from Hazlitt's contributions to Hunt's *Examiner* started from 1814 (Thorpe 489), an important part of Keats's early reading, and it was probably also around that time that Keats read *Essay on the Principles of Human Action* (W. J. Bate 1964: 256). When Hazlitt gave the *Lectures on the English Poets* from January to March 1818, Keats attended almost all of them, and though he did not go to the later *Lectures on the English Comic Writers* delivered from November 1818 to January 1819, he read the manuscript (*KL* II:24). Keats also had a copy of *Characters of Shakespear's Plays* which he marked and annotated. Other writings of Hazlitt's Keats has mentioned include Hazlitt's essay on Southey in May 1817 (*KL* I:137–8, 144) and one of Hazlitt's contributions to the *Edinburgh Review* (*KL* I:301), which he must have read regularly. So it can be assumed that his reading was not restricted to the above pieces of which there is some record.

Hazlitt appears only once in Keats's poetry, in the opening surreal scene of the epistle to J. H. Reynolds: 'Voltaire with casque and shield and habergeon, / And Alexander with his night-cap on – / Old Socrates a tying his cravat; / And Hazlitt playing with Miss Edgeworth's cat' (7–10).[6] This 'theatre of the absurd' does not tell much except for Keats's familiarity with Hazlitt's attack on the bluestockings. In Keats's prose, however, Hazlitt, whose style is highly regarded by Keats, figures more prominently. In May 1817, Keats mentions Hazlitt's article on Southey's *Letter to William Smith* twice in his letters, commenting admiringly that the conclusion is rendered 'with such a Thunderclap' and 'appears to me like a Whale's back in the Sea of Prose' (*KL* I:138). Later, reading Hazlitt's *Lectures on the English Comic Writers* in manuscript, Keats describes its style with the 'usual abrupt manner, and fiery laconiscism' (*KL* II:24) in his letter on 2 January 1819. When reporting to his brother about Hazlitt's fiery retaliation on Gifford in March 1819, Keats remarks, 'He hath a demon as he himself says of Lord Byron' (*KL* II:76). Keats's enthusiastic review on Kean, also the best Shakespearean actor according to Hazlitt, in 21 December 1817 *Champion*, around the time of the negative capability letter, not only resembles Hazlitt's spontaneous style but adopts his vocabulary, so that one sentence can be 'easily mistakable for one of Hazlitt's' (Bromwich 367): 'There is an indescribable gusto in [Kean's] voice, by which we feel that the utterer is thinking of the past and the future, while speaking of the instant' (*KPB*: 530). 'Gusto' is easily recognizable, and the sentence is also very close to Hazlitt's comments on Shakespeare: 'He had "a mind reflecting ages past," and present' (V:47), and 'The passions are in a state of projection. Years are melted down to moments, and every instant teems with fate' (V:51).

Such borrowings are numerous in Keats's letters.[7] One of Keats's poetic axioms, 'if Poetry comes not as naturally as the Leaves to a tree it had better not come at all' (*KL* I:238–9), is reminiscent of Hazlitt's claim in 'On Posthumous Fame': 'It is . . . one characteristic mark of the highest class of excellence to appear to come naturally from the mind of the author, without consciousness or effort' (IV:24). What Keats describes as '[t]he innumerable compositions and decompositions which take place between the intellect and its thousand materials before it arrives at that trembling delicate and snail-horn perception of Beauty' (*KL* I:264–5) find similar expressions in Hazlitt's lecture 'On Shakespeare and Milton', where he comments on the characterization of Shakespeare with 'In Shakespeare there is a continual composition and decomposition of its elements' (V:51). Even in Keats's verse, 'the mighty dead' (I:21) in the opening stanza of *Endymion* has been used by Hazlitt in his essay

'On Classical Education' (IV:5) in *The Round Table*. Many of Keats's favourite words, such as 'truth', 'beauty', 'speculation', 'disagreeable' and 'evaporate', are often employed by Hazlitt as well, but they are more likely words of currency in their time. All these clues may lead us to the most important ideas of Hazlitt that Keats has imbibed. A particularly relevant case is Keats's comment on West's painting made in the negative capability letter, which was also criticized by Hazlitt.

Death on the Pale Horse and 'Gusto'

Hazlitt first quotes the laudatory advertisement on the painting, ready to be polemical: 'The general effect proposed to be excited by this picture is the terrible sublime . . . until lost in the opposite extremes of pity and horror' (XVIII:136). The tragic cathartic effect it claims fails to convey itself to Hazlitt, who comments that the 'Death' painted by West 'has not the calm, still, majestic form of Death, killing by a look, – withering by a touch. His presence does not make the still air cold. . . . The horse . . . is not "pale," but white'; in summary, 'there is no gusto, no imagination in Mr. West's colouring' (XVIII:138). Keats's view on the painting comes very close:

> It is a wonderful picture, when West's age is considered; But there is nothing to be intense upon; no women one feels mad to kiss; no face swelling into reality. the excellence of every Art is its intensity, capable of making all disagreeables evaporate, from their being in close relationship with Beauty & Truth – Examine King Lear & you will find this examplified throughout; but in this picture we have unpleasantness without any momentous depth of speculation excited, in which to bury its repulsiveness – (*KL* I:192)

What Keats has complained of in the painting is also its deficiency of 'the terrible sublime' the advertisement has falsely claimed for it. Further, both Keats and Hazlitt have emphasized an almost magical, dynamic force which invigorates the object with life, by rendering an intense experience of it in its most characteristic capacity. This force derives from the artist but is powerful enough to pass on not only to the object but to the spectator. Hazlitt calls the force 'gusto', while Keats describes such a quality in art as 'intensity'. By 'gusto', Hazlitt means 'power or passion defining any object':

> [T]here is hardly any object entirely devoid of expression, without some character of power belonging to it, some precise association with pleasure or pain: and it is in giving this truth of character from the truth of feeling, whether in the highest or the lowest degree, but always in the highest degree of which the subject is capable, that gusto consists. (IV:77)

What is original about this signature phrase of Hazlitt's is that he turns it from the quality of the critic into that of the artist and his artistic object. Hazlitt first gives the premise, that every object has a 'truth of character', which is emphasized to be dynamic as the distinctive 'character of power', for it is foremost emotional, subjected to pleasure or pain in different degrees the gradation of which in turn characterizes it. The task of the artist is to discern this 'truth of character', and this ability stems from his emotional capacity, 'the truth of feeling', which is essentially a sympathetic imagination that enables him to enter into the emotional existence of his object and to find out the 'highest degree' it is emotionally capable of. Such an emotional interaction produces a magnetism between the artist, his object and the spectator, and gusto is the maximum energy that can be generated in this interaction. When Keats writes that 'The Sun, the Moon, the Sea and Men and Women who are creatures of impulse are poetical and have about them an unchangeable attribute' (*KL* I:387) whereas the camelion poet has none, he is expressing a similar thought: that the camelion poet needs to 'continually' transfigure himself into these 'creatures of impulse', so as to bring out their respective 'truth of character'.

West's painting wants gusto, in that it fails to render the truth of the character of Death, but only gives it a form, a form that, Hazlitt satirizes, 'would cut a figure in an undertaker's shop' (XVIII:138) but does not have the essence to 'kill by a look' or 'wither by a touch'. In Keats's terms, it lacks intensity, so that its unpleasantness remains stagnant, dwelling on itself without being transformed into its opposite, 'Beauty & Truth', thus having in it 'no women one feels mad to kiss; no face swelling into reality'.

Hazlitt has illustrated gusto in a similar manner, describing it as 'the living principle' (IV:77) of an object. With gusto, Michaelangelo's 'limbs' convey 'moral grandeur, and even . . . intellectual dignity', while Correggio's hands suggest 'sentiment', so that 'we always wish to touch them'. Gusto gives non-human objects life too: 'the winds seemed to sing through the rustling branches of the trees' in Titian's landscape, and Rembrandt's 'furs and stuffs are proof against a Russian winter' (IV:78). In contrast, Raphael's 'trees are like sprigs of grass stuck in a book of botanical specimens', and Claude's 'trees are perfectly beautiful, but quite immovable', for the reason that 'he painted . . . with . . . an abstraction of the gross, tangible impression'. Abstraction results from his lack of sympathetic imagination for his landscapes: 'they resemble a mirror or a microscope', which calls to mind the distinction M. H. Abrams makes between the mirror and the lamp, because 'he saw the atmosphere, but he did not feel it'. Then Hazlitt digs deeper into the reason for such an unimaginative imitation of nature: 'his eye wanted imagination: it did not strongly sympathise with his other faculties' (IV:79). As Bate rightly points out, Hazlitt's belief in the associative perception of the senses finds the most eloquent expression in Keats's poetry characterized by 'empathic imagery' (1964: 253). Equally important, the synaesthetic nature of gusto indicates a relish in the fullness of

experience which inspires the artist to feel with all the senses the concrete
particularity of his object.

This is exactly what West's *Death on the Pale Horse* lacks. In choosing such
a subject to paint, Hazlitt comments, West seeks to represent '[t]he moral attri-
butes of death', or 'powers and effects of an infinitely wide and general descrip-
tion, which no individual or physical form can possibly represent' (XVIII:137).
Hazlitt then proposes his version of objective correlative:

> The only way in which the painter of genius can represent the force of moral
> truth, is by translating it into an artificial language of his own, – by substitut-
> ing hieroglyphics for words, and presenting the closest and most striking
> affinities his fancy and observation can suggest between the general idea and
> the visible illustration of it. (XVIII:138)

Hazlitt here clearly expresses the notion that truth is not found in abstraction
or generality, but is always embodied in the tangible and the concrete, and only
by finding the perceptible 'hieroglyphics' of truth, can an artist convey and
render it with gusto.

On this point, Hazlitt touches upon something quite relevant to negative
capability, though he has not quite spelled it out: since 'Death is a mighty
abstraction', and West, instead of finding its 'visible illustration', intends to con-
vey 'the moral impression' of it, what he does can only be to impose an abstract
conception on an abstract object. In this sense, West is caught in a deeper pit-
fall, because, Hazlitt suggests, 'The less definite the conception, the less bodily,
the more vast, unformed, and unsubstantial, the nearer does it approach to
some resemblance of that omnipresent, lasting, universal, irresistible principle'
of death (XVIII:137). In its indication of the paradox between an indefinite
conception and a more truthful imitation, this statement strikes a note quite
resonant with negative capability, though Hazlitt is dealing with a specific topic
of the representation of death. It is unlikely that Keats has developed his
thoughts on negative capability from this single statement, but Hazlitt's attribu-
tion of the failure of the artistic representation to the artist's 'definite concep-
tion' is certainly relevant to Keats's notion. Whether this was Keats's point of
departure or not, he has reached further than Hazlitt on this point.

In West's case, the definiteness of his conception is both the cause and effect
of its abstraction. The absence of concreteness makes the artist self-regarding,
and egotism in turn enforces abstraction. In consequence, Hazlitt remarks,
'Mr. West's vicarious egotism obtrudes itself . . . offensively' (XVIII:138) in
painting Christ and other figures. While the advertisement claims that 'the
painter has attempted to excite the strongest degree of pity', Hazlitt points
out that this is exactly where West 'has principally failed'. West's lack of sym-
pathy for the figures is comparable with Claude's seeing the landscape without
feeling it, for the egotism of an artist gets in the way of his entering into the

particular, emotional state of his objects, which is what gusto composes of. Consequently, West's figures 'are not likely to excite any sympathy in the beholders' (XVIII:139), for without gusto, the painting does not possess the dynamism between the artist and the viewer.

To go back to the advertisement for the painting, West fails to produce 'the terrible sublime' which it claims to be 'lost in the opposite extremes of pity and horror', exactly because he lacks the sympathy to feel the 'pity and horror' of his objects, thus handicapping this paradoxical transformation of 'the terrible' into a tragic catharsis. Both Hazlitt and Keats have recognized the failure of the enterprise, but neither of them has denied the rightness of such an endeavour. Hazlitt believes that '[o]bjects in themselves disagreeable or indifferent, often please in the imitation' (IV:72), while Keats has also indicated the ability of an intense artistic work to transform the 'disagreeables' into their opposite 'Beauty & Truth'. Hazlitt clearly illustrates what makes this paradoxical transformation possible:

> Imitation renders an object, displeasing in itself, a source of pleasure, not by repetition of the same idea, but by suggesting new ideas, by detecting new properties, and endless shades of difference, just as a close and continued contemplation of the object itself would do. (IV:73–4)

The 'close and continued contemplation of the object' indicates not only a close observation of its concrete reality, but an involvement with its existence that is intense enough to achieve an imaginary identification with it, by which only the artist can gain insight into its 'truth of character', which is not its static present condition, but its potential in different circumstances imaginable, in which its more profound nature is revealed. This insight is comparable to 'the momentous depth of speculation' 'excited' by unpleasantness in Keatisan terms, and both the transformation of the 'disagreeables' into 'Beauty & Truth' and the excitement of speculation are accomplished by intensity.

Hazlitt therefore believes that 'imitation interests . . . by exciting a more intense perception of truth, and calling out the powers of observation and comparison' (IV:75). An artist has to be perspicacious to be able to discover 'new properties' others have not seen and to discriminate the subtlest 'shades of differences' others have not noticed, but Hazlitt emphasizes that for a great artist, such discoveries and discriminations are never performed in an aloof, judgemental manner. Hazlitt is clearly aware that '[t]he pursuit of art is liable to be carried to a contrary excess, as where it produces a rage for the *picturesque*' (IV:74), which is a reversal of the means to the end, and can only be avoided by a deep attachment to the experiential life itself, as Hazlitt expresses it:

> [T]he study of the *ideal* in art, if separated from the study of nature, may have the effect . . . of producing dissatisfaction and contempt for everything but

itself . . .; but to the genuine artist, truth, nature, beauty, are almost different names for the same thing. (IV:75)

Keats's interchangeable 'beauty' and 'truth' may very well be influenced by Hazlitt's view expressed here, and both of their usages indicate an ideal of art in marrying 'beauty', the aesthetic, with 'truth', the experiential, for 'true genius, though it has new sources of pleasure opened to it, does not lose its sympathy with humanity' (IV:76), Hazlitt stresses. When Keats observes that '[t]hough a quarrel in the streets is a thing to be hated, the energies displayed in it are fine' for '[t]his is the very thing in which consists poetry' (*KL* II:80–1), what he delights in is exactly 'the sympathy with humanity'. Only this sympathy can prevent the artist from carrying his talent 'to a singular excess' (IV:76), Hazlitt warns, his wording and idea adapted by Keats to one of his poetic axioms, 'Poetry should surprise by a fine excess and not by Singularity' (*KL* I:238).

The Hazlittean conception of gusto, therefore, with its apparent suggestions of spontaneity and passion, involves their paradoxical opposites at the same time. It stresses the artist's strong emotional involvement, but the nature of the involvement is essentially sympathetic. It sees the mind as an agent free to re-create nature with imaginativeness, but the imaginativeness derives from the full participation of the senses in the concrete particularity of the empirical world. Hazlitt's aesthetic idea of gusto is deeply rooted in his philosophical belief in disinterestedness, which constitutes another important part of his influence on Keats in the formation of negative capability.

An Essay on the Principles of Human Action and 'Disinterestedness'

The central argument in *An Essay on the Principles of Human Action*, as the sub-title goes, 'in defence of the natural disinterestedness of the human mind' (I:1), lays the groundwork for Hazlitt's later criticism. We do not know whether this book is the main reason for Keats to think about asking for Hazlitt's advice in metaphysics, but Keats owned the book and also used the word 'disinterest-edness' quite often.[8] An interesting example is Keats's description of his sister-in-law as 'the most disinterrested woman I ever knew', commenting that '[t]o see an entirely disinterrested Girl quite happy is the most pleasant and extraor-dinary thing in the world – it depends upon a thousand Circumstances', one of which may be '[w]omen must want Imagination' (*KL* I:293). I do not intend to discuss the possible sexist indication here, but to draw attention to a closely-knit connection in Keats's mind of disinterestedness and imagination, which is a key argument in *An Essay on the Principles of Human Action*.

In his book, Hazlitt starts from the premise that '[t]he objects in which the mind is interested may be either past or present, or future'. The interests in the present and the past are respectively based on 'consciousness', or 'sensation'; and 'memory', which 'I cannot have in the past, or present feelings of others' and are thus self-oriented. Therefore, '[i]t is only from the interest excited in him by future objects that man becomes a moral agent, or is denominated self-ish, or the contrary' (I:1), because the interests in the future cannot be achieved from 'consciousness' or 'memory' but only from 'imagination', which is defined by Hazlitt as,

> The imagination, by means of which alone I can anticipate future objects, or be interested in them, must carry me out of myself into the feelings of others by one and the same process by which I am thrown forward as it were into my future being, and interested in it. I could not love myself, if I were not capable of loving others. Self-love, used in this sense, is in it's fundamental principle the same with disinterested benevolence. (I:1–2)

Imagination in the Hazlittean sense, therefore, is the decisive factor in his argument for the 'natural disinterestedness' of the mind, and with this definition, Keats's peculiar association of Georgiana's rare disinterestedness and women's usual lack of imagination can be easily understood.

This not altogether common usage of the word 'imagination' encapsulates several fundamental principles of Hazlitt's. In arguing that imagination is the only force to make the mind 'a moral agent' because it is the only means of constructing future interests, Hazlitt has first to make the distinction between the interests of the mind in the future and those in the present and past, since he has conceded that the interests in the present and past are controlled by 'consciousness' and 'memory', which operate only on the self. As he puts it,

> I have not the same sort of exclusive, or mechanical self-interest in my future being or welfare, because I have no distinct faculty giving me a direct present interest in my future sensations, and none at all in those of others. (I:1)

Conversely, 'the doctrine of the natural selfishness' (I:2) bases its argument on the premise that selves in the past, present and future are one and the same, all of whose interests are determined by external sensations received by no other but the self. Denying that the same faculties work for future interests, Hazlitt at the same time rejects 'the supposition of the absolute, metaphysical identity of my individual being', and the consequent 'wild and absurd notion' that 'whatever can be affirmed of that principle at any time must be strictly and logically true of it at all times' (I:4). Following this train of logic, the hypothesis of self-interest in itself confirms the role of imagination, for

> with this faculty enabling him to throw himself forward into the future, to anticipate unreal events and to be affected by his own imaginary interest, he

must necessarily be capable in a greater or less degree of entering into the feelings and interests of others and of being consequently influenced by them. (I:21)

Therefore, by differentiating the volition of the human mind for future actions from its passivity for the past and present with the factor of imagination, Hazlitt has disproved the assumption of a fixed self-identity that is merely mechanically reactive, and associated the moral capacity of the mind with its imagination of the other including the future self, which became the founding principle for his subsequent consistent criticism of egotism. More relevantly, Hazlitt's 'imagination' provides the strongest metaphysical ground for Keats's idea of negative capability, the openness of which recognizes the fluidity of one's self-identity in the first place.

Further, by affirming the mind's capacity of 'imagination' of the unactual, Hazlitt clearly suggests that the nature of the mind is voluntary rather than mechanical, as he argues:

All voluntary action . . . or effort of the mind to produce a certain event must relate to the future . . . . But that which is future, which does not yet exist can excite no interest in itself, nor act upon the mind in any way but by means of the imagination. The direct primary motive, or impulse which determines the mind to the volition of any thing must therefore in all cases depend on the *idea* of that thing as conceived of by the imagination. (I:8)

The volition of the mind is essential to Hazlitt's general argument, without which he cannot refute the notion of the natural self-interestedness which reduces the mind to a passive receptacle of external sensations. Since the mind is creative in its capability of imagination of 'the idea' of the thing rather than being possessed only by the sensation of the thing itself, Hazlitt continues to argue that human actions are motivated by the conception of the idea, regardless of whether the self or the other is the recipient of the actions:

[I]f we admit that there is something in the very idea of good, or evil, which naturally excites desire or aversion, which is in itself the proper motive of action, which impels the mind to pursue the one and to avoid the other by a true moral necessity, then it cannot be indifferent to me whether I believe that any being will be made happy or miserable in consequence of my actions, whether this be myself or another. I naturally desire and pursue my own good . . . simply from my having an idea of it sufficiently warm and vivid to excite in me an emotion of interest, or passion; and I love and pursue the good of others . . . for just the same reason. (I:12)

The mind has the ability to make disinterested moral judgements because imagination enables it to conceive of the idea of good or evil, yet the idea is not abstract, but 'sufficiently warm and vivid' to 'excite' the 'desire' for good or 'aversion' to evil. Rather than being directly motivated by pre-existing ideas of good and evil, imagination is immediately provoked by 'our natural desire of happiness and fear of pain' (I:18), our emotional properties, which enable the mind to conceive of the ideas, as he clarifies:

> When I say . . . that the human mind is naturally benevolent, this does not refer to any innate abstract idea of good in general, or to an instinctive desire of general indefinite unknown good but to the natural connection between the idea of happiness and the desire of it, independently of any particular attachment to the person who is to feel it. (I:12)

It is worth noting that in making his point of the natural inclination of the imagination to the idea of benevolence, Hazlitt is not given to the admission of innate ideas. Instead of suggesting that the mind by nature leans to the idea of good, he shifts the moral 'good' to the emotional 'happiness', thus attributing the mind's natural disinterestedness to its emotional capacity. Hazlitt's concept of imagination, therefore, encapsulates his fundamental beliefs that the human mind is other-regarding, open to change, freely-willing, and emotive.

Clearly, when Hazlitt wrote the book, his chief target was the prevailing empiricist doctrine that the nature of the mind is purely mechanical and self-interested, but in his refusal to admit innate ideas, he has made it clear that he is not taking an opposite rationalist stand either. His basic philosophical stance is characteristically non-conforming. *An Essay on the Principles of Human Action* is only the first and the least polemical of the philosophical writings to which he devoted himself chiefly in his earlier years. In his 1809 *Prospectus of a History of English Philosophy* and 1812 *Lectures on English Philosophy*, he attacks 'the material or *modern* philosophy' much more explicitly and vehemently. His attitude is clearly seen from his summary of it at the beginning of his lectures: 'all thought is to be resolved into sensation, all morality into the love of pleasure, and all action into mechanical impulse' (II:124). In Hazlitt's view, empiricism goes from one extreme, that of scholastic rationalism, to the other: 'We despised "experience" altogether before; now we would have nothing but "experience," and that of the grossest kind' (II:125). In essence, it is empiricism's sole concern for physical and mechanical nature and its complete dismissal of the intellectual and emotive power of the human mind that Hazlitt is mostly against, as he puts at the top of his philosophical principles:

I. . . . That *the mind itself is not material,* or that the phenomena of thought and feeling do not originate in the common properties of what is called matter.

II. That *the understanding or intellectual power of the mind is entirely distinct from simple perception or sensation.* [his italics] (II:116)

Hazlitt puts the volition of the mind as the most important point for the same reason that he has expressed in his *Essay on the Principles of Human Action*, that it defends the disinterested nature of the human mind, as he reiterates here: 'The question . . . whether there is a moral sense, is reducible to this: whether the mind can understand or conceive, or be affected by, any thing beyond its own physical or mechanical feelings' (II:220). Imagination thus is again stressed as the central force that enables the mind to get beyond self-love and feel sympathy for others. Sympathy for Hazlitt, however, is a very different concept from the empiricist one, which is taken as resulting from 'the general recollection of the sufferings to which . . . I myself may be exposed' (II:223), or self-love in essence. Hazlitt is strongly against this empiricist twist in distorting sympathy into another form of self-love, defying it explicitly: 'In feeling compassion for another . . . it was not for myself that I was concerned, but for the sufferer' (II:224). Much later, in 'On Reason and Imagination', Hazlitt expresses his view on the connection between passion and sympathy more succinctly: 'Men act from passion; and we can only judge of passion by sympathy' (XII:45); their connection is made possible by imagination: 'Passion . . . is the essence, the chief ingredient in moral truth; and the warmth of passion is sure to kindle the light of imagination on the objects around it' (XII:46). For Hazlitt, therefore, it is passion that begets compassion by the power of imagination, and together they form the basis of one's moral sense. The emotive and sympathetic nature of the human mind remains at the core of Hazlitt's philosophical beliefs from the beginning to the end.

Not only has Hazlitt remained a fervent critic of 'modern' philosophy, but he has repeatedly expressed a low regard for the leading empiricists, Locke in particular. He claims to have 'never derived either pleasure or profit' (XII:224) from Locke's *Essay on the Human Understanding*, and one of his essays is entitled 'Mr. Locke A Great Plagiarist' (XX:69–81), referring to his debt to the work of Hobbes. The German idealism at the other end of the spectrum is not commented on in a favourable light by Hazlitt either. Though he does quote Kant's '*The mind alone is formative*' (II:153) to counter the empiricist doctrine that ideas are formed exclusively from sensations, he nevertheless describes Kant's system as that which 'appears to us the most wilful and monstrous absurdity that ever was invented' (XVI:123).

To both the prevailing empiricism and idealism, then, Hazlitt is more a dissenter than an advocate, but for all his critical assertions, one wonders how much he has imbibed the spirit of his age unconsciously at the same time, for his firm belief in the concreteness of the experiential world *is* empirical, if not empiricist, and his faith in the 'formative' power of the mind *is* idealistic, if not strictly Kantian. To have a clearer idea of Hazlitt's exposure to his philosophical contemporaries, we can take a glance at Hazlitt's readings in the field of philosophy, to which many critics have offered helpful clues. P. P. Howe's and Ralph M. Wardle's biographies record Hazlitt's early readings of Berkeley,

Hume and Hartley (Howe 50; Wardle 46). René Wellek claims that Hazlitt's knowledge of philosophy was 'confined to the English empirical tradition and kindred French authors' (209), while John Kinnaird in his book on Hazlitt stresses the 'provincialism' in his reading: 'his most grievous limitation is his ignorance of . . . all philosophy beyond British empiricism and its French successors (with the one great exception of Kant, and he knew Kant mainly through Coleridge and through Willich's bad translation)' (50). Bromwich also states that Hazlitt 'had not investigated Kant thoroughly' (240), and '[t]hat he read Kant at all is more than we know; if he did, it was likely to have been Willich's volume of selections' (29). Uttara Natarajan agrees that 'his reading is of his own compatriots, among them, Hobbes, Locke, Hartley, Burke, and Hume' (1998, 3), and '[h]is reading of the Germans in translation is limited and even cursory' (1998: 5).

A few other figures stand behind Hazlitt's idea of disinterestedness. In his attack on Helvetius's theory of self-love, Hazlitt describes Helvetius's view that 'morality "is an affair of the five senses"' as a proposition which any 'man of the world, possessed of the least common sense, would treat with as much contempt and incredulity as Shaftesbury or Hutcheson' (II:221). As Bromwich points out, in his defense of natural disinterestedness Hazlitt 'evidently has in mind, though he does not name them, Adam Smith and such scholars of the affections as Shaftesbury and Hutcheson' (48). Shaftesbury believes that 'Our Passions and Affections' 'are certain, whatever the *Objects* may be, on which they are employ'd' (I:272). Hutcheson also states clearly that 'Virtue is not pursued from the Interest of Self-love of the Pursuer, or any Motives of his own Advantage' (102). Adam Smith, too, regards 'pity or compassion' as 'original passions of human nature' (1), though his approach to sympathy as imagined from the self exposed to the same situation is disapproved of by Hazlitt (I:80). Moreover, Shaftesbury and Hutcheson are the chief proponents of disinterestedness not only in moral philosophy but in aesthetics, though of course the most influential contemporary advocate of aesthetic disinterestedness is Kant. Critics may be right that Hazlitt did not have an accurate knowledge of Kant, but he would have at least come upon Kant's basic argument about 'the pure disinterested satisfaction in the judgment of taste' (91).

With these different pieces of evidence, these critics have not drawn exactly identical conclusions on the genealogy of Hazlitt's philosophical ideas, but all of them have stressed a mixture of different 'isms' in Hazlitt. Bate places Hazlitt's genealogy in the 'psychological tradition of eighteenth-century British empiricism' (1964: 239) or 'a union of eighteenth-century English empiricism and emotional intuitionalism' (1970: 282). James Engell's version is slightly more elaborate: Hazlitt 'represents a complete blending . . . of the British traditions of empirical psychology, associationism, intuitionalism, common sense, sympathy, moral thought, and interest in genius' (197). Bromwich describes Hazlitt more precisely as 'a thinker committed to the procedures of empirical philosophy but convinced that the tradition ought to be revised' (29). Natarajan's conclusion emphasizes the ambivalence within Hazlitt: 'Coleridge's engagement with German idealism is notorious, but Hazlitt is a proponent of what we must call British idealism. . . . Hazlitt's idealism is evolving, not from the Germans, but from the empiricist tradition dominant in Britain' (1998: 3).

Putting their conclusions together, we also need to note that though Hazlitt is versed in and has written profusely on philosophy, he is not doctrinaire, and this enables him to embrace various aspects of distinct philosophical schools even though he has not adopted any of these philosophical systems as a whole. In this sense, he exemplifies a congenial spirit with Keats's negatively capable mind. His objections to empiricism's sole reliance on the mechanical processing of the sense data and its complete denial of the mind's intellectual capability of reasoning and abstraction, for example, do not make him an opponent of emotion and concreteness. Rather, he is against the extreme position taken by the empiricists, which does not mean that his stance lies at the other extreme. Quite the contrary, while maintaining that the mind possesses the power of reasoning and abstraction, he holds that emotion and concreteness are the ground for it. As he puts it, 'I hate people who have no notion of any thing but generalities . . . . They stick to the table of contents, and never open the volume of the mind. They are for having maps, not pictures of the world we live in' (XII:44). What he aims at is a more balanced view: 'We must improve our concrete experience of persons and things into the contemplation of general rules and principles; but without being grounded in individual facts and feelings, we shall end as we began, in ignorance' (XII:46). Similarly, when he objects to the empiricist principle of association, what he is against is its exclusive claim, as he puts it, '[t]hat the only principle of connection between one idea and another is *association*' (XX:75), rather than the validity of the association principle itself. In fact, he believes that imagination, the key function of the mind, 'is an *associating* principle' (XII:51).

Hazlitt's approach to philosophy, therefore, is more commonsensical, emotive, and intuitive than theoretical, deductive and dogmatic. 'True philosophy', Hazlitt writes, 'is softened by feeling, and owes allegiance to nature' (XX:374). In his integrating contemporary philosophies without fully accepting any of them, he exemplifies the capability of holding contradictory principles in his mind. As Bromwich rightly describes him:

> He could not belong wholeheartedly to any one age however all-disposing its spirit. The critic of an intellectual movement who was himself . . . committed to the premises of that movement, he had the faculty of holding two opposed ideas in his mind at the same time. (22)

Whether Keats studied Hazlitt's philosophical essays thoroughly or not, he had followed Hazlitt's writings closely enough to know Hazlitt's basic principles, which, especially around the time when he was writing *Endymion* with its thoughts on 'self-destroying' 'fellowship' (I:799, 779), must have fermented those germane ideas in his mind and helped formulate them into more mature shapes. On the other hand, Keats is not simply borrowing Hazlitt's ideas without developing them into his own. When Hazlitt argues that the human mind must possess the power of imagination, he is making a philosophical argument for a general mental faculty. When Keats affirms that 'What the imagination seizes as Beauty must be truth' (*KL* I:184), he has taken off from Hazlitt's philosophical ground to the poetic realm, where imagination becomes imaginativeness, or poetic imagination, which, by its intensity, is able to achieve a higher truth than actuality.

Similarly, Keats's idea of disinterestedness, most definitely drawn from Hazlitt, does not altogether coincide with Hazlitt's argument. Undoubtedly, Hazlitt's philosophical speculation about the disinterestedness of the human mind gives confirmation to Keats, who, with his natural bent to sympathetic imagination, claimed that 'if a Sparrow come before [his] Window', he could 'take part in its existence and pick about the Gravel' (*KL* I:186). Yet unlike Hazlitt who discusses disinterestedness as a metaphysical issue, Keats contemplates it in the actual world, which gives him a very different perspective: 'Very few men have ever arrived at a complete disinterestedness of Mind: very few have been influenced by a pure desire of the benefit of others' (*KL* II:79). Reflecting on his own detachment from others' misfortune, he finds that he himself is no exception: 'I perceive how far I am from any humble standard of disinterestedness' (*KL* II:79); and he continues more grimly, 'I have no doubt that thousands of people never heard of have had hearts comp[l]etely disinterested: I can remember but two – Socrates and Jesus' (*KL* II:80). On the other hand, neither does Keats believe in what he calls the 'perfectibility' of the world, that 'Mankind may be made happy' 'by the persevering endeavours of a seldom appearing Socrates' (*KL* II:101). The absence of absolute disinterestedness thus does not lead to despair, but becomes the premise for the acceptance of the soul-making world as necessary to forge every particular human being. '[A]xioms in philosophy are not axioms until they are proved upon our pulses' (*KL* I:279); here Keats is testing Hazlitt's metaphysical principle of natural disinterestedness on the pulses of life, and reconciles it with actual human experience.

For all the 'demon' in himself, Hazlitt, at least in his philosophical argument, has not made the demonic side of human nature an essential point. Keats, on the other hand, is explicit about this:

[T]here lives not the Man who may not be cut up, aye hashed to pieces on his weakest side. The best of Men have but a portion of good in them – a kind of spiritual yeast in their frames which creates the ferment of existence – by which a Man is propell'd to act and strive and buffet with Circumstance. (*KL* I:210)

As Bailey recollects of Keats, 'he was uniformly the apologist for poor, frail human nature, & allowed for people's faults more than any man I ever knew' (*KC* II:274). It is the sober view of human nature that makes Keats a disinterested sympathizer with humanity, and convinces him of the human potential that this soul-making world of circumstances inevitably endows humanity with. Thus, he also believes that despite the rarity of completely disinterested men, 'there is an ellectric fire in human nature tending to purify – so that among these human creature[s] there is continually some birth of new heroism' (*KL* II:80). This purifying fire exists only because the human heart, constantly tortured by the antagonistic world of pains and troubles, nevertheless refuses to succumb to it. It is therefore Keats's firm belief in the fortitude of the human heart that makes his stark view of human nature tragic instead of pessimistic, and his unwavering faith in the holiness of the heart's affections supplies the most powerful support to Hazlitt's philosophical argument for the creative and emotive nature of the human mind. Like Hazlitt stresses time and again, Keats never forgets that 'the heart' is the 'seat of the human Passions' (*KL* II:103).

Keats's wording calls to mind again a statement of Hazlitt, that the religion of Christ is 'the religion of the heart', and Christ 'made the affections of the heart the sole seat of morality' (VI:184). Disinterestedness and emotion, or passion and compassion, are the two leading principles of Hazlitt not only in philosophy but in other fields. So does he base his aesthetics on these two key factors and form the notion of gusto, which applies to his views on poetry and literature as well.

Lectures on the English Poets and Dramatic Poetry

Hazlitt defines poetry as follows: 'it is the natural impression of any object or event, by its vividness exciting an involuntary movement of imagination and passion, and producing, by sympathy, a certain modulation of the voice, or sounds, expressing it' (V:1). The definition makes the experience of nature the firm ground of poetry, but it also gives weight to a passionate and imaginative expression of this experience which in turn evokes sympathy in the reader. 'Passion' and 'imagination': these two key words clearly assert Hazlitt's departure from the Neoclassic poetics. Hazlitt affirms in the first place that poetry 'is an imitation of nature', but rather than being 'One clear, unchanged, and universal light', 'nature' is at the same time human nature, a significant part of which is 'the imagination and the passions' (V:3). While poetry is the mirror held up to nature, it is 'seen through the medium of passion and imagination, not divested of that medium by means of literal truth or abstract reason' (V:8). The implied target is the Neoclassic unimaginative accuracy and unfeeling rationality, and this anti-Neoclassic undertone comes up again when he makes the point that progress, accelerated by such Neoclassic values, poses a threat to poetic imagination: 'the progress of knowledge and refinement has a tendency to circumscribe the limits of the imagination, and to clip the wings of poetry' (V:9). The phrasing is familiar: 'Philosophy will clip an Angel's wings, / Conquer all mysteries by rule and line' ('Lamia' II:234–5). 'Lamia' is certainly not the only poem in which Keats questions 'literal truth' and 'abstract reason', though it poses the questions in a more ambiguous manner than the other poems. In the much earlier 'Sleep and Poetry', for instance, Keats's antagonism towards the Neoclassicists is unreserved, attacking them as 'closely wed / To musty laws lined out with wretched rule / And compass vile' (194–5). In it, Hazlitt's influence is already perceptible; his 'Dr. Johnson and Pope would have converted [Milton's] vaulting Pegasus into a rocking horse' (IV:40) is translated into 'They sway'd about upon a rocking horse, / And thought it Pegasus' (186–7). What Hazlitt and Keats have both manifested is a typical Romantic reaction to Neoclassicism, memorably expressed by Charles Lamb in his description of Newton, the Neoclassic enlightener of the universe, as the one who 'destroyed all the poetry of the rainbow by reducing it to the prismatic colours' (*KPA* 645).

This Romantic elevation of feeling and spontaneity, important as it is, is not peculiarly Hazlittean. It is rather a pervasive spirit of the age that shaped both Hazlitt and Keats and their contemporaries and was at the same time shaped by all of them. Hazlitt's influence upon Keats can be probed from this premise, but extends to a direction that goes exactly against the main current of their time. Indeed, Hazlitt sees poetry as first and foremost an expression of emotion, which 'relates to whatever gives immediate pleasure or pain to the human mind' (V:1), with the human heart at its centre: 'Poetry is the universal language which the heart holds with nature and itself' (V:1). However, Hazlitt also makes it clear that poetry is not an expression of the poet's own feelings. Instead, 'the poet does no more than describe what all the others think and act', including 'the vain, the ambitious, the proud, the choleric man, the hero and the coward, the beggar and the king, the rich and the poor, the young and the old' (V:2). The poet Hazlitt describes is exactly a camelion poet, whose emotional capacity is characterized by a powerful sympathetic imagination. Therefore, 'a mere delineation of natural feelings', Hazlitt stresses, does not '[constitute] the ultimate end and aim of poetry, without the heightenings of the imagination' (V:3), which, by its sympathetic nature, transcends egotistical emotional expressiveness. Conversely, imagination is also enkindled by passion, and together they create a dynamic force for poetry, as Hazlitt illustrates:

> Poetry puts a spirit of life and motion into the universe. It describes the flowing, not the fixed. It does not define the limits of sense, or analyze the distinctions of the understanding, but signifies the excess of the imagination beyond the actual or ordinary impression of any object or feeling. The poetical impression of any object is that uneasy, exquisite sense of beauty or power that cannot be contained within itself; that is impatient of all limit; that . . .

strives to link itself to some other image of kindred beauty or grandeur; to enshrine itself . . . in the highest forms of fancy, and to relieve the aching sense of pleasure by expressing it in the boldest manner, and by the most striking examples of the same quality in other instances. (V:3)

The passage outlines several key points in Hazlitt's views on poetry. First, Hazlitt sees poetry, as he does visual art, as an imaginatively illuminating lamp instead of a mechanically reflective mirror. Second, Hazlitt indicates that poetry with gusto treats a subject that is sublime rather than beautiful, and thus creates a more intense and violent emotional effect, though he again refers to the sublime in loose terms as the 'uneasy, exquisite sense of beauty'. As Abrams points out in *The Mirror and the Lamp*, Longinus's influence 'underlies the typical romantic theory of poetry in general' (132) and 'the Longinian emphasis on critical responsiveness and "enthrallment," rather than judgment' is particularly evident in Hazlitt's idea of gusto (134–5), while 'the image-and-intensity aspect of the Longinian heritage' is found in Keats 'more than . . . his contemporaries' (136). The more immediate source for Hazlitt's association of poetic imagination with the sublime may be Burke, an important part of Hazlitt's early reading (Bromwich 288; Woolf 159). Further, Hazlitt also highlights in this passage that the dynamic nature of poetic imagination makes it associative, reaching out to other 'kindred' images, thus broadening the realm of poetry. According to Hazlitt, poetic imagination 'is that faculty which represents objects, not as they are in themselves, but as they are moulded by other thoughts and feelings, into an infinite variety of shapes and combinations of power' (V:4). The Hazlittean sense of poetic imagination thus is essentially dramatic, just as his definition of poetry has already indicated a higher status for dramatic poetry than lyrical, for dramatic poetry fuses the poet's passion with imagination most intimately, and in turn engenders the strongest sense of sympathy in the reader with its gusto.

According to Hazlitt, dramatic poetry 'is the closest imitation of nature; . . . it brings forward certain characters to act and speak for themselves, in the most trying and singular circumstances' (XVIII:305). Consequently, the dramatic poet 'must not only identify himself with each, but must take part with all by turns . . .; must not only have [their] passions rooted in his mind, but must be alive to every circumstance affecting them'. In other words, the poetic imagination has to be wrought to the most thorough extent in dramatic poetry, which springs from particularly intense passions: 'it is from the excess of passion that he must borrow the activity of his imagination' (XVIII:306). Dramatic poetry brings passion and imagination into the fullest play.

If the spirit of Hazlitt's age is characterized by empiricism in philosophy and by the *Lyrical Ballads* in poetry, then as he is chiefly an opponent of 'modern' philosophy, so is Hazlitt a critic of this new school of lyrical poetry. As shown above, Hazlitt's often harsh criticism of his poetic contemporaries is not a matter of personal taste but consistent with his perennial philosophical and aesthetic values. According to Hazlitt, the fact that the *Lyrical Ballads* was produced at this particular historical moment is not merely a coincidence. The age they live in, Hazlitt comments, can be labelled as 'critical, didactic, paradoxical, romantic, but it is not dramatic' (XVIII:302). Its 'poverty' in dramatic achievements has to be attributed to the French Revolution, for in such a sweeping movement, Hazlitt explains:

> Our attention has been turned, by the current of events, to the general nature of men and things; and we cannot call it heartily back to individual caprices, or head-strong passions, which are the nerves and sinews of Comedy and Tragedy. (XVIII:304)

Individual emotions become insignificant, for 'the hugest private sorrow looks dwarfish' in face of 'the large vicissitudes of human affairs', while 'the general progress of intellect' takes the place of interest in specific, concrete human lives. 'In a word, literature and civilization have abstracted man from himself so far, that his existence is no longer *dramatic*', and in accordance with such a context with its 'bias to abstraction' (XVIII:305), 'we have no dramatic poets' (XVIII:306), for dramatic poetry 'is essentially individual and concrete' (XVIII:305).

That is why, Hazlitt argues, this new school of poetry 'had its origin in the French revolution' (V:161). Tracing its development to its reaction against the Neoclassic poetry which Hazlitt also disparages, calling it 'the most trite, insipid, and mechanical of all things', Hazlitt disapproves of the poetry of his contemporaries for going to the other extreme, owing to the impact of the French Revolution: 'it rose . . . from the most servile imitation and tamest commonplace, to the utmost pitch of singularity and paradox' (V:161). 'Singularity', we remember from Hazlitt's artistic criticism, results from the lack of sympathy with humanity and the overwhelming interest in the self. So is it in poetry, which Hazlitt sees as rooted in the egotism of his poetic contemporaries, further incensed by the French Revolution:

> They were for bringing poetry back to its primitive simplicity and state of nature, as he was for bringing society back to the savage state: so that the only thing remarkable left in the world by this change, would be the persons who had produced it. A thorough adept in this school of poetry and philanthropy is jealous of all excellence but his own. He does not even like to share his reputation with his subject . . . . His egotism is in some aspects a madness; for he scorns even the admiration of himself. (V:163)

Egotism then is a disease of revolution, evolved from the burgeoning sense of the self in face of the infinite possibilities of creation promised by this revolutionary age, and exacerbated into an interest not in creating, but in playing the role of creator. Hazlitt therefore sums up:

> The great fault of a modern school of poetry is, that it is an experiment to reduce poetry to a mere effusion of natural sensibility; or what is worse, to divest it both of imaginary splendour and human passion, to surround the meanest objects with the morbid feelings and devouring egotism of the writers' own minds. (V:53)

'Modern' poetry, therefore, fails to conform to Hazlitt's two basic principles of poetry, imagination and passion, for the 'natural sensibility' stems from involuntary movements of mind that are unimaginative, and excessive feelings, because of their egotistic nature, only become 'morbid' instead of passionate. Hazlitt's objection to his poetic contemporaries thus parallels his denunciation of 'modern' philosophers, in both of which he finds the human mind reduced to a container of immediate sensations and human passions distorted into self-love that he is adamantly against.

As the leading lyrical poet of his time, Wordsworth also becomes the most prominent failure as a dramatic poet. Hazlitt criticizes Wordsworth, a poet of feeling as he is, as one who 'sees all things in his own mind; he contemplates effects in their causes, and passions in their principles' (XIX:10). Even when Wordsworth sympathizes, '[h]e only sympathises with those simple forms of feeling, which mingle at once with his own identity, or with the stream of general humanity' (XIX:11). All these weaknesses point to the same problem: 'An intense intellectual egotism swallows up everything. Even the dialogues . . . are soliloquies of the same character' (XIX:11). Hazlitt thus concludes, 'the evident scope and tendency of Mr. Wordsworth's mind is the reverse of dramatic', and continues more incisively: 'It is as if there were nothing but himself and the universe. He lives in the busy solitude of his own heart' (XIX:11). Years later, Hazlitt came back to the subject with the same view, though adopting a milder tone: Wordsworth 'is not a man to go out of himself into the feelings of any one else; much less, to act the part of a variety of characters', and he 'has none of the bye-play, the varying points of view, the venturous magnanimity of dramatic fiction' (XVIII:308).

Following Hazlitt's writings closely, Keats would have been familiar with these views of Hazlitt's on contemporary poetry and poets, which, especially when he started out as a young and obscure poet, would be a crucial force leading him to look at these then probably larger-than-life figures more objectively and critically. Keats's changing views towards them, Wordsworth in particular, in the course of his career confirm Hazlitt's influence, though they also result from his own quick maturing.

At the beginning of his career, not only did Keats write two markedly Wordsworthian sonnets, 'O Solitude! if I must with thee dwell' and 'To one who has been long in city pent', but he exalted Wordsworth as the first of the 'Great spirits' who 'now on earth are sojourning', and when knowing Haydon was about to send this sonnet to Wordsworth, he wrote to Haydon, the very idea 'put me out of breath' (*KL* I:118). Wordsworth is the leading figure of the present 'fairer season' (221) in 'Sleep and Poetry', and *The Excursion* is one of the 'three things to rejoice at in this Age' (*KL* I:203). Later, after entering the circles of men of letters but feeling 'quite disgusted with' them, Keats continued to regard Wordsworth as the poet extraordinary: 'I . . . will never know another except Wordsworth – no not even Byron' (*KL* I:169). In the letter in February 1818, around the time he attended Hazlitt's *Lectures on the English Poets*, however, he compares modern poets to 'an Elector of Hanover' with 'his petty state', and ancient poets, 'Emperors of vast provinces', claiming: 'I will have no more of Wordsworth . . . . Why should we be owls, when we can be Eagles? . . . . Why with Wordsworths "Matthew with a bough of wilding in his hand" when we can have Jacques "under an oak &c"' (*KL* I:224). Keats's radical change of attitude might have something to do with actual meetings with Wordsworth, who 'has left a bad impression wherever he visited in Town – by his egotism, Vanity and bigotry' (*KL* I:237), and who had also slighted Keats's 'Hymn to Pan' as 'a Very pretty piece of Paganism' (*KC* II:144), but Hazlitt's view has definitely played an important role here, though it is not accepted wholesale either.

Hazlitt's sharp criticism of Wordsworth's 'Gipsies' in a note of his essay 'On Manner', for example, is duly noticed and carefully considered by Keats:

> [W]ith respect to Wordsworth's Gipseys I think he is right and yet I think Hazlitt is right[9] and yet I think Wordsworth is rightest . . . . It is a bold thing to say and I would not say it in print – but it seems to me that if Wordsworth had though[t] a little deeper at that Moment he would not have written the Poem at all – I should judge it to <has> have been written in one of the most comfortable Moods of his Life – it is a kind of sketchy intellectual Landscape – not a search after Truth – nor is it fair to attack him on such a subject – for it is with the Critic as with the poet had Hazlitt thought a little deeper and been in a good temper he would never have spied an imaginary fault there. (*KL* I:173–4)

Keats's criticism of 'Gipsies', though tentative out of his deep respect for the poet, cuts to the core of the problem. The 'comfortable Mood' reveals its emotional indifference, and the 'sketchy intellectual Landscape' suggests 'a palpable design' with which the poet envelops his self and 'bullies' others. In this sense, he concurs with Hazlitt's overall critical attitude. On the other hand, Keats cannot fully accept Hazlitt's ill-humoured criticism here, because Hazlitt's 'bad temper' is more than anything else aroused by Wordsworth's coat-turning conservatism:

> Mr. Wordsworth, who has written a sonnet to the King on the good that he has done in the last fifty years, has made an attack on a set of gipsies for

having done nothing in four and twenty hours . . . . We did not expect this
turn from Mr. Wordsworth, whom we had considered as the prince of poetic
idlers, and patron of the philosophy of indolence, who formerly insisted on
our spending our time 'in a wise passiveness'. Mr. W. will excuse us if we are
not converted to his recantation of his original doctrine; for he who changes
his opinion loses his authority. We did not look for this Sunday-school phil-
osophy from him . . . . We hate the doctrine of utility, even in a philosopher,
and much more in a poet. (IV:45–6n)

For all its penetrating insights, Hazlitt's invective is biased by his attack on
Wordsworth's political stand when criticizing the poem, thus picking on 'an
imaginary fault'. That Keats cannot fully accept Hazlitt's attitude is again a
proof of his being 'the apologist for poor, frail human nature', for whom Hazlitt
might seem too exacting and intolerant here. He himself has been ever cau-
tious not to let his critical judgement of Wordsworth the poet be taken over by
his increasing disappointment in Wordsworth the man.

After meeting Wordsworth and having gained an unfavourable impression of
his personality, Keats still insisted, 'yet he is a great Poet if not a Philosopher'
(*KL* I:237); but on this point he would wrestle for quite a while, most fully
exemplified in his long letter to Reynolds on 3 May 1818, in which Keats con-
templates 'Wordsworth's genius' and 'as a help, in the manner of gold being
the meridian Line of worldly wealth, – how he differs from Milton':

> [H]ere I have nothing but surmises, from an uncertainty whether Miltons
> apparently less anxiety for Humanity proceeds from his seeing further or no
> than Wordsworth: And whether Wordsworth has in truth epic passion<s>,
> and martyrs himself to the human heart, the main region of his song –
> In regard to his genius alone – we find what he says true as far as we have
> experienced and we can judge no further but by larger experience – for
> axioms in philosophy are not axioms until they are proved upon our pulses:
> (*KL* I:278–9)

By comparing Wordsworth with Milton, Keats is evaluating not only two individ-
ual poets, but also the poetry of their respective times, and at the same time
pondering his own position and direction. Feeling that Milton shows 'less anx-
iety for humanity' at least apparently, Keats seems inclined to contemporary
poetry, which puts humanity at its centre and explores its experience to a deeper
level. Yet he cannot decide whether Milton's more optimistic outlook results
from deeper vision, or from a less profound understanding of the human
heart. On the other hand, while affirming that Wordsworth has made the
human heart 'the main region' of his poetry, Keats is also bothered by the
question whether the passions in his poetry are truly 'epic' ones, or passions
going beyond the personal levels. What is going on in his mind is very much a

debate with the critic he admires on the worth of the poetry of the past and present.

Keats then gets off the subject for a while, but his mind is obviously taken up by it, so he comes back:

> I will return to Wordsworth – whether or no he has an extended vision or a circumscribed grandeur – whether he is an eagle in his nest, or on the wing – And to be more explicit and to show you how tall I stand by the giant, I will put down a simile of human life as far as I now perceive it; that is, to the point to which I say we both have arrived at – (*KL* I:280)

Interestingly, the figure for Wordsworth now becomes 'an eagle' instead of 'an owl', but Keats is still reserved about whether Wordsworth, with the power of an eagle, has flown out of the nest of egotism. At this stage, with his own growth, Keats has become bold enough to measure his own poetry against Wordsworth's 'giant' achievement, and in doing so, he also indicates that he is moving towards a non–egotistical direction of poetry that is not evident in Wordsworth. Then follows the famous comparison of human life to 'a large Mansion of Many Apartments', a Keatsian version of the stages of growth outlined in 'Tintern Abbey': moving from 'the infant or thoughtless Chamber' to 'the Chamber of Maiden-Thought', one of the effects is

> that tremendous one of sharpening one's vision into the <head> heart and nature of Man – of convincing ones nerves that the World is full of Misery and Heartbreak, Pain, Sickness and oppression – whereby This Chamber of Maiden Thought becomes gradually darken'd and at the same time on all sides of it many doors are set open – but all dark – all leading to dark passages – We see not the ballance of good and evil. We are in a Mist – *We* are now in that state – We feel the 'burden of the Mystery,' To this point was Wordsworth come, as far as I can conceive when he wrote 'Tintern Abbey' and it seems to me that his Genius is explorative of those dark Passages. Now if we live, and go on thinking, we too shall explore them. he is a Genius and superior [to] us, in so far as he can, more than we, make discoveries, and shed a light in them – (*KL* I:280–1)

In describing his own experience as having gone through similar paths and arrived at a similar state, Keats at the same time recognizes that Wordsworth has explored the human heart in a way that is not peculiarly individual. Therefore he continues, 'Here I must think Wordsworth is deeper than Milton', but adds, 'though I think it has depended more upon the general and gregarious advance of intellect, than individual greatness of Mind' (*KL* I:281). But the conclusion still seems unsatisfactory, so Keats modifies it: '[Milton] did not think into the human heart, as Wordsworth has done – Yet Milton as a Philosop<h>er, had sure as great powers as Wordsworth' (*KL* I:282).

Characteristically, Keats leaves his questions unresolved, whether Milton's philosophy is limited in not probing deep enough into the human heart, and whether Wordsworth's passions lack grandeur in being circumscribed by egotism. He has expressed doubts on both sides, but ends up in uncertainties about these doubts. By doing so, he is able to see the strengths and weaknesses of both sides, thus opening the questions up to the contemplation of how to bring together contemporary poetry and tradition, the depth and the scale, the intricacy and the grandeur. Though his awareness of the problems with contemporary poetry owes much to Hazlitt, Keats also recognizes the aspects of Wordsworth's genius more readily than Hazlitt, probably because he feels the predicament facing a modern poet more keenly than the critic. Several months later, in the camelion poet letter, Keats clearly asserts that he himself belongs to the kind of poets 'distinguished from the wordsworthian or egotisical sublime', but it should also be noted that he does not make any further critical judgement, simply setting it apart as 'a thing per se and stands alone' (*KL* I:387).

Wordsworth is the only contemporary poet Keats continues to hold in awe even after having a clear-sighted view of his weakness. Apparently, Keats is also familiar with some of Coleridge's poetry and prose, but is not acquainted with the man except for the two-mile walk in April 1819 in which Coleridge 'broached a thousand things', from 'Nightingales' to 'Metaphysics', from 'Nightmare' to 'Mermaids' (*KL* II:88–9). To judge by how Keats uses Coleridge in the negative capability passage as 'an instance' of 'being incapable of remaining content with half knowledge', he may have formed his impression from Hazlitt's opinion of Coleridge as well as his own readings.

Hazlitt censures Coleridge even more strongly than he does Wordsworth, perhaps because of his 'first acquaintance' with him. Coleridge, in Hazlitt's description, though 'with great talents, has, by an ambition to be everything, become nothing. His metaphysics have been a dead weight on the wings of his imagination – while his imagination has run away with his reason and common sense' (XVI:137). His 'irritable reaching after fact & reason' accounts for his failure as a dramatic poet, for '[h]e is a florid poet, and an ingenious metaphysician, who mistakes scholastic speculations for the intricate windings of the passions, and assigns possible reasons instead of actual motives for the excesses of his characters' (XVIII:309).

If Hazlitt's comments on Wordsworth and Coleridge sound harsh, his criticism of Byron is relentless. Nevertheless, Byron is undoubtedly, in Keats's words, one of the 'literary kings' (*KL* II:16) of their time. In his adolescent years, Keats had dedicated a sonnet to him ('Byron, how sweetly sad thy melody'), and had imitated his look and dress (*KC* II:211), but Byron's halo disappeared rather quickly. Hazlitt's attitude towards Byron, again, is pertinent.

Hazlitt finds Byron's poetry 'more intolerable than even Mr. Wordsworth's arbitrary egotism and pampered self-sufficiency' (XIX:36). Though in his

'Critical List of Authors' Hazlitt describes the 'distinguishing quality' of Byron as 'intensity of conception and expression' (IX:244), he still maintains that Byron is 'a pampered egotist' (XI:77). Not denying Byron's poetry is passionate, Hazlitt sees that his passion is 'of a mind preying upon itself', and thus is 'the ruling passion and moody abstraction of a single mind, as if it would make itself the centre of the universe' (V:153). The Byronic egotism is slashed together with the Wordsworthian one by Hazlitt:

> Mr. Wordsworth, to salve his own self-love, makes the merest toy of his own mind, – the most insignificant object he can meet with, – of as much importance as the universe: Lord Byron would persuade us that the universe itself is not worth his or our notice; and yet he would expect us to be occupied with him. (XIX:36)

That Keats had outgrown his adolescent idolatry is already evident in *Sleep and Poetry*, where Byron is implied to be one of 'the poets Polyphemes / Disturbing the grand sea' (234–5). In his letter talking about the difference between modern and ancient poets where he asserts that he would have no more of Wordsworth, Keats rejects at the same time 'the 4th Book of Childe Harold' (*KL* I:225) which was about to be published. When his own poetry has come of age, in his letter of 20 September 1819, Keats can afford to make critical evaluations of his early idol by talking about the 'great difference' between Byron and himself: 'He describes what he sees – I describe what I imagine – Mine is the hardest task' (*KL* II:200), which is much in line with Hazlitt's opinion on modern poetry in general as 'a mere effusion of natural sensibility'.

On the other hand, it is not all that easy to dismiss the poetic king because of his stunning success and popularity. It must have been an annoying experience when Keats had to hear his guardian Richard Abbey, who had called him 'either Mad or a Fool' (*KC* I:307) when he gave up the career of a surgeon to be a poet, read him 'some extracts from Don Juan' and tell him 'the fellow says true things now & then' (*KL* II:192).[10] In *The Fall of Hyperion*, the poet most anxiously distinguishes himself from 'large self worshipers, / And careless hectorers in proud bad verse' (I:207–8), an even more vehement tone than that of Hazlitt's 'pampered egotist', and claims feverishly: 'Though I breathe death with them it will be life / To see them sprawl before me into graves' (I:209–10). It is then not difficult to understand why Keats, for all his difference from Byron, is not insulated from his influence. At places in 'Lamia', Keats's sarcastic tone is conspicuously Byronic, and in 'The Jealousies', itself a satirical poem, Keats even satirizes the master of satire himself by parodying his poem to Lady Byron, 'Fare Thee Well' (609–11). Such Byronic traces, however, are but insignificant in Keats's poetry. After all, the identity of Byron 'presses upon'[11] Keats much more as that of the man than the poet. Once in his letter Keats reflects, 'there are two distinct tempers of mind in which we judge of things – the worldly, theatrical and pantomimical; and the unearthly, spiritual and etherial', and Byron, together with Napoleon, are exemplars of the first group (*KL* I:395). In a letter written later, when Keats ponders that 'A Man's life of any worth is a continual allegory', he thinks of Byron again: 'Lord Byron cuts a figure – but he is not figurative – Shakspeare led a life of Allegory; his works are the comments on it – ' (*KL* II:67). Ironically, it is the very theatricality of Byron the man that denies Byron the poet the dramatic quality, and the paradox between the self-identity of the poet and the impersonality of his work cannot be better demonstrated than by the contrast between Byron and Shakespeare.

Keats's increasingly heightened awareness of this paradox can be seen in his view of Shelley's poetry as well, though he could not have been influenced by Hazlitt on this account, for Hazlitt's criticism of Shelley was not published until 1821 and 1824. Unsurprisingly, in Hazlitt's eyes, the insubstantiality of Shelley's poetry deprives his poetry of the dramatic quality in the first place: 'Mr. Shelley's style is to poetry what astrology is to natural science – a passionate dream, a straining after impossibilities, a record of fond conjectures, a confused embodying of vague abstractions' (XVI:265). Hazlitt does not hesitate to recognize that Shelley 'was a man of genius' (XVI:266) with 'the true sources of strength and beauty', but he criticizes Shelley for setting the goal of poetry in 'a high spirit of metaphysical philosophy' (XVI:265). Consequently, Hazlitt comments,

> If some casual and interesting idea touched his feelings or struck his fancy, he expressed it in pleasing and unaffected verse: but give him a larger subject, and time to reflect, and he was sure to get entangled in a system. (XVI:266)

This may very well be translated into Keats's terms, that Shelley is incapable of being in the uncertainties and mysteries of this world without reaching after a metaphysical concept, only he soars higher than Coleridge, as Hazlitt writes, '"beyond the visible diurnal sphere," to the strange, the improbable, and the impossible' (XVI:265).

Shelley is the only major Romantic poet Keats was really acquainted with, through their common connection with Leigh Hunt. At the end of the negative capability letter, mentioning that 'Shelley's poem is out & there are words about its being objected too, as much as Queen Mab was', Keats laments, 'Poor Shelley I think he has his Quota of good qualities' (*KL* I:194), the compliment betraying more sympathy than esteem. Yet because of their closer age and roughly equal status as poets, Shelley's criticism of *Endymion*[12] may have sounded a bit harsh to Keats:

> I have lately read your Endymion again <for> & ever with a new sense of the treasures of poetry it contains, <bu> though treasures poured forth with

indistinct profusion – This, people in general will not endure, & that is the cause of the comparatively few copies which have been sold. (*KL* II:311)

Replying to the letter, Keats criticizes Shelley's *The Cenci* in return:

There is only one part of it I am judge of; the Poetry, and dramatic effect, which by many spirits now a days is considered the mammon. A modern work it is said must have a purpose, which may be the God – *an artist* must serve Mammon – he must have 'self concentration' selfishness perhaps. You I am sure will forgive me for sincerely remarking that you might curb your magnanimity and be more of an artist, and 'load every rift' of your subject with ore. (*KL* II:322–3)

Without knowing Hazlitt's attitude, Keats expresses a similar opinion: that Shelley, with his high spirit, always strives for 'a system' above human experience while an artist must fix his attention on 'the diurnal visible sphere'. For the virtuous philosopher, the 'purpose' of poetry dominates, but the camelion poet must find his Muse in Mammon, the demon of this world, for dramatic poetry is nourished only by worldly copiousness. Granted that he has a possible psychological need to get even, Keats is not making a criticism for its own sake. It is in a sense a recapitulation of the contrast between the theatrical Byron and the allegorical Shakespeare which illustrates the paradox between the artist's self and the self-less art, and here the paradox is explored further. The dramatic poet has to have 'self concentration', or an intense self-experience, before he can enter into the beings of various others under diverse circumstances. On the other hand, in artistic creation, the self also needs to be curbed; or its profusion only defeats the artistic work of intensity. Unlike Shakespeare's magnanimity, which is artistic, Shelley's is personal. In his deeper insight into the paradox of the artist's 'selfishness' and artistic 'magnanimity', Keats goes one step further than Hazlitt in understanding dramatic poetry. All these insights, after all, derive from the ever-present 'meridian Line' in his mind – not Milton but Shakespeare, who is the camelion poet having 'as much delight in conceiving an Iago as an Imogen'. But even in finding this 'meridian Line', Keats is deeply indebted to Hazlitt.

Shakespeare's 'Generic Quality'

Hazlitt's admiration for, and championship of, Shakespeare, like his censure of his poetic contemporaries, are rooted in his high regard for dramatic poetry, the ideal of which, in Hazlitt's mind, is realized by Shakespeare, who represents a perfect combination of passion and imagination as the requisite qualities of a dramatic genius.

Hazlitt's attitude can be clearly seen in 'On Shakspeare and Milton', one of his *Lectures on the English Poets*, where he compares Shakespeare with the other three 'greatest names in English poetry', Chaucer, Spenser and Milton. 'Chaucer excels as the poet of manners, or of real life; Spenser, as the poet of romance . . . . Milton, as the poet of morality', but Shakespeare, 'as the poet of nature (in the largest use of the term)', surpasses the other three's excellence by being all inclusive. While 'imagination . . . was common to them all', the driving force of imagination is different in each:

> [T]he . . . moving power . . . in Chaucer, was habit, or inveterate prejudice; in Spenser, novelty, and the love of the marvellous; in Shakspeare, it was the force of passion, combined with every variety of possible circumstances; and in Milton, only with the highest. (V:46)

Not only is Shakespeare's imagination passionate in nature, but the passions are dramatic, belonging to the imaginary characters in various dramatic situations. In Hazlitt's mind, each of these poets has a distinctive greatness, but Shakespeare is distinctive in accommodating all the others' greatness: 'The characteristic of Chaucer is intensity; of Spenser, remoteness; of Milton, elevation; of Shakspeare, every thing' (V:46–7). This is his key point, so Hazlitt stresses it again: 'the great distinction of Shakspeare's genius was its virtually including the genius of all the great men of his age, and not his differing from them in one accidental particular' (V:47). If as Harold Bloom suggests, what Hazlitt says of Milton's 'distinct' greatness, that 'the nearer it approaches to others, becomes more distinct from them' (V:58), can be called 'positive capability' (1973: 34), then the all-encompassing genius of Shakespeare Hazlitt describes is exactly 'negative' capability.

As Shakespeare embraces various great writers, so is he capable of containing the vast diversity of human experience within his plays. Hazlitt thus writes:

> The striking peculiarity of Shakspeare's mind was its generic quality, its power of communication with all other minds – so that it contained a universe of thought and feeling within itself, and had no one peculiar bias, or exclusive excellence more than another. He was just like any other man, but that he was like all other men. He was the least of an egotist that it was possible to be. He was nothing in himself; but he was all that others were, or that they could become. He not only had in himself the germs of every faculty and feeling, but he could follow them by anticipation, intuitively, into all their conceivable ramifications, through every change of fortune or conflict of passion, or turn of thought. He had 'a mind reflecting ages past,' and present: – all the people that ever lived are there . . . . His genius shone equally on the evil and on the good, on the wise and the foolish, the monarch and the beggar . . . . He was like the genius of humanity, changing places with all of us at pleasure, and playing with our purposes as with his own. (V:47)

The whole passage can be read side by side with Keats's description of the camelion poet, who 'has no self' and is at the same time 'every thing and nothing', who can thus freely metamorphosize into diverse other beings, and whose sympathetic identification is disinterested in being able to enjoy both sides of the opposites, 'foul or fair, high or low, rich or poor, mean or elevated'. Shakespeare's powerful dramatic imagination that is at once sympathetic and disinterested is the most significant aspect of Hazlitt's Shakespearean criticism to have inspired Keats on his way to formulating negative capability.

In Hazlitt's commentaries on Shakespeare, he highlights time and again the non-egotistical nature of Shakespeare's passion and imagination. The source of Shakespeare's dramatic imagination is sympathetic identification: 'The poet may be said, for the time, to identify himself with the character he wishes to represent, and to pass from one to another, like the same soul successively animating different bodies'. The nature of his imagination therefore is fundamentally other-regarding: 'he throws his imagination out of himself, and makes every word appear to proceed from the mouth of the person in whose name it is given' (V:50). The non-egotistical nature of imagination also allows it to be 'plastic', for it has the disinterested capacity to '[unite] the most opposite extremes' (V:53). This is very close to Keats's notion of intensity, which is characterized by bringing together irreconcilable contraries.

As Shakespeare's imagination is dramatic in nature, so are his passions. Hazlitt comments: 'His plays alone are properly expressions of the passions, not descriptions of them'. If the passions are 'described', they are still possessed by the author, but in Shakespeare, the passions are 'expressed' as they truly belong to the dramatic characters that are thus endowed with lives of their own. Therefore, '[h]is characters are real beings of flesh and blood; they speak like men, not like authors . . . . In the world of his imagination, every thing has a life, a place, and being of its own!' (V:50). The root of this, Hazlitt stresses, is that the passion in Shakespeare is non-egotistic: 'It is not some one habitual feeling or sentiment preying upon itself, growing out of itself, and moulding every thing to itself', like that exemplified in contemporary poetry. Instead, 'it is passion modified by passion, by all the other feelings to which the individual is liable, and to which others are liable with him'. Passions in Shakespeare, therefore, undergo constant interactions and conflicts, and instead of remaining static, they are always 'in a state of projection' (V:51).

Shakespeare's dramatic characters thus are beings constantly shaped by the dramatic experience which reveals 'the highest degree' of the 'truth of character' they are capable of, or, in other words, characters of gusto. To illustrate this, Hazlitt compares Shakespeare's characterization with that of Chaucer and Milton, and summarizes, 'Chaucer's characters are narrative, Shakspeare's dramatic, Milton's epic'. By 'narrative', Hazlitt refers to the stasis and the absence of the plastic. As he explains it, Chaucer's characters 'are like portraits or physiognomical studies, with the distinguishing features marked with inconceivable truth and precision, but that preserve the same unaltered air and attitude'. On the other hand, Shakespeare's characters are 'put into action, where every nerve and muscle is displayed in the struggle with others, with all the effect of collision and contrast, with every variety of light and shade'. They are thus dynamic, subjected to changes of unpredictable kinds, because they are conceived in intense dramatic conflicts which in turn bring out their profound and intricate traits. As complex representations, they have to be exposed to experience to betray their nature, so to speak. Thus, while Chaucer 'answered for his characters himself', '[i]n Shakspeare they are introduced upon the stage, are liable to be asked all sorts of questions, and are forced to answer for themselves' (V:51).

Then Hazlitt adopts a set of chemical metaphors to further illustrate their differences:

> In Chaucer we perceive a fixed essence of character. In Shakspeare there is a continual composition and decomposition of its elements, a fermentation of every particle in the whole mass, by its alternate affinity or antipathy to other principles which are brought in contact with it. Till the experiment is tried, we do not know the result, the turn which the character will take in its new circumstances. Milton took only a few simple principles of character, and raised them to the utmost conceivable grandeur, and refined them from every base alloy. (V:51)

The interest of the passage not only lies in the wording of 'composition and decomposition' which is later borrowed by Keats, but in the metaphor of a chemical process that Keats had also used in his letter to Bailey written in November 1817, before the lecture of Hazlitt was given:

> Men of Genius are great as certain ethereal Chemicals operating on the Mass of neutral intellect – by[13] they have not any individuality, any deter-mined Character. I would call the top and head of those who have a proper self Men of Power – (*KL* I:184)

Coincidentally, as Hazlitt uses 'fermentation' and 'refinement' to illustrate the 'direct contrast' (IV:56) between Shakespeare and Milton, Keats also adopts a chemical metaphor to convey a similar difference between a non-egotistic personality and one with distinct individuality. Milton, a man 'of power', is described by Hazlitt as marked by his 'originality', 'the power of [whose] mind is stamped on every line' (V:58). While Shakespeare's genius is peculiar in its ability to ferment the growth of other elements, Milton's power lies in refining other elements to create a purified proper self. As Hazlitt expresses it: 'Milton has borrowed more than any other writer, and exhausted every source of imitation . . . yet he is perfectly distinct from every other writer' (V:58).

In this lecture, Hazlitt also points out that the generally experiential nature of Shakespeare's genius is correspondingly conveyed in his 'hieroglyphical' language, which 'translates thoughts into visible images'. His metaphors, similarly, 'are the building, and not the scaffolding to thought' (V:55). To someone like Keats whose imagination is characteristically embodied in the full richness of the senses, this view of Hazlitt must have created a deep impression, and in his essay on Kean, Keats uses the very phrase of 'Shakespearian hieroglyphics' (*KPB* 530).

Keats evidently knows this lecture of Hazlitt well; it encapsulates those views of Hazlitt's on Shakespeare that are scattered through his other writings consistently. The other concentrated but more elaborate writing of Hazlitt on Shakespeare is his *Characters of Shakespear's Plays*, which Keats has underlined with marginalia. The essays contained in this collection can be described by Hazlitt's own word of gusto, each of them endeavouring to bring out the 'truth of character' of a particular play from his own 'truth of feeling'. For instance, he comments on *Hamlet*:

> It is the one of Shakespear's plays that we think of the oftenest, because it abounds most in striking reflections on human life, and because the distresses of Hamlet are transferred, by the turn of his mind, to the general account of humanity. (IV:233)

Thus, '[i]t is *we* who are Hamlet' (IV:232). According to Hazlitt, 'Shakespear had more magnanimity than any other poet, and he has shewn more of it in this play than in any other', in that '[t]here is no attempt to force an interest: every thing is left for time and circumstances to unfold' (IV:233). The Hazlittean 'magnanimity' then has a very similar connotation to the Keatsian 'enormous' negative capability. Further, Hazlitt also emphasizes that this very magnanimous indefiniteness of moral and philosophical purpose in Shakespeare contains a higher poetic truth, as he puts it:

> In one sense, Shakespear was no moralist at all: in another, he was the greatest of all moralists. He was a moralist in the same sense in which nature is one. He taught what he had learnt from her. He shewed the greatest knowledge of humanity with the greatest fellow-feeling for it. (IV:347)

Keats's 'Presider'

Keats began to study Shakespeare carefully from the spring of 1817, and became a committed bardolater in the most profound sense. His admiration for Hazlitt developed concomitantly, and the two influences interacted with and reinforced each other. It was Hazlitt's views of Shakespeare that Keats found the most congenial and which consequently shed most light on his own, and in reading Shakespeare closely Keats also came to understand Hazlitt's overall critical stance more thoroughly. The dramatic genius of Shakespeare which Hazlitt had persistently expounded entered into Keats's thoughts so deeply that it developed into a Shakespearean poetic ideal that he himself strove for, which was epitomized in his conception of negative capability inspired by the thought that Shakespeare possessed it 'so enormously'. This was indeed a more intellectual reflection on Shakespeare, but like Keats's other 'axioms', it evolved from the deep affections of his heart. It was Keats's ardent bardolatry that paved the way for his later understanding of Shakespeare 'to his depths' (*KL* I:239).

Keats's reverence for Shakespeare is most famously expressed in his letter to Haydon on 10 May 1817: 'I remember your saying that you had notions of a good Genius presiding over you – I have of late had the same thought . . . . Is it too daring to Fancy Shakspeare this Presider?' (*KL* I:141–2). The letter was written from Margate, when he left London to start the composition of *Endymion*, and Shakespeare did 'preside over' his whole trip. When Keats had just arrived at Southampton on 15 April, he wrote to his brothers, 'I felt rather lonely this Morning at breakfast so I went and unbox'd a Shakspeare' (see Figure 1.1),[14] and then quoting *The Tempest* obliquely, he adds, 'There's my Comfort' (*KL* I:128). Two days later, he wrote to Reynolds that he 'found a head of Shakspeare which [he] had not before seen', and '[liking] it extremely', he hung it over his books (*KL* I:130). He tells Haydon about this portrait again in the letter in which he fancies Shakespeare his presider:

> When in the Isle of W<h>ight I met with a Shakspeare in the Passage of the House at which I lodged – it comes nearer to my idea of him than any I have seen – I was but there a Week yet the old Woman made me take it with me though I went off in a hurry – Do you not think this is ominous of good? (*KL* I:142)

At the end of the letter, Keats readily takes Haydon's advice of 'dont despair' and 'read Shakespeare' (*KL* I:135), promising, 'I never quite despair and I read Shakspeare – indeed I shall I think never read any other Book much . . . . I am very near Agreeing with Hazlit that Shakspeare is enough for us' (*KL* I:143).

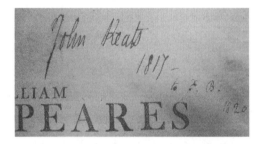

FIGURE 1.1   Keats's inscription in Shakespeare's First Folio

The trip almost became a spiritual homage to Shakespeare. Even the new coastal surrounding reminded Keats of his presider: 'the passage in Lear – "Do you not hear the Sea?" – has haunted me intensely' (*KL* I:132). Keats writes to Reynolds in the same letter that, inspired by the haunting ghost of *Lear*, he had composed the sonnet 'On the Sea' and 'slept the better . . . for it' (*KL* I:133). When he continued the letter the following day, noticing the date was 18 April, his thoughts turned to Shakespeare again: 'On the 23rd was Shakespeare born – now If I should receive a Letter from you and another from my Brothers on that day 't would be a parlous good thing' (*KL* I:133). Keats then exclaims, 'Whenever you write say a Word or two on some Passage in Shakespeare that may have come rather new to you; which must be continually happening, notwithstandᵍ that we read the same Play forty times' (*KL* I:133), and then cites two examples from *The Tempest* to demonstrate it. In the same letter are also found echoes of *A Midsummer Night's Dream* and *The Merry Wives of Windsor*.

Keats's letters, especially around this time, are saturated in quotations from and reminiscences of Shakespeare, in which *King Lear* and *Hamlet* emerge as the most frequent, and *The Tempest* probably ranks third. In his letter to Reynolds on 22 November 1817, he tells him that in his current stay at Burford Bridge, 'one of the three Books I have with me is Shakespear's Poems'[15] (see Figure 1.2), and expresses to Reynolds the exhilaration of reading them again: 'I neer found so many beauties in the sonnets – they seem to be full of fine things said unintentionally – in the intensity of working out conceits – Is this to be borne? Hark ye!' (*KL* I:188); he subsequently quotes Sonnet 12. The exhilaration, however, is accompanied with a sense of anxiety: 'He has left nothing to say about nothing or any thing', and again, 'He overwhelms a genuine Lover of Poesy with all manner of abuse' (*KL* I:189). Keats then cites *Love's Labour's Lost, Venus and Adonis*, Sonnets 17, 19, 21 and ends the letter by jumbling lines from *I Henry IV, The Merry Wives of Windsor, Troilus and Cressida, King John*, and *Romeo and Juliet*.

While his immersion in Shakespeare grew deeper, Keats also became more keenly aware of the nature of Shakespeare's genius. Writing to Hunt on 10 May 1817, Keats picks up a topic of controversy on Shakespeare's religious belief from an argument Haydon and Shelley had had back in January. Without any intention to settle the dispute, Keats offers one piece of evidence for each side, giving two quotes respectively from *Measure for Measure* and *Twelfth Night*, with 'the one for, the other against' (*KL* I:138). It was revealing that the argument had stayed in his mind for months, which must be one of the first occasions for him to be struck that both sides of the debate could find support from the works of the same poet, and yet neither of them could prove anything definite about the poet's proper self. This remarkable capacity of Shakespeare's to assume completely opposite personalities and metamorphosize himself into the dramatic personae began to sink into Keats's mind, and he would contemplate later that it is self-annihilation that makes it possible for the poet to entertain

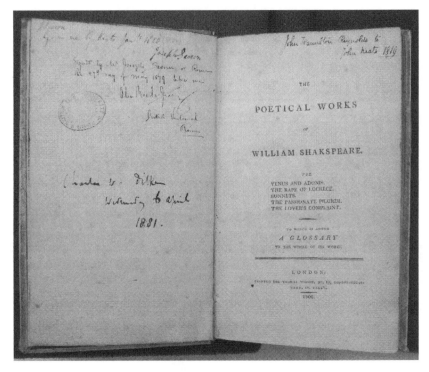

FIGURE 1.2 Keats's copy of *The Poetic Works of William Shakspeare*

contradictions. The 'poetical character' 'has no self'; 'it enjoys light and shade', with as much 'relish of the dark side of things' as 'taste for the bright one'.

Thus Keats's reading of Shakespeare, together with his exposure to Hazlitt's Shakespeare criticism, fermented his growth, and along with his own maturation, his thoughts on Shakespeare also became more reflective and increasingly bound up with his own contemplations over the roles of the poet and poetry. This gradual change became especially evident after he had finished *Endymion*, when Shakespeare led him to the thoughts centred on negative capability. In the same letter, we remember, Keats has pondered the 'intensity' of *Lear* as an exemplification of 'the excellence of every Art'. In about a month's time, he re-read the play and wrote the sonnet 'On Sitting Down to Read *King Lear* Once Again' (see Figure 1.3). He related this to Bailey on 23 January 1818, 'I sat down to read King Lear yesterday, and felt the greatness of the thing up to the writing of a Sonnet preparatory thereto' (*KL* I:212),[16] and to his brothers again on the same day:

> I think a little change has taken place in my intellect lately – I cannot bear to be uninterested or unemployed, I, who for so long a time, have been addicted

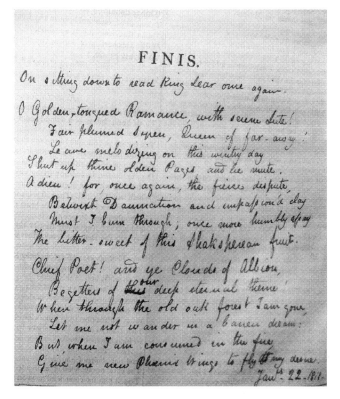

FIGURE 1.3   'On Sitting Down to Read *King Lear* Once Again' in Keats's Folio

to passiveness – Nothing is finer for the purposes of great productions, than a very gradual ripening of the intellectual powers – As an instance of this – observe – I sat down yesterday to read King Lear once again the thing appeared to demand the prologue of a Sonnet, I wrote it & began to read – (*KL* I:214)

His intellectual ripening, taking place in the process of his own poetic creation, was nourished by his intense absorption of Shakespeare along the way, and in turn, it also brought him deeper insights into the bard. Yet a month later, in his letter to Taylor dated 27 February, Keats writes, 'thank God I can read and perhaps understand Shakspeare to his depths' (*KL* I:239).

Direct quotations from or allusions to Shakespeare became less dense in Keats's later letters, but the bardolatry persisted, with its impact growing more profound and pervasive almost as an indispensable part of the life experience. Writing to Bailey on 13 March 1818 on the contemplation that 'Ethereal thing may . . . be . . . real, divided under three heads', 'Things real', 'Things semireal' and 'no things', Keats puts 'passages of Shakspeare' together with 'existences of Sun Moon & Stars' as 'Things real' (*KL* I:242–3). The thought is reiterated to Bailey in his letter dated 14 August 1819: 'I am convinced more and more every day that (except the human friend Philosopher) a fine writer is the most genuine Being in the World', and Shakespeare is again the first example coming to his mind to illustrate this: 'Shakspeare and the paradise Lost every day become greater wonders to me' (*KL* II:139).

Meanwhile, Shakespeare continued to be regarded by Keats as an auspicious force not only for his poetic creation but for his daily life. After George and Georgiana had emigrated, John wrote to them on 16 December 1818, 'sometimes I fancy an immense separation, and sometimes . . . a direct communication of spirit with you'. He made a proposition:

> [W]hen I tell you that I shall read a passage of Shakspeare every Sunday at ten o Clock – you read one [a]t the same time and we shall be as near each other as blind bodies can be in the same room. (*KL* II:5)

Though not really practicing it, Keats began to write in a like manner in his correspondence with them, by including minute details of his life in his letters so that they could continue to feel this spiritual closeness with each other. Such details are often associated with his presider, as if that is the most telling part of his life. In the letter on 14 February 1819, Keats tells them, 'I am sitting opposite the Shakspeare I brought from the Isle of wight – and I never look at it but the silk tassels on it give me as much pleasure as the face of the Poet itself' (*KL* II:62). When the journal letter proceeds to 12 March, after giving them a precise description of his present posture of writing, he continues, 'Could I see the same thing done of any great Man long since dead it would be a great delight: as to know in what position Shakspeare sat when he began "To be or not to be"' (*KL* II:73). In Keats's life, Shakespeare has indeed become a 'Thing real', so much so that his mind can drift to Shakespeare even in his love letters. Writing to Fanny Brawne in February 1820, Keats wonders in amusement, 'what would Rousseau have said at seeing our little correspondence! What would his Ladies have said!', but he dismisses the Romantic hero immediately: 'I don't care much – I would sooner have Shakspeare's opinion about the matter'[17] (*KL* II:266).

While Shakespeare became increasingly bound up with his very existence, Keats, with his own keener awareness of human sufferings, came to perceive his presider as having had a similar experience which made him the great tragic poet. In his journal letter on 19 February 1819, Keats muses, 'A Man's life of any worth is a continual allegory – and very few eyes can see the Mystery of his life – a life like the scriptures, figurative'. Then he contrasts Shakespeare, who transformed miseries of life into great tragedies, with Byron, who posed as a misanthrope within and without his poetry: 'Lord Byron cuts a figure – but he is not figurative – Shakspeare led a life of Allegory; his works are the comments on it – ' (*KL* II:67). Later in 1819, in his letter dated 9 June, judging that Boiardo 'was a noble Poet of Romance; not a miserable and mighty Poet of the human Heart', Keats sees Shakespeare as the exemplar of a poet whose soul is made by this tormenting world: 'The middle age of Shakspeare was all couded over; his days were not more happy than Hamlet's who is perhaps more like Shakspeare himself in his common every day Life than any other of his Characters' (*KL* II:115–6).

As Keats fancied, his short creative life, especially the most formative period, was presided over by Shakespeare, but Shakespeare meant for him much more than just a 'good genius' of poetry. As much as Keats owed his aesthetic understandings of Shakespeare to Hazlitt, his bardolatry became most intimately involved with his whole existence both as a poet and as a human being. His veneration of Shakespeare was thorough and unreserved, not confined to any particular plays or poems. But one play stood out much more prominently than others as his most significant presider, particularly in the formation of negative capability. To understand negative capability to its depths, we must re-read the play as Keats did time and again.

Chapter 2

King Lear and Negative Capability

The Romantic Restoration

King Lear has a towering stature among Shakespeare's plays. That Keats should feel closest to it is no more surprising than if he had found, say, *Hamlet* the most congenial of the plays, as many Romantics did. At the same time, there is one significant fact about *Lear* that needs to be taken into account: unlike other Shakespearean plays, *Lear* was experiencing a dramatic change in its fortunes in Keats's lifetime. The happy-ever-after *Lear* adapted by Nahum Tate that had dominated the stage for more than a hundred years began to suffer fierce attacks from the leading critics of Keats's time, through whose influence the play was gradually restored to something closer to Shakespeare's tragedy during the first half of the nineteenth century (Muir 1972: xli). There was even an anecdotal interlude as part of this process: the play was suspended in theatres for a decade from 1811 when the insanity of George III was finally announced, for it was too dangerously reminiscent of the contemporary royal circumstances (J. Bate ~~and Jackson~~ 93).

Tate's adaptation of *Lear* in 1681 is 'notorious' (Muir 1972: xl), but he is only one of many who have found the play too catastrophic to accept. He however took actions to revise it. The resistance to the catastrophe is most famously expressed by Dr. Johnson, one of the most important advocates of Tate's adaptation: 'I was many years ago so shocked by *Cordelia*'s death, that I know not whether I ever endured to read again the last scenes of the play' (161–2). What Dr. Johnson does not know as he concludes his essay on *Lear* with this comment is that he has put his finger on the central issue of *Lear* criticism for the centuries to come, which only shows that the shock Dr. Johnson experienced is not peculiar to the Neoclassical age.

Dr. Johnson explains his resistance to the catastrophe with typically Neoclassical logic:

A play in which the wicked prosper, and the virtuous miscarry, may doubtless be good, because it is a just representation of the common events of human life: but since all reasonable beings naturally love justice, I cannot easily be persuaded, that the observation of justice makes a play worse; or, that if other excellencies are equal, the audience will not always rise better pleased from the final triumph of persecuted virtue. (161)

Johnson has revealed here, interestingly enough, that it is not because the ending fails to '[hold] up . . . a faithful mirrour of manners and of life' (11) that he cannot accept it, but because it violates poetic justice. After all, for Dr. Johnson, 'the greatest graces of a play, are to copy nature *and* [emphasis mine] instruct life' (30). The popularity of Tate's adaptation is simply the dramatic illustration of the Neoclassic values most famously promoted by Dr. Johnson, who, mainly because of this stress on the moralizing significance of a drama to 'instruct life', became the archenemy of the Romantics as a commentator on Shakespeare in the century to come. The turn of the tide for *Lear* during the Romantic period exemplifies the change of values and taste from the eighteenth to the nineteenth century most dramatically. What Dr. Johnson had expressed about *Lear* became the very ground for the Romantics to turn over and restart from.

The catastrophe that shook Johnson was found to be powerful and inevitable by the Romantics. Schlegel is 'the first major commentator' (Harris and Scott II:89) to defend Shakespeare's ending, and Lamb soon follows by vehemently attacking Tate's adaptation: 'A happy ending!. . . . If [Lear] is to live and be happy after, if he could sustain this world's burden after, why all this pudder and preparation, – why torment us with all this unnecessary sympathy?' (Lamb 299). *Shakespearean Criticism* represents the nineteenth century as '[marking] an abrupt turning point' (Harris and Scott II:89) in *Lear*'s fate, but of course, none of these historical changes can be literally 'abrupt'. Coleridge was baffled over the 'monstrosity' (Coleridge I:52) of Goneril and Regan, and uneasy about the blinding of Gloucester (Coleridge I:59), and he accepted the play only on the ground that '*Lear* is the only serious performance of Shakespeare the interest and situations of which are derived from the assumption of a gross improbability' (Coleridge I:53). The persistence of Neoclassical values can still be felt, though Coleridge is among the leading figures in the Romantic period to change the fortunes of *Lear*, recognizing the titanic quality of the play as 'more terrific than any a Michael Angelo inspired by a Dante could have conceived' (Coleridge I:59).

As one of the most receptive English poets, Keats was attentive to the intellectual currents of his time and would have been familiar with the significant criticisms on Shakespeare initiated and rejected by his contemporaries. His strong interest in *Lear* cannot be taken out of a context in which an enthusiastic reappraisal of the play was taking place. And not only *Lear*, but Shakespeare in general, was experiencing a resurgence in Keats's lifetime, though for the Romantics Shakespeare 'is the Poet . . . rather than the playwright' (Shaaber 247). Among the most important Romantic critics of Shakespeare and of *Lear*, Keats took most from the critic he admired in his reading of *Lear*, as he did in his views on Shakespeare in general. After all, it is Hazlitt who unequivocally claims *Lear* to be 'the best of all Shakespear's plays' (IV:257).

The distinguishing quality of *Lear*, according to Hazlitt, is 'the greatest depth of passion' (IV:233), one of Hazlitt's key words in aesthetics which parallels Keats's 'intensity'. But this is not a new discovery, for the sweeping emotional power of *Lear* is uncontroversial. Even the Neoclassical archenemy recognized it, and in a most memorable way:

> The Tragedy of *Lear* is deservedly celebrated among the dramas of *Shakespeare.* There is perhaps no play which keeps the attention so strongly fixed; which so much agitates our passions and interests our curiosity. The artful involutions of distinct interests, the striking opposition of contrary characters, the sudden changes of fortune, and the quick succession of events, fill the mind with a perpetual tumult of indignation, pity, and hope. There is no scene which does not contribute to the aggravation of the distress or conduct of the action, and scarce a line which does not conduce to the progress of the scene. So powerful is the current of the poet's imagination, that the mind, which once ventures within it, is hurried irresistibly along. (Johnson 159–160)

Coleridge gives a similar description in a figurative mode: 'Of all Shakspeare's plays Macbeth is the most rapid, Hamlet the slowest, in movement. Lear combines length with rapidity, – like the hurricane and the whirlpool, absorbing while it advances' (Coleridge I:49).

Despite their common recognition of the emotional power *Lear* possesses, however, Johnson and Coleridge acknowledge this power in a very different way from Hazlitt. They both struggle to detach themselves from it by making moralistic analyses, while Hazlitt does not wrestle with this sweeping emotional experience but actively immerses himself in it. This attitude is shown at the very opening of his essay on *Lear*:

> We wish that we could pass this play over, and say nothing about it. All that we can say must fall far short of the subject; or even of what we ourselves conceive of it. To attempt to give a description of the play itself or of its effect upon the mind, is mere impertinence. (IV:257)

This readiness to submit oneself to the dramatic experience bespeaks an important critical attitude of Hazlitt, one which is experiential instead of deductive, receptive rather than judgemental. Only after making this reservation does Hazlitt start to comment on *Lear*, sticking to the critical stance he has established. He thus goes directly into the source and nature of *Lear*'s emotional power: 'the passion . . . is that which strikes its root deepest into the human heart; of which the bond is the hardest to be unloosed; and the cancelling and tearing to pieces of which gives the greatest revulsion to the frame' (IV:257–8). When he closes the piece by drawing some general artistic principles out of

Lear, he again maintains that 'the greatest strength of genius is shewn in describing the strongest passions' (IV:271). For Hazlitt, therefore, *Lear* is the best of Shakespeare's plays because Shakespeare, being 'the most in earnest' (IV:257) himself in this play, brings out the most passionate feelings the characters are capable of by his own fully exerted imagination. *Lear* is an epitome of gusto.

Hazlitt's view of *Lear* is consistent with his high regard for 'tragic poetry' as 'the most impassioned species' of verse, because it

> strives to carry on the feeling to the utmost point of sublimity or pathos, by all the force of comparison or contrast; loses the sense of present suffering in the imaginary exaggeration of it; exhausts the terror or pity by an unlimited indulgence of it; . . . and in the rapid whirl of events, lifts us from the depths of woe to the highest contemplations on human life. (V:5)

This comment on tragedy is based upon his general notion of imitation: 'Objects in themselves disagreeable or indifferent, often please in the imitation' (IV:72). One also remembers that he criticizes West's *Death on the Pale Horse* for failing to transform the 'disagreeable' into the pleasant because of its abstraction and absence of sympathy. *Lear*, on the contrary, triumphs in tragic catharsis because of its strong passions. Hazlitt's idea of deriving aesthetic pleasure from 'disagreeable' objects, similarly expressed by Keats as the evaporation of the 'disagreeables' into 'Beauty & Truth', can be traced to Hume, though the source of all of them goes further back to Aristotle's idea of tragic catharsis.

Hume in his essay 'On Tragedy' has inquired into the nature of the pleasure experienced at tragedy, and even used the same word 'disagreeable':

> It seems an unaccountable pleasure, which the spectators of a well-written tragedy receive from sorrow, terror, anxiety, and other passions, that are in themselves disagreeable and uneasy. The more they are touched and affected, the more are they delighted . . . . They are pleased in proportion as they are afflicted. (216–7)

The explanation Hume offers is that the passion excited by the painful circumstance in reality 'is so smoothed, and softened, and mollified, when raised by the finer arts, that it affords the highest entertainment' (223). However, Hume carefully adds, the disagreeables cannot be overstretched:

> An action, represented in tragedy, may be too bloody and atrocious. It may excite such movements of horror as will not soften into pleasure; and the greatest energy of expression, bestowed on descriptions of that nature, serves only to augment our uneasiness. (224)

Hume here is chiefly discussing violent actions of a spectacular kind, but the general effect he describes can very well apply to the predominant reception of

Lear as a tragedy that excites too much 'horror' to be 'softened', 'augmenting' too much 'uneasiness' to be alleviated. Hazlitt's view of tragedy, however, does not set any limit to the degree of the imaginary pain, but indicates that it is the most intense suffering due to 'disagreeables' that excites the most passionate tragic joy: 'sublimity and pathos' need to be carried 'to the utmost point', so that 'the terror or pity' can be 'exhausted' 'by an unlimited indulgence'. Hazlitt's divergence from Hume here is crucial in understanding his unreserved commendation of *Lear*, because the emotional devastation of the play is the very indication of its ultimate artistic accomplishment. This view is clearly revealed in his comment on the catastrophe of the play: 'The concluding events are sad, painfully sad; but their pathos is extreme. The oppression of the feelings is relieved by the very interest we take in the misfortunes of others, and by the reflections to which they give birth' (IV:270).

Hazlitt's defense of Shakespeare's catastrophe is therefore not only based, like Schlegel's or Lamb's, on its dramatic inevitability, but even more on the paradoxical power of such a catastrophe to transform itself into a cathartic power. Only by such a catastrophic dramatic experience and emotional 'oppression', can sympathy be inspired to the extreme degree needed to counteract the devastation and so allow 'the reflections' or deeper insights to be achieved. This paradox that Hazlitt finds in *Lear* could not be recognized by Johnson or Coleridge, for they resisted this 'oppression of the feelings' in the first place. Neither is it truly acknowledged by Lamb, though he is recognized by his friend as 'a better authority than [Johnson and Schlegel]' (Hazlitt IV:270). In his fervent objection to the staging of Shakespeare, especially *Lear*, Lamb betrays his idealistic reading of *Lear* and the refusal of the ugly, agonizing actuality that is indispensable in *Lear*:

> [T]o see Lear acted, – to see an old man tottering about the stage with a walking-stick, turned out of doors by his daughters in a rainy night, has nothing in it but what is painful and disgusting . . . . The greatness of Lear is not in corporal dimension, but in intellectual. (298)

Lamb has in fact expressed the common tendency of his contemporaries to romanticize Shakespeare and to overlook his darker, realistic side. For Hazlitt, however, the 'painful and disgusting' is an absolute artistic necessity, without which 'the greatest depth of passion' would lose its force. He reiterates this at the end of the essay when he generalizes from *Lear*:

> That the circumstance which balances the pleasure against the pain in tragedy is, that in proportion to the greatness of the evil, is our sense and desire of the opposite good excited; and that our sympathy with actual suffering is lost in the strong impulse given to our natural affections, and carried away with the swelling tide of passion, that gushes and relieves the heart. (IV:271–2)

Significantly, Hazlitt points out that it is exactly 'the pain' that provokes the equally strong 'pleasure', 'the greatness of the evil' that propels the powerful longing for good, and it is this very opposition that produces 'the greatest depth of passion' in *Lear*, which enables the audience to be emotionally involved in the dramatic experience to such a passionate degree that their passion in turn becomes cathartic and 'relieves' the pain.

If we look back on Keats's most explicit reference to *Lear*, out of which his articulation of negative capability develops, we will find how close Keats's view is to Hazlitt's: 'the excellence of every Art is its intensity, capable of making all disagreeables evaporate, from their being in close relationship with Beauty & Truth – Examine King Lear[1] & you will find this examplified throughout'. Keats has also noted the opposition of the 'disagreeables' and 'Beauty & Truth' as an indispensable quality of *Lear*, and that they are paradoxically related because of 'intensity', which parallels Hazlitt's 'gusto'. Both Keats's notion of 'intensity' and Hazlitt's idea of 'gusto' indicate an overwhelming effect of the artistic work to transport the reader or the viewer out of the familiar experience of the self into the otherness of the aesthetic experience, even when this otherness is confrontational and oppositional. Imagination in the Hazlittean sense, or sympathetic imagination, thus plays an essential role in both their notions and their readings of *Lear*. Further, since these remarks are made in connection with West's *Death on the Pale Horse*, Keats's comment on the painting also indicates his opinion on *Lear*: 'there is nothing to be intense upon; no women one feels mad to kiss; no face swelling into reality . . . . We have unpleasantness without any momentous depth of speculation excited, in which to bury its repulsiveness'. So Keats stresses again that only intensity can 'bury' the 'unpleasantness' of the disagreeables, and transform it into 'momentous depth of speculation', which comes very close to 'the reflections' Hazlitt believes the catastrophic end of *Lear* brings forth that are able to 'relieve' the 'oppression of the feelings'.

It is difficult to decide to what extent Keats's idea about *Lear* was influenced by Hazlitt and to what extent he simply found Hazlitt's view affinitive, but Keats's reading of Hazlitt's commentary on *Lear* provides some clue. In Keats's copy of Hazlitt's *Characters of Shakespear's Plays*,[2] his markings and annotations suggest an overwhelming interest in Hazlitt's view on *Lear*; except for one comment put at the end of the essay on *The Tempest*, all of them are found in the piece on *Lear*. One of Keats's marginalia is particularly revealing. At the side of Hazlitt's observation, 'That the greatest strength of genius is shewn in describing the strongest passions: for the power of the imagination, in works of invention must be in proportion to the force of the natural impressions, which are the subject of them', two crosses are put and the following comment is made by Keats:

If we compare the Passions to different tons and hogsheads of wine in a vast cellar – thus it is – the poet by one cup should know the scope of any particular wine without getting intoxicated – this is the highest exertion of Power, and the next step is to paint from memory of gone self storm. (Lowell II:589)

Though the two crosses seem to convey Keats's hearty consent to Hazlitt that 'the strongest passions' make the greatest poetic intensity, he has taken Hazlitt's point yet further. What Keats adds here is reflected from the perspective of a poet rather than a critic, and he is, while reading Hazlitt, also dialoguing with the greatest poet in English history, contemplating the creative process that has produced his greatest play. It reads much like a Keatsian version of 'spontaneous overflow of powerful feelings recollected in tranquility', but it suggests a closer connection to what T. S. Eliot was to propound about 'impersonality' a hundred years later. Keats has perceived a paradox in poetic creation: only by the disinterested imaginative power of the poet can passion in poetry be produced. Intensity is the product, but disinterestedness is the process.

Like Hazlitt, Keats is also trying to infer some universal artistic principles from the accomplishment of *Lear*. His thoughts start from the most striking quality of *Lear*, its intensity, pondering what composes this intensity, reflecting on the necessity of disagreeables, and understanding that intensity is only achieved in the tension and the paradox of the disagreeables and 'Beauty & Truth'. But that is not enough. As a poet, Keats still needs to apply this to his own creative process. His thoughts take several turns, and seem to find a moment of epiphany when they arrive at the quality of a great artist: 'several things dovetailed in my mind, & at once it struck me, what quality went to form a Man of Achievement especially in Literature & which Shakespeare possessed so enormously – I mean *Negative Capability*.'

To understand how *Lear* gave rise to the idea of negative capability, we need to first consider Keats's continuous reflections on the play.

'The Bitter-Sweet of This Shaksperean Fruit'

This letter was written in December 1817, about a month after the first draft of *Endymion* was finished, which was dated 28 November (*KL* I:187n). Incidentally, many other references Keats made to *Lear* are also closely bound up with his writing of *Endymion*. Earlier that year, when Keats went to the Isle of Wight to start *Endymion* in April, as soon as he arrived, *Lear* leapt to his mind from the surrounding seascape: 'the passage in Lear – "Do you not hear the Sea?" – has haunted me intensely', and the sonnet 'On the Sea' was promptly composed. The writing of *Endymion*, however, turned out to be far less prompt than the ideal plan laid down at the beginning of the poem. On 11 May, not even a month after he had started it, Keats tells Haydon in the same letter where he fancies Shakespeare as his presider, 'truth is I have been in such a state of Mind as to read over my Lines and hate them' (*KL* I:141), and adopts Edgar's language again to express his frustration: 'I am "one that gathers Samphire dreadful trade" the Cliff of Poesy Towers above me – yet when, Tom who meets with some of Pope's Homer in Plutarch's Lives reads some of those to me they seem like Mice to mine' (*KL* I:141). When *Endymion* was finally finished, his comment on West's painting written at the end of 1817 shows that *Lear* was not only still 'haunting' him, but had become for him a reference point for artistic works in general. More revealingly, just a month later, while Keats was preparing *Endymion* for the press, he chose to re-read *Lear* at the same time. On 23 January 1818, Keats wrote to Bailey, 'Tom is getting stronger but his Spitting of blood continues', which is followed by a dash that leads into: 'I sat down to read King Lear yesterday, and felt the greatness of the thing up to the writing of a Sonnet preparatory thereto' (*KL* I:212). That is how the sonnet 'On Sitting Down to Read *King Lear* Once Again' came to be. Remarkably, just as when *Lear* came to summon him in the springtime it had produced 'On the Sea', now it came again as an inspirational force urging him to poetic expression.

Keats bought his seven-volume Shakespeare in April 1817 and took it to the Isle of Wight, so it was quite natural for him to echo Edgar's lines, if he happened to be reading the play just at that time; though it was probably not his first reading, since *Lear* emerged in one of his earliest poems, 'Imitation of Spenser', written in 1814: 'I could e'en Dido of her grief beguile; / Or rob from aged Lear his bitter teen' (21–2). 'On the Sea', for all its close association with an immediate setting which is easily reminiscent of the cliff scene in *Lear*, still carries touches of sublimity that suggest Keats's quick absorption of the play. Moreover, the sense of sublimity is particularly conjured up by imitating the 'old shadowy sound' (4) of the sea, which is analogous to what Edgar does for his blind father, thus making the poem an appropriate prologue to a greater poetic endeavour which was about to begin.

If the opening of *Endymion* by *Lear* was simply fortuitous, then the conclusion by it was a very conscious quest for inspiration made by a reflective mind. As Keats told his brothers, this re-reading was 'an instance' of 'a very gradual ripening of the intellectual powers' 'for the purposes of great productions'. For Keats, by then, *Lear* became not only an exemplar of artistic intensity, but a symbol for his own intellectual growth and poetic creativity. There seemed to be an inexhaustible source of energy in the tragedy that could be constantly drawn on by the poet: in the process of reading and reflecting on the play the poet matured, and his maturing brought him back to the play which promised yet further nourishment. This interplay between the tragedy and the poet took place during the process of composing *Endymion*, without the experience of which the tragedy might very well have remained an artistic accomplishment external to him perceived by a passive mind. As already manifested in his thoughts on negative capability and on Hazlitt's commentary on the play, Keats was reading *Lear* particularly as a poet, whose eyes were constantly on its creative process while reflecting on his own. It seems a wonder how a young poet could have written his first ambitious poem with such a great tragedy haunting his mind from beginning to end.

Endymion was written, in Keats's own words, as 'a test, a trial of my Powers of Imagination and chiefly of my invention' (*KL* I:169). When the trial was done, he concluded that it was 'a feverish attempt, rather than a deed accomplished' (*KPS* 102). The conclusion is reached in the preface he wrote for *Endymion* on 10 April 1818, in which he also attributes the problem with *Endymion* to his immaturity, or, the process of growing out of immaturity, which corresponds to the 'gradual ripening' he told his brothers about several months back:

> The imagination of a boy is healthy, and the mature imagination of a man is healthy; but there is a space of life between, in which the soul is in a ferment, the character undecided, the way of life uncertain, the ambition thick-sighted: thence proceeds mawkishness. (*KPS* 102–3)

Given the fact that the poem was written with the example of *Lear* constantly in mind, it is not unreasonable to surmise that the frustration Keats had experienced in writing it and after its finish was directly related to his reading and re-reading of *Lear*. But it is not simply a matter of the anxiety of influence, as shown in his letter to John Taylor on 27 February, written when he was copying *Endymion* for its publication:

> If Endymion serves me as a Pioneer perhaps I ought to be content. I have great reason to be content, for thank God I can read and perhaps understand Shakspeare to his depths, and I have I am sure many friends, who, if I fail, will attribute any change in my Life and Temper to Humbleness rather than to Pride – to a cowering under the Wings of great Poets rather than a Bitterness that I am not appreciated. I am anxious to get Endymion printed that I may forget it and proceed. (*KL* I:239)

Endymion is a product of apprenticeship, the very significance of which lies in failure rather than success. As Keats came to see in retrospect:

> In Endymion, I leaped headlong into the Sea, and thereby have become better acquainted with the Soundings, the quicksands, & the rocks, than if I had <stayed> stayed upon the green shore, and piped a silly pipe, and took tea & comfortable advice. (*KL* I:374)

Being 'a severe critic on his own Works' (*KL* I:373), Keats actually realized the nature of its failure more clearly than his commentators, both friendly and hostile ones. As he writes in the preface, 'there is not a fiercer hell than the failure in a great object' (*KPS* 102).

Appropriately enough, his own criticism of *Endymion* is more fully revealed in no other place than the sonnet he wrote on the re-reading of *Lear*, which, by juxtaposing his *Endymion* with *Lear*, conveys poetically how the writing of the former had led him to the understanding of the latter 'to [its] depth', and how he was about to 'proceed' from where he had failed in *Endymion*: 'O golden-tongued Romance, with serene lute! / Fair plumed syren, queen of far-away! / Leave melodizing on this wintry day, / Shut up thine olden pages, and be mute' (1–4). The contrast between romance and tragedy is brought home to him only after he has tried his own hand with a romance, the failure of which brings him a deeper insight into the accomplishment of the tragedy of *Lear*: 'Adieu! for, once again, the fierce dispute / Betwixt damnation and impassion'd clay / Must I burn through; once more humbly assay / The bitter-sweet of this Shaksperean fruit' (5–8). In bidding farewell to romance and turning away to tragedy, the poet abandons serenity for fierceness, the beautiful for the sublime, which is revealed as soon as *Lear* comes into his poetic vision. The mood immediately shifts to one of violence, and words and images suggesting opposition and tension ('fierce dispute', damnation and purgation, bitter-sweetness) are introduced to capture the mood of the tragedy itself. Moreover, the 'dispute' may also be read as a description of the re-reading experience itself, which at once aggravates the hellish feeling of his own failure and inspires him to new creative endeavours. Then he evokes his bard:

> Chief Poet! and ye clouds of Albion,
> Begetters of our deep eternal theme!
> When through the old oak forest I am gone,
> Let me not wander in a barren dream:
> But, when I am consumed in the fire,
> Give me new phoenix wings to fly at my desire. (9–14)

Contrary to the romance which is 'golden-tongued' and 'far-away', Shakespeare, or *Lear*, as its association with 'Albion' suggests, is rooted in the human world that is immediate and historical, and can thus at the same time convey 'our deep eternal theme'. The oppositional force is again brought into play, but the paradox has shifted to the creative process. In the abundant images of birth ('fruit', 'begetter' and 'barren'), the young poet's anxiety for new poetic inspiration is clearly felt: an anxiety which, he has now become clearly aware, can only be attained by a painful process of transformation, as embodied in the burning images, of the clay hardened and to be shaped into a well-wrought urn, and of the phoenix burned to ashes and born anew, by going through the antagonistic forces of agony and purgation in the fire.

What this sonnet expresses poetically about the re-reading of *Lear* is consistent with his reflection on the play made about a month earlier in prose.

The intensity he assigns to *Lear* in his December letter is conveyed here by violent and massive images, and the tension between the 'disagreeables' and 'Beauty & Truth' that composes its intensity is captured by images of conflict that dominate the poem. More importantly, the chief motif of the sonnet is also a creative one, just as his statements about *Lear* in prose are also made from the perspective of a poet. The creative motif is directly provoked by his completion of the apprenticeship in *Endymion*.

All these thoughts are compressed in his succinct comment on *Lear* made in the negative capability letter, and the letter can be re-read in this light. The 'intensity' of *Lear* was not fully taken in by Keats until he had tried a long poem of a very different nature. It was almost from what he had failed to do in *Endymion* that he came to understand what *Lear* had achieved. *Endymion* was written with resolution and perseverance, but it was also written as a long poem for the long poem's sake, as Keats was perfectly aware when he started out: 'I must make 4000 Lines of one bare circumstance and fill them with Poetry' (*KL* I:169–70). In doing so, he violated one of his own 'axioms' on poetry, 'if Poetry comes not as naturally as the Leaves to a tree it had better not come at all' (*KL* I:238–9); but of course, this very axiom was not discovered until after the practice of *Endymion*. His romance may, as Woodhouse observes when vehemently defending Keats against the reviewers, 'contain more beauties, more poetry . . . and . . . much more promise of excellence' if compared with Shakespeare's earliest work *Venus and Adonis* (*KL* I:383), but in essence it comes short of a higher artistic demand of intensity as exemplified in *Lear*, for it does not have a solid experiential foundation in the human world which is by nature contradictory and diverse, and therefore is in want of tension and limited in dimension. Dwelling on the gigantic tragic force of *Lear* with his own 'thing of beauty' at the back of his mind, Keats easily perceives the lameness of West's painting which stands at the other extreme of failing intensity by being only 'repulsive' without exciting the opposite pleasure and 'speculation'.

His restless mind then passes from West to Haydon, then on to some other people in the artistic or literary circles that he has recently met, whom he describes to his brothers:

[T]hey only served to convince me, how superior humour is to wit in respect to enjoyment – These men say things which make one start, without making one feel, they are all alike; their manners are alike; they all know fashionables; they have a mannerism in their very eating & drinking, in their mere handling a Decanter – They talked of Kean & his low company – Would I were with that company instead of yours said I to myself! (*KL* I:193)

As he talks about his resentment of these men and compares wit unfavourably to humour, Keats's mind seems to be taken up by the capability of the ego to feel for the external world: if humour requires self-mockery and humbleness, then wit tends to be self-important and unsympathetic. He then relates that he 'had not a dispute but a disquisition with Dilke', whom he later characterizes as one 'who cannot feel he has a personal identity unless he has made up his Mind about every thing' (*KL* II:213). From the different kinds of egotism exemplified by Dilke and these men of wit, and probably also from the association of Kean with Shakespeare, Keats's train of thought turns to the quality of a great artist, as he has just articulated it in relation to the 'excellence' of *Lear* in contrast to the weakness of his own *Endymion* and West's painting. So he continues, as we have already seen:

> [S]everal things dovetailed in my mind, & at once it struck me, what quality went to form a Man of Achievement especially in Literature & which Shakespeare posessed so enormously – I mean *Negative Capability*, that is when man is capable of being in uncertainties, Mysteries, doubts, without any irritable reaching after fact & reason – Coleridge, for instance, would let go by a fine isolated verisimilitude caught from the Penetralium of mystery, from being incapable of remaining content with half knowledge. This pursued through Volumes would perhaps take us no further than this, that with a great poet the sense of Beauty overcomes every other consideration, or rather obliterates all consideration.

Obviously, the present thought on negative capability is not a result of 'consequitive' thinking, but its coherence with his contemplation of *Lear* and his other random reflections can still be perceived. The men of wit and Dilke acted as they did because their minds inhabit the narrow realm of the ego, a fortress guarded by all the values with which the ego is secure. Such a mind will never be able to produce an artistic work as great as *Lear*, which dramatizes a world of fierce opposition and runs on an immense scale far surpassing one's own familiar world. To conceive this tragic world where the beautiful and the disagreeable coexist takes a magnanimous mind, which is only nourished by actively exposing itself to the actual complexity and vastness of human experience itself. In the process of its composition, therefore, this mind has to be capable of suspending its moral judgement and getting rid of any philosophical certitude, since the artistic 'Beauty' 'overcomes every other consideration'. At the same time, to bring this complex and diverse dramatic world to life, or to render it 'truth', the mind of the artist should also possess a metamorphic quality, which will enable it to sympathize with and transfigure itself into each particular character. Such a magnanimous and metamorphic mind is termed by Keats as possessing 'negative capability', which entails, essentially, the capability of opening one's self to others, and of opening one's moral and philosophical considerations to actual experience, both of which will enable the artist to produce an artistic world rich and diverse, intense and plastic, which expresses a higher aesthetic concern.

Some of these points might not have been clearly formulated when Keats wrote the negative capability letter, but they are more fully expressed in his letter on 'the camelion poet', who, Keats explicitly asserts, 'has no self', and who 'is continually in for – and filling some other Body'. The camelion poet is an artist of negative capability, who is capable of staying in artistic 'speculation', or 'uncertainties, Mysteries, doubts', unlike 'the virtuous philosopher' who cannot help the 'irritable reaching after fact & reason'. Such a poet is characterized by his capability of enjoying completely opposite aspects of life, 'be it foul or fair, high or low, rich or poor, mean or elevated', which are the very qualities that compose intensity. Negative capability is also distinguished from the 'wordsworthian or egotistical sublime', thus giving full weight to its quality of self-'annihilation'. The very epithet of 'camelion' conveys Keats's clear awareness of the necessary metamorphic quality of a poet, which is only indicated in the negative capability letter. Thus, the disinterested, dramatic quality of a poet as the core of negative capability is expressed much more confidently and elaborately in the 'camelion poet' letter than almost a year before. This letter was written on 27 October 1818 to Woodhouse in reply to his anxiety over Keats's reaction to the severe criticism of *Endymion*, and not many days before Keats had just re-read *Lear* yet again.

In Keats's Folio, the date recording the re-reading, 'Sunday Evening Oct.4, 1818', is found at the side of Edgar's 'poore Tom' which is underlined (see Figures 2.1 and 2.2),[3] and Keats's letters confirm that it is around this time that the 'Poor Tom' in his own life 'gets weaker every day' (*KL* I:375). When Keats refers to his previous re-reading, we remember, it is preceded by an abrupt dash cutting short the situation of the sick Tom, and the gap made by the dash there is now bridged by this annotation. There is no way of knowing whether the camelion poet letter is directly provoked by his re-reading of *Lear* at this time, but, obviously, for a young man who picked up the tragedy again at the side of his dying brother, the tragedy was much more than just an artistic exemplar. *Lear* as the symbol for Keats had become increasingly richer, and had by now even acquired an autobiographical significance. It was almost like a personal companion that he could turn to whenever he needed emotional consolation. How could a tragedy as catastrophic as *Lear* offer solace to a young man who was experiencing the immediacy and cruelty of death by witnessing another young life dear to him wasting away? We do not know, for Keats rarely relates his personal troubles in his letters. But when *Lear* is next referred to in Keats's letters, his thoughts there shed much light on what had driven him to re-read *Lear* time and again when his own life came to crisis.

'Man is originally "a poor forked creature" subject to the same mischances as the beasts of the forest, destined to hardships and disquietude of some kind or other' (*KL* II:101): Keats quotes Lear's own words in his contemplation of the condition of human life which leads to his thoughts on 'the vale of Soul-making'. It is not surprising that the renaming of the world from the 'common

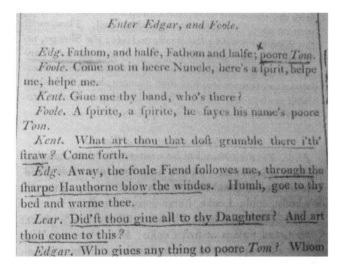

FIGURE 2.1   Keats's markings in *King Lear*: another re-reading

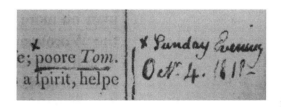

FIGURE 2.2   Keats's marginalia in *King Lear*: another re-reading

cognomen' of 'a vale of tears' is prompted by Lear's speech. After all, 'disagreeables' is one of the key words Keats has adopted to describe the play. But if back then the 'disagreeable' world of *Lear* was still perceived as an artistic necessity, by now it has become internalized as a way of life. Keats has read the tragedy when he was experiencing terrible pain in his own life, and he has now willingly accepted the tragic condition of human life for its paradoxical force of making a soul. Keats is not repudiating negative capability as many critics believe, nor is he contradicting his claim that a poet has no self. Instead, he is making the observation from a different level. Only a human being with a 'soul', which is not made until one has plunged oneself into actual human experience, can become a poet in the first place, for the artistic world cannot but be built on the very ground of human experience, as he has already realized from his failure in *Endymion*: 'That which is creative must create itself' (*KL* I:374). On the other hand, in the creative process, to endow this experiential world with life, or poetic truth, and to transform it into artistic beauty, the poet needs to be negatively capable, to purge away his personal self and become disinterested and dramatic. Paradoxically, however, negative capability cannot be obtained until after the soul has been made, for it is impossible for a poet to relish both the dark and the bright without first keenly experiencing both the fair and the foul. Negative capability is not only an artistic quality but also a human value, and the two levels have converged here in this letter written in April 1819, the spring of the great odes.

In this light, the tragedy of *Lear* itself can be read as a soul-making process. Its dramatic world is indeed 'a world of pains and troubles', in which 'the heart' of the characters in the play 'must feel and suffer in a thousand diverse ways', but its 'excellence' lies exactly in presenting such a world to a relentlessly truthful degree, without which the opposed qualities of beauty and truth cannot achieve equal intensity. At the same time, the heart of the reader also has to go through this tragic world in agony, but it is this agonizing process that awakens the heart and transforms it into a soul. With his dying brother at his side, Keats may be momentarily relieved from immediate pain by immersing himself in the dramatic world, but more likely, since the world of *Lear* is no less painful than real life, he may be seeking for strength to face the human tragedy by experiencing the poetic tragedy that dramatizes the worst possibilities in human life. In coming back to *Lear* time and again, symbolically, Keats was not only 'making' his soul, but tempering and whetting it.

'Intensity' and 'the Fierce Dispute'

Since *Lear* has such a unique significance for Keats in so many different ways, his aesthetic ideas, centred on negative capability and developed in this period along with his reading and re-readings of the play, must be explored from within the play itself. Though the reflections Keats makes on the play, recorded in prose and verse over a period of two years, are continuous and consistent, their connections to the play itself have never been fully explicated, and they are usually expressed as impromptu comments, condensed but elusive. When scrutinizing the terms Keats has adopted to refer to the play, one is still faced with a gap between the terms and the play itself. When Keats uses 'intensity' to describe the 'excellence' of *Lear*, how does the word apply to the play? What in the play answers to such terms as 'the disagreeables', or 'unpleasantness' and 'repulsiveness', and in what sense are they closely bound up with 'Beauty & Truth', or 'excite' 'depth of speculation', so that they can 'evaporate' or be 'buried'? What in the play inspires his compressed poetic designation of the play as 'the bitter-sweet of this Shaksperean fruit' that conveys 'our deep eternal theme'? And, how did he read the play so that he came to the realization that the play was conceived by a poet of 'enormous' negative capability, who, 'camelion'-like, could sample the whole 'cellar' of the wine of 'Passions' yet remain sober? When he returns to the play as a spring of emotional consolation and a 'vale of soul-making', what in the play offers the solace and how does it form the soul? We need to re-read the play to explore how it exemplifies these Keatsian terms and ideas, and, in turn, to illuminate these terms and ideas by their dramatic exemplifications in the play.

I shall first come back to the most direct reference Keats makes to the play, the passage where he refers to it with the key word 'intensity', which is 'capable of making all disagreeables evaporate, from their being in close relationship with Beauty & Truth'. At first glance, it seems difficult to reconcile Keats's comment with the play, and nowhere else does the play seem to speak against Keats more strongly than in its catastrophe, which is disagreeable to an unbearable degree, yet the impact of which does not seem to evaporate at all but overwhelms the audience. That is why Johnson's reaction to the ending is 'not of an age, but for all time'. It might be easy to recognize the lameness of Tate's art, but it would be hard not to share the shock Johnson experienced at the ending. When critics of later ages argue about the meaning of the catastrophe, they have but demonstrated again how upset they are by the way in which the play concludes.

The catastrophe, when Lear comes back to the stage with the dead Cordelia in his arms, is shocking, especially when it has been preceded by the reunion of father and daughter, which seems finally to have redeemed all Lear's sufferings; and the shock is aggravated by the complete absence of justification for such a malevolent fate. Cordelia's death directly brings forth the doubt about the nature of the universe, as Lear asks in agony, 'Why should a dog, a horse, a rat, have life, / And thou no breath at all?' (V.iii.305–6),[4] and Lear's death, an immediate consequence of the death of Cordelia, would seem to deny the significance of his former sufferings, making all his struggles futile. True, convention has it that tragedies conclude in deaths and comedies in weddings, but rarely do tragedies end in deaths that offer no redemption for the sufferings in life, thus stripping away consolations of any kind, moral or philosophical. In terms of the emotional impact of the ending, Johnson speaks for us all, for Cordelia's death is shockingly painful, and each time Lear is deceived by an illusion that she has come back to life, we wish with Lear that it was true. The deaths of Hamlet, Othello or Macbeth arouse deep pity and regret, but none of them is so cruel and disturbing as that of Cordelia, which, because of her simple and truthful goodness, tortures the audience with the longing for her to live, and the longing for what she embodies to persist. If it were not for her 'being in close relationship with Beauty & Truth', the catastrophe would not have felt so 'disagreeable'.

On the other hand, it is just in her death that 'Beauty & Truth' is perceived in a sharp clarity and experienced in painful poignancy. Both the disagreeable and the beautiful and truthful are pushed to extremes in the catastrophe, and their 'relationship' becomes closest, their 'dispute' 'fiercest'. Thus wrought to the most violent degree, the tension, however, is left unresolved. The disagreeables have not exactly evaporated, but coexist with the opposites they are simultaneously transformed into. The emotional devastation brought by the ending is so powerful exactly because it is two-fold: the shock and the pain brought by Cordelia's death by no means disappear, but they are experienced together with the clear realization of her worth brought home by suffering from the pain of being deprived of her, and thus with a sense of deep compassion for Lear by being brought to feel with him the pain of losing her. Incidentally, Keats's markings of the play also suggest a strong interest in Cordelia, whose extended speeches concentrated in Act IV, Scene iv, where she first returns to the stage, and the reunion scene are almost all underlined by Keats.[5]

Only by being able to perceive such a 'bittersweetness' of the catastrophe, can one yield to its experience instead of resisting it, and paradoxically, this perception cannot be gained without first allowing oneself to be taken over by the dramatic experience. Tate had to revise the ending, Johnson could not '[endure] to read again the last scenes', and many more cannot accept the catastrophe without first attempting to justify it poetically. Hence the interpretation of Cordelia as the Christ figure, regarding her death as symbolic of redemption and salvation, or on the other end, the reading of the play as an expression of nihilism chiefly based on the dark vision presented in the catastrophe. Both bespeak an inability to submit to the artistic experience, to stay 'in uncertainties, Mysteries, doubts, without any irritable reaching after fact & reason'.[6] By coming back to the play time and again and thus throwing himself into the dramatic experience, by being 'burned through' 'the fierce dispute' time and again, Keats approached what he saw as the negatively capable mind of Shakespeare, and in this catastrophe where the dispute reaches the fiercest degree, the 'enormous' negative capability of Shakespeare is most clearly felt, for only a poet who can embrace completely antagonistic visions without trying to unify them into a consistent 'philosophy' can give such an ending to the play. And only by understanding the ending of the play as a deliberate refusal to offer any easy resolution to the 'deep, eternal theme' of human life can we approach Keats's conception of negative capability, which, by the full participation in the artistic experience, 'overcomes' 'considerations' of poetic or philosophical justice. The tragic intensity, in this case, 'obliterates all other consideration'.

Artistic intensity, however, is not Keats's sole concern. This is the play Keats chose to return to when he was confronted with miseries in his own life, the one he associates with 'the vale of soul-making'; and the catastrophe, more than any other place in the play, can answer to his needs. By presenting such a relentlessly agonizing experience so powerfully, the catastrophe 'excites' 'momentous depth of speculation' about the truth of human life, stripping away any illusion one might entertain about it, and thus enabling one to 'cast a cold eye' on human reality unblinkingly, so to speak. Emblematic of the real world 'of pains and troubles', the catastrophic end of the play offers an imaginary occasion of extreme agonies for one to 'feel and suffer', and in this 'schooling' process, to have the soul shaped and fortified. Keats's markings indicate his keen emotional and meditative attention to the last scene; they become dense once Lear comes back onstage and are concentrated on almost every word Lear delivers afterwards, from the intensely agonizing 'Howl' to his brief, distracted turns such as 'Aye, so I think' (see Figure 2.3).

The catastrophe sheds much light on the Keatsian term of 'intensity' as imbued with poetic and human significance. It entails a thorough exploration of the tragic aspects of human experience, and a full expression of it without reducing it to metaphysical transcendence or resolution. Composed of discordant and conflicting forces, it is the poetic exertion of an artist's negatively capable mind, which has the intrepidity to encounter the darkest reality and the magnitude to embrace disturbing complexity.

All these ideas of Keats's are most prominently exemplified in the catastrophe, but they are manifested 'throughout', as Keats reminds us. Part of the force of the catastrophe derives from its violent plunge into disaster from the hard-won fulfilment in the preceding reconciliation scene between Lear and Cordelia which, in its turn, achieves an unparalleled touching tenderness by its sharp contrast to the former scenes of sound and fury with Lear raging in the external and internal storms. Those scenes of madness and chaos, again, grow from the collapse of the opening world of order and control thinly veiling menace and crisis. It is a play in which tensions are built up immediately and constantly, and they almost never slacken, not even when the play ends. These dramatic tensions offer multiple perspectives to observe 'intensity' in the Keatsian sense, which provide different pathways to reach the core of negative capability.

The play opens in the casual exchange between Kent and Gloucester, when Edmund is brought in and introduced. Then it soon shifts to a solemn and

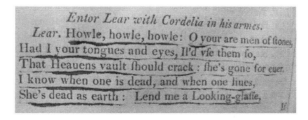

FIGURE 2.3   Keats's markings in *King Lear*, V.iii.

ceremonious mode when the king comes in, but the celebratory tone is much at odds with its 'darker purpose' (I.i.34) of the division of the kingdom, which, though already settled, is to be preceded on Lear's command by a love contest. Two daughters compete with each other in their fervent declarations of loyalty, whereas the third, whom the king fondly calls 'our joy' (I.i.81) and for whom he is ready with a 'more opulent' (I.i.85) portion, speaks 'nothing' (I.i.86). The ceremony then plunges straight into disaster, which is signalled in the echo of the blank 'nothing', breaks out in Lear's furious curses on Cordelia, and fully explodes in his banishing the interfering Kent. The play then subsides into a quieter mood, but the quietness is surrounded by a sinister air when the two daughters are found to be already conspiring as soon as turning their backs, thus piling up for the next conflict which is soon to come to the surface.

The dramatic intensity manifests itself in Lear's curses on Cordelia and Kent, which is the first chunk of continuous marking in Keats's copy. But as Coleridge rightly points out in his pioneer analysis of the opening scene, the conflicting elements leading to the intensity 'on which the whole tragedy is founded, are all prepared for, and will to the retrospect be found implied in' (I:50) the preceding part of the opening. Hazlitt notes on the first appearance of Cordelia to the similar effect: 'the story is almost told in the first words she utters' (IV:258). This preparation, however, is provided in a cryptic way, where the conflicts, instead of emerging to the surface, are only felt in curiously distorted forms, as Johnson describes in puzzlement: 'The King has already divided his kingdom, and yet when he enters he examines his daughters, to discover in what proportions he should divide it' (154). What lies behind this curious behaviour, as Coleridge sees, is '[Lear's] intense desire to be intensely beloved' (I:49) and '[his] *moral* incapability of resigning the sovereign power in the very moment of disposing of it' (I:54), and this drama of consciousness unfolded in the opening is exactly what the whole play is developed from. On the other hand, when Johnson concludes from his bafflement that '[t]here is something of obscurity or inaccuracy in this preparatory scene' (154), his word 'obscurity', though missing its point, does capture the way in which this opening is executed. Without the deliberately 'obscure' indications and tortuous manifestations of the conflicts, the following moment when the conflicts break out would be deflated in its energy and could not achieve such a drastic effect. The sharp turns of the dramatic course are built upon the sudden veering of emotion from anxiety for love to unexpected disappointment, interwoven with the contradictions between truth and falsity, form and substance, feeling and speech, intention and consequence. Without the complex psychology within Lear himself, the sharp disparity between Cordelia and her sisters, the confrontation of Lear's pride with Cordelia's equal measure of obstinacy to truthfulness, the contrast of the blindness of Lear in passion with the clear judgement of Kent in anxiety for Lear, the moment of intensity could not be accomplished. In turn, all these dark currents pushing forward to the flood of passions are only revealed when

Lear breaks out and thus, while giving us a strong sense of injustice, also arouses deep pity. The moment of intensity is defined by its violent destructive energy, but is buttressed with its pregnancy of emotions that run in these undercurrents.

The dramatic action reaches the next climactic point in the last scene of the first act, when Goneril makes her first open challenge and Lear bursts out again in curses, but as Hazlitt observes,

> [F]ine as is this burst of rage and indignation at the first blow aimed at his hopes and expectations, it is nothing near so fine as what follows from his double disappointment . . . when both his daughters turn against his age and weakness. (IV:263)

In Keats's Folio, both parts are heavily marked, with almost all of Lear's speeches underlined or side-marked (see Figure 2.4). Indeed, the latter scene is a much more elaborate parallel of the former, working on the conflict of the same nature, but more controlled in its gradual accumulation of the conflict which makes its release more overwhelming. Lear's outburst at Goneril in Act I Scene iv is almost as sudden and unexpected as his cursing of Cordelia in the opening, but in the latter scene he has been desperately struggling with his temper throughout. The whole scene is a pendulum swinging from Lear's adamant refusal to believe in his daughters' malice to his daughters' insistence on stripping away his illusions one after another; as Hazlitt describes it: 'His keen passions seem whetted on their stony hearts' (IV:260). Lear is already enraged when he rushes from Goneril to Regan, and the sudden departure of Regan

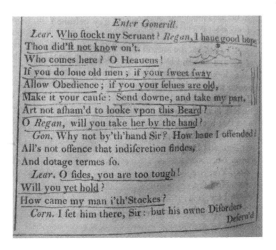

FIGURE 2.4 Keats's markings in *King Lear*, II.iv.

gives the first sign that Lear finds 'strange' (II.iv.1) at the opening of this scene, when he is greeted by Kent in the stocks. In his fierce denial of the fact that Kent presents to him, Lear shows his desperate resistance to the reality that is facing him, when he is yet again affronted by 'both he and she' (II.iv.12) who refuse even to speak to him. Finally managing to bring them out, Lear speaks to Regan sometimes in rage, sometimes with goodwill, seeking her pity for the wrong he has received from Goneril at one moment, charging her with violation of her natural obligation at another, when Goneril promptly arrives to break the last straw of his patience. The tempo quickens in the chorus of the two daughters' meanness, and the emotional effect overwhelms us when Lear has to plead to them in turn in humiliation. As the only scene where Lear is together with his two daughters onstage other than the opening of the play, it presents a hideous reversal: the king has turned from the endower to the beggar, while his daughters who have competed to make a more ardent pledge of loyalty now beat each other in their capacity of outrageous mercilessness. In their naked bargaining of the number of the knights Lear insists on keeping, the tension between pity for Lear and the relentlessness of his daughters reaches an unbearably sharp degree, when Lear finally breaks out and breaks down:

> O, reason not the need! Our basest beggars
> Are in the poorest thing superfluous.
> Allow not nature more than nature needs,
> Man's life's as cheap as beast's. Thou art a lady;
> If only to go warm were gorgeous,
> Why, nature needs not what thou gorgeous wear'st,
> Which scarcely keeps thee warm. But, for true need –
> You heavens, give me that patience, patience I need! (II.iv.259–66)

In a purely dramatic sense, this scene can be regarded as the most intense in the whole play, with the conflict between Lear and his two daughters brought out into the fiercest contention. What has been latent about the two daughters is now exposed to full light, their disguises peeled off layer by layer, until their true faces are revealed in a glaring clarity. The Keatsian term 'disagreeable' easily comes to mind when one thinks of this scene, though in a very different sense from that in the catastrophe. The disagreeables here are produced by the unbearable 'repulsiveness' of Goneril and Regan, while those in the ending are caused by the emotional devastation brought by Cordelia's death and Lear's end. These two kinds of disagreeables, however, are but the double faces of the same coin, for the offensiveness felt at human evil flipped to its reverse side is the instinctive clinging to human good. As the emotional devastation in the catastrophe provokes opposite aspirations, here, too, this extreme 'repulsiveness' of his daughters paradoxically highlights the pathos of Lear. The strong antipathy to such daughters calls forth equally strong sympathy for Lear, which is exactly what brings the ever acquiescent Gloucester to risk his life to come to the king's rescue. The pity is further sharpened in the disparity between the present situation and the opening scene, and in retrospect, the daughters' shameless claim of love mocks at Lear's headstrong rashness in cruel irony. In presenting the daughters' horrifying remorselessness to such a truthful degree, the scene forces the audience to dwell on the darkest corners hidden in human nature, but it brings them to keenly feel the natural inclination of human beings to sympathy at the same time. Thus the 'disagreeables' here, as those in the catastrophe, though still prevailing instead of 'evaporating', also evoke opposite forces and by transcending their actual ugliness, generate artistic intensity. In a sense, the artistic power of this scene relies on Goneril's and Regan's remarkable capability of heartlessness, which indeed manifests an extraordinary negative capability of its creator, for he has to have 'as much delight in conceiving [a Goneril and a Regan] as a [Cordelia]'.

It is on this basis of 'repulsiveness' that the following scenes of Lear in the storm are developed, which are thus rendered with a dramatic inevitability that gives credibility to their wild energy and sweeping power that run beyond the natural bounds. Without much development of actual dramatic conflicts, these scenes manage to convey a fierce intensity almost solely by Lear's outpourings, thus transforming the dramatic intensity into a poetic one. With the eye of a poet, it is only natural for Keats to be particularly rapt by these scenes of poetic intensity, and his markings cover not only literally all of Lear's speeches in verse in these storm scenes (see Figure 2.5), but almost every single delivery of Lear in prose as well, not excepting 'I will keep still with my philosopher' (III.iv.164) and 'Come, good Athenian' (III.iv.168).[7] One of Keats's marginalia is also pertinent, though not put in the storm scenes themselves. Below the conspiring prose of Goneril and Regan at the end of the opening scene, which is also underlined, Keats writes:

How finely is the brief of Lear's character sketched in this conference – from this point does Shakespeare spur him out to the mighty grapple – 'the seeded pride that hath to this maturity blowne up' Shakespeare doth scatter abroad on the winds of Passion, where the germs take buoyant root in stormy Air, suck lightning sap, and become voiced dragons – self-will and pride and wrath are taken at a rebound by his giant hand and mounted to the Clouds – there to remain and thunder evermore –

By employing such images as 'the winds of Passion', 'stormy Air', 'lightning' and 'thunder' to paint Lear's 'mighty grapple', Keats here adopts a language that is resonant with the mood of the storm scenes, and 'voiced dragons' does capture the furious, massive poetic power of Lear's speeches in these scenes. Ironically, however, Lear's 'dragon'-like voice is only gained by his 'mighty grapple', the extreme psychological and physical sufferings concentrated in

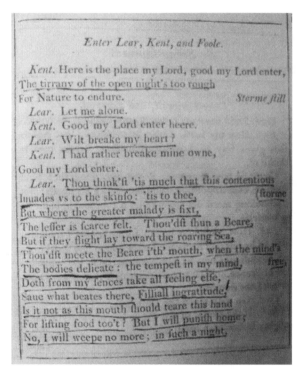

FIGURE 2.5   Keats's markings in *King Lear*, III.iv.

these scenes. The poetic intensity of these scenes, therefore, derives from the intensity of Lear's experience, without which Lear's wild railings would become but loud, hollow sounds.

As Lear concludes his last speech in the preceding scene with 'I shall go mad!' (II.iv.281) when the tempest sets in, the following scenes operate on the interaction between the violence and disorder in the natural realm and the human world, which correspond to and reinforce each other. As soon as Lear enters the scene, he bellows that wild nature would '[s]mite flat the thick rotundity o' the world' (III.ii.7), demonstrating at the same time the fearfully destructive energy for vengeance within himself. Immediately afterwards, he starts to accuse heaven of being unjust for sending forth physical afflictions to him as his daughters' 'servile ministers' (III.ii.20), while he is emotionally afflicted by them. Refusing to submit to the frightening natural elements, Lear is at the same time contending with the tumultuousness of his own mind. Pouring out his emotional pain with all his might in speeches as wrathful as the tempest, Lear, however, is also pleading to 'be the pattern of all patience': 'I will say nothing' (III.ii.36). But soon he is drawn back to the irrepressible fury and

pain caused by his 'pelican' (III.iv.72) daughters, thus again imploring the gods
to punish them, complaining pitiably, 'I am a man / More sinned against than
sinning' (III.ii.57–8). In this see-saw movement of the tortured heart between
defiance and self-pity, Lear is simultaneously caught in a physical predicament
he has never experienced before. Obsessed with '[t]he tempest in [his] mind'
(III.iv.13), he throws himself into the 'contentious storm' (III.iv.7), attempting
to exorcize his internal pain by exposing himself to external suffering. Yet, just
as his internal pain cannot be relieved by the external storm, his physical suffer-
ing cannot be denied despite his extreme emotional agony. The exigencies
of the body in fact momentarily drive him out of his own mind and give him
glimpses of the others outside his self, thus bringing him to ask the Fool, 'Art
cold?' (III.ii.66), and to meditate on the feelings of '[p]oor naked wretches'
(III.iv.29). All these contentions come together when poor Tom runs out of the
hovel. Lear immediately projects an alter ego on him, 'Hast thou given all to thy
two daughters?' (III.iv.49), but also finds him an ultimate alien other, '[n]oble
philosopher' (III.iv.160), as Lear calls him, who inspires Lear with insights of
cynical wisdom, culminating in his first extended prose speech, which is also
the speech Keats quotes in his soul-making letter:

> Is man no more
> than this? Consider him well. Thou owest the worm no silk, the
> beast no hide, the sheep no wool, that cat no perfume. Ha! here's
> three on's are sophisticated! Thou art the thing itself; unaccommodated
> man is no more but such a poor, bare, forked
> animal as thou art. (III.iv.95–100)

When Lear is brought out of the storm into the shelter in III.vi, these various
contending forces are found to be wrought together in a fiercer tension, yet
have also merged more seamlessly with the discordance becoming less percep-
tible. When Lear holds the imaginary trial of his invisible daughters with the
'[f]alse [justicers]' (III.vi.51),[8] his mind has finally taken its departure from
a too painful reality, and the boundary between the actual and the illusory
becomes radically blurred. The stormy world becomes Lear's deranged mind,
and the poetic intensity becomes interior.

The poetic intensity of these scenes, demonstrated particularly in Lear's
speeches, therefore, is achieved by the cruel physical and emotional pain that
Lear is experiencing at this stage, which, in turn, becomes the powerful impetus
for his defiance, thus instilling full vigour and energy into his voice. It is in
the unrestrained emotional power of Lear's speeches that his refusal to suc-
cumb to external afflictions is most clearly felt, and his majesty is thus most
forcefully demonstrated in these scenes where he becomes deprived of not only
the actual kingship, but of the satisfaction of his most basic human needs. As
he reflects, 'The art of our necessities is strange, / That can make vile things

precious' (III.ii.68–9). The closeness of these lines and Lear's experience in gen-
eral to Keats's thoughts on the soul-making world is too striking to miss. On the
other hand, Lear's defiance and majesty are also blended with self-obsession,
incoherence and confusion, all of which record the vivid movements of a mind
undergoing immense shock and pain. It is these discordant but truthful strug-
gles of the heart that make Lear's shattered, labyrinthine mind accessible to
the audience, bringing them to feel what Lear feels. These scenes, consequently,
are both awe-inspiring and heart-wrenching, because their fierce energy is
charged with deep pathos. The intensity is demonstrated in the poetic sense, but
it is the experiential and the emotional depth that gives the poetry the intense
voice.

On the other hand, underneath the main current of the plot concerned with
Lear, which does not have much actual dramatic development in the storm
scenes, Gloucester's story progresses with more striking vicissitudes. It is during
these scenes that Gloucester resolves to stand up for Lear, which leads to his
blinding at the end of this act, which concludes the violence of these scenes
with a finishing touch. It is one of the most terrible moments in the play, more
'disagreeable' than the confrontation between Lear and his two daughters at
the end of the previous act, and in one sense even more immediately horrible
than the catastrophe. If in the treatment of their father Goneril and Regan, as
well as Cornwall who plays the leading role in this scene, are still restrained by
the last residue of civilization in and around them, then their potential for
bestiality is fully released in their mutilation of Gloucester. And if the death of
Cordelia still involves some haphazard forces of a malevolent fate beyond
human control and understanding, then the blinding of Gloucester is undoubt-
edly an action of human will without any accidental or supernatural interven-
tion, thus producing unmitigated horror.

Not surprisingly, the scene 'shocks the virtuous philosopher', for whom
Johnson again becomes the spokesman. After defending Shakespeare's por-
trayal of the sisters on the ground that 'the cruelty of the daughters is an histor-
ical fact' (160), he continues:

> But I am not able to apologise with equal plausibility for the extrusion of
> *Gloucester*'s eyes, which seems an act too horrid to be endured in dramatick
> exhibition, and such as must always compel the mind to relieve its distress by
> incredulity. (160)

Coleridge, too, for all his admiration of the bard, finds it difficult to swallow
this scene: 'What can I say of this scene? My reluctance to think Shakespeare
wrong, and yet – ' (I:59), leaving his notes of this scene unfinished. It is indeed
a 'horrid' scene, even in the purely spectacular sense. *Oedipus Rex*, of course,
presents the same 'horrid' sight, but the eyes are plucked out by Oedipus him-
self, which makes the fundamental difference. What produces the horror of this

scene in *Lear* is exactly the fact that the violence is inflicted upon a victim whose offense is his 'betrayal' of these children whose relentlessness he could no longer bear, and the violence is conceived and performed by the same children. In Coleridge's notes, a line is later added to the above-quoted comment, 'Necessary to harmonise their [Goneril's and Regan's] cruelty to their father' (I:59). One wonders how long Coleridge had wrestled with this scene, but even the later note still indicates an effort of self-conviction 'from being incapable of remaining content with half knowledge', as if the only means to persuade himself out of the instinctive resistance is to resort to 'consequitive' reasoning.

The only way to reconcile the ultimate disagreeables of the scene is actually to stop being a 'virtuous philosopher', to release the mind from the 'incredulity', or in Coleridge's own words, to 'suspend the disbelief' in the possibility of such foulness. Moreover, the foulness of the scene, it is significant to realize, is not dwelt upon for its own sake, nor is Shakespeare equivocal about the monstrosity of the act. It is not a horror scene created for the effect of the grotesque, but presented together with its opposite 'Beauty & Truth', thus bringing about a two-fold effect of both extreme terror and extreme pity. In creating such an effect, Gloucester's long speech in this scene is crucial, which is underlined throughout by Keats (see Figure 2.6):

Because I would not see thy cruel nails
Pluck out his poor old eyes; nor thy fierce sister
In his anointed flesh stick boarish fangs.
The sea, with such a storm as his bare head

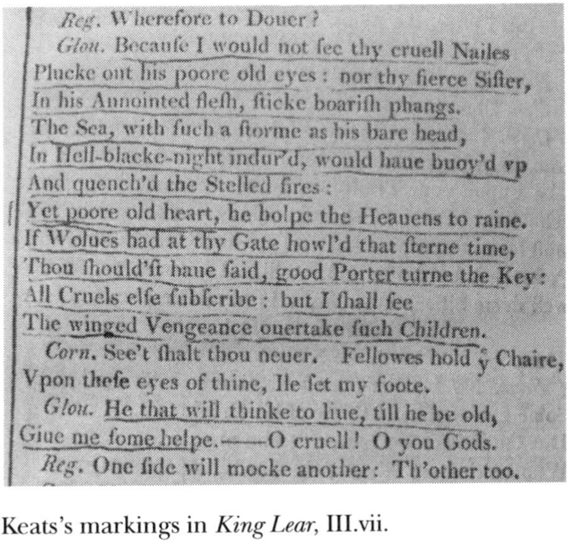

Reg. Wherefore to Douer?
Glou. Becauſe I would not ſee thy cruell Nailes
Plucke out his poore old eyes: nor thy fierce Siſter,
In his Annointed fleſh, ſticke boariſh phangs.
The Sea, with ſuch a ſtorme as his bare head,
In Hell-blacke-night indur'd, would haue buoy'd vp
And quench'd the Stelled fires:
Yet poore old heart, he holpe the Heauens to raine.
If Wolues had at thy Gate howl'd that ſterne time,
Thou ſhould'ſt haue ſaid, good Porter turne the Key:
All Cruels elſe ſubſcribe: but I ſhall ſee
The winged Vengeance ouertake ſuch Children.
Corn. See't ſhalt thou neuer. Fellowes hold ỳ Chaire,
Vpon theſe eyes of thine, Ile ſet my foote.
Glou. He that will thinke to liue, till he be old,
Giue me ſome helpe.——O cruell! O you Gods.
Reg. One ſide will mocke another: Th'other too.

FIGURE 2.6 Keats's markings in *King Lear*, III.vii.

In hell-black night endured, would have buoyed up,
And quenched the stelléd fires.
Yet, poor old heart, he holp the heavens to rage.
If wolves had at thy gate howled that dern time,
Thou shouldst have said 'Good porter, turn the key.'
All cruels else subscribed. But I shall see
The wingéd vengeance overtake such children. (III.vii.57–67)

The speech is delivered to accuse Regan and Cornwall, but it simultaneously explains the motives that have driven him to take such a dangerous action. What Gloucester expresses is to be echoed by Cordelia when she later learns about the afflictions of Lear on this night, 'Mine enemy's dog, / Though he had bit me, should have stood that night/Against my fire' (IV.vii.36–8). What they both manifest is an instinctive inclination to kindness in human nature that will spontaneously yield to compassion at the sight of a sufferer, even when one's own interest may be threatened by relieving the sufferer. The intensity of sympathy is powerful enough to overwhelm the egotistical concern, and that is why Gloucester, being customarily compliant, can risk his life to help Lear. It is against the eyes of such a person that Cornwall '[sets his] foot' (III.vii.69), which makes the scene particularly horrifying, for it not only performs a terribly atrocious action, but also plunges the audience into an abysmal darkness by bringing them face to face with what heinousness human nature is capable of. On the other hand, it is exactly such a shocking cruelty that provokes its counter forces, which are equally unforeseen, as shown when Cornwall's own servant who is not involved in the plot in any way stands up to kill Cornwall, and when other servants who are not even significant enough to have their proper names in the play risk their lives to help Gloucester. They are merely spectators as the audience are, but they have chosen to stand with Gloucester as Gloucester has done with Lear. The horror of the scene, therefore, is at once reinforced by and poised against such forces of natural and simple good represented by both Gloucester himself and these servants. With them, the audience, too, just as they will feel a natural sympathy with the good at the death of Cordelia, will in this scene experience an instinctive repugnance for monstrosity in witnessing this utter horror. It is with the same surge of sympathy that Keats in the sonnet inspired by the play evokes this scene: 'O ye who have your eyeballs vext and tir'd, / Feast them upon the wideness of the sea' ('On the Sea' 9–10).

This scene plunges the play to the lowest point, with both Lear and Gloucester at the nadir of their fates. From here on, the play picks up gradually, with Edgar coming together with Gloucester, though in disguise, Cordelia returning to avenge Lear, and even Albany beginning to turn against Goneril, all of which seem to suggest some hope that justice is after all about to prevail. Lear, however, has been absent all the while, and when he comes back, the faint hope is immediately shattered in his perfectly developed mad eloquence blending 'matter' with 'impertinency' (IV.vi.168). It is also in this scene that Lear and Gloucester appear onstage together, the two intertwining plots of the play finally converging. It is a long scene of large scope, moving from Gloucester's attempted suicide and Edgar's rescue of him to Lear's uncurbed wild speeches, with the former part resembling a fantasy in exemplifying the magically deceptive power of imagination, while the latter approaches the theatre of the absurd in Lear's adept shifting between '[r]eason' and 'madness' (IV.vi.169). Ironically discordant as they are, the two parts are joined with each other, thus binding the whole scene in tension and ambivalence. On the other hand, the first part with Gloucester and Edgar poses a sharp contrast with the blinding scene, offering warmth and comfort in the midst of the darkness, while the latter part when Lear is '[a]s mad as the vexed sea' (IV.iv.2) will be similarly pacified and tranquilized by the immediately following reunion of Lear and Cordelia. The oppositions within and without this scene make it particularly intense, and intense on various levels. The first part of this scene is the one which 'haunted' Keats in his trip to the Isle of Wight, and the latter part focusing on Lear is found to be densely marked by him, sometimes underscored or side-marked with double lines, and a few even with triple lines (see Figure 2.7).

The particular line 'haunting' Keats is Edgar's 'Hark, do you hear the sea?' (IV.vi.4), and his following extended description of the imaginary cliff is the

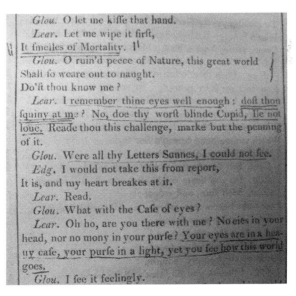

FIGURE 2.7 Keats's markings in *King Lear*, IV.vi.

passage that directly provoked Keats's sonnet 'On the Sea', which is alluded to again in his letter to Haydon when revealing his frustration about *Endymion*:

> How fearful
> And dizzy 'tis, to cast one's eyes so low!
> The crows and choughs that wing the midway air
> Show scarce so gross as beetles. Halfway down
> Hangs one that gathers sampire, dreadful trade!
> Methinks he seems no bigger than his head.
> The fishermen, that walk upon the beach,
> Appear like mice; and yond tall anchoring bark,
> Diminished to her cock; her cock, a buoy
> Almost too small for sight. The murmuring surge,
> That on the unnumbered idle pebble chafes,
> Cannot be heard so high. I'll look no more,
> Lest my brain turn, and the deficient sight
> Topple down headlong. (IV. vi.11–24)

On the same passage, Johnson expresses a very different opinion:

> This description has been much admired since the time of *Addison*, who has remarked, with a poor attempt at pleasantry, that *he who can read it without being giddy has a very good head, or a very bad one.* The description is certainly not mean, but I am far from thinking it wrought to the utmost excellence of poetry. He that looks from a precipice finds himself assailed by one great and dreadful image of irresistible destruction. But this overwhelming idea is dissipated and enfeebled from the instant that the mind can restore itself to the observation of particulars, and diffuse its attention to distinct objects. (158–9)

Johnson's insistence on a sober, literal-minded stance certainly forms an interesting contrast with the poetic inspiration Keats finds in it. But whether the passage in itself is a poetic feat is beside the point, for, as a speech delivered by a dramatic character in a particular dramatic situation, its poetic merit is bound up with its dramatic relevance, and Edgar's speech here is effective because its poetic power intensifies the dramatic context. For his father who is bent on ending his life from the supposed cliff Edgar can only conjure up a fictional one and, to save his father's life, he cannot afford to fail in this deception. It is a deception analogous to a poetic endeavour, for all he can resort to are imagination and words. His speech is powerful not simply because it is graphic, but because its poetic 'conceit' is called up from the depth of Edgar's imaginative resources out of his anxiety to 'cure' his father of 'despair' (IV.vi.33,34), to light up and console his father's world which has become 'All dark and comfortless'

(III.vii.88). It is by this poetic cliff that Gloucester is rescued from complete hopelessness, and the audience too delivered from the abysmal blinding scene.

But this poetic consolation is promptly cut short when Lear runs onstage crowned with wild flowers. As soon as Lear starts speaking, the stage turns into a world of chaos; all order falls apart and is swept away. His first utterance is an unfaltering declaration of his majesty, 'I am the king himself' (IV.vi.84), but soon follows a completely opposite assertion of his humanity, 'They told me I was everything. 'Tis a lie, I am not ague-proof' (IV.vi.102–3). The same violent swing of attitude repeats itself when he first affirms his identity to Gloucester, 'Aye, every inch a king!' (IV.vi.105), and then replies to Gloucester's request to 'kiss that hand' (IV.vi.130) with 'Let me wipe it first; it smells of mortality' (IV.vi.131). Not only is his self-perception vacillating from the extreme of his natural kingship to the other of his human fallibility, but the world outside the self is turned upside down in his denial of any distinctions. 'Adultery' (IV.vi.108) is no sin; 'Let copulation thrive' (IV.vi.112), for the human world is only the animal world in disguise, where his lawful daughters are no 'kinder' (IV.vi.113) than Gloucester's illegitimate son: 'Down from the waist they are Centaurs, / Though women all above' (IV.vi.121–2). Justice is arbitrary: 'Change places and, handy-dandy, which is the justice, which is the thief?' (IV.vi.148–9); 'thou [who lashes] that whore' only 'hotly lusts to use her in that kind / For which thou whip'st her'; and '[t]he usurer hangs the cozener' (IV.vi.155–7). Therefore, 'None does offend, none, I say, none; I'll able 'em.' (IV.vi.162).

In this monologic outburst of cynicism, Lear still finds his 'imagination' 'sweetened' (IV.vi.128) by the blind Gloucester. When Gloucester moans that he can only 'see' the world 'feelingly' (IV.vi.145), quibbling on 'seeing' and 'feeling' to indicate his actual blindness as well as his pessimistic world view, Lear impatiently retorts, 'What, art mad? A man may see how this world goes with no eyes' (IV.vi.146–7), and then elaborates more sardonically: 'Get thee glass eyes; / And, like a scurvy politician, seem / To see the things thou dost not. Now, now, now, now!' (IV.vi.164–6). The cynical and violent tone, however, suddenly gives way to sincerity and sympathy:

If thou wilt weep my fortunes, take my eyes.
I know thee well enough; thy name is Gloucester:
Thou must be patient. We came crying hither;
Thou knows't, the first time that we smell the air,
We wail and cry. (IV.vi.170–4)

The two streams of the play run into one now in Lear's recognition of Gloucester, and the collective address of 'we' binds the two fathers together as the common sufferers of ill fortunes. The solemn, sorrowful voice goes on, 'When we are born, we cry that we are come / To this great stage of fools' (IV.vi.176–7), but then takes a sharp turn again and bursts out into violence, 'And when I have stol'n upon these sons-in-law, / Then, kill, kill, kill, kill, kill, kill!' (IV.vi.180–1).

This is the last scene before Lear is restored to his senses, and by its invincible energy it brings the poetic intensity of the storm scenes to fulfilment. In this scene, Lear has lifted himself from painful reality to an almost ecstatic state of freedom unrestrained by reason in either matter or form. After breaking the fetters of logic and refinement, he has now achieved an unprecedented poetic power, undauntedly inveighing against the limitation of himself and the absurdity of the world. In a sense, this whole scene is a display of poetic power, first that of Edgar, then of Lear, but if the former part is poetically intense for its healing effect, then the latter achieves its intensity by its destructive power. As Lear's onstage spectators, Gloucester wails, 'O ruined piece of nature! This great world / Shall so wear out to nought' (IV.vi.132–3), and Edgar in his aside tells the audience, 'my heart breaks at it' (IV.vi.139). Together, they have expressed the closely fused 'bittersweet' effect of this scene: in Lear's frenzied celebration of the bitter wisdom he has gained, what is simultaneously called up is the terrible vicissitudes he has gone through, and thus his greatest poetic triumph is saturated in the pathos of his tragic fate.

Appropriately enough, this scene is immediately followed by his reconciliation with Cordelia, what Hazlitt calls 'the most affecting part' (IV:268) of the play. Simple and short as it is, its beauty and sorrow are intense enough to counterbalance the unrestrained Dionysian power of the preceding scene. His wild energy soothed in sleep, Lear wakes up to find Cordelia at his side. With a heart long accustomed to suffering, he can only conceive of the reunion as a consequence of death: 'You do me wrong to take me out o' the grave. / Thou art a soul in bliss; but I am bound / Upon a wheel of fire, that mine own tears / Do scald like molten lead' (IV.vii.45–8). The sight of Cordelia immediately brings back 'the fierce dispute / Betwixt damnation and impassion'd clay', torturing him with guilt and grief. The restoration of his senses follows in a painfully gradual process, first inquiring of Cordelia, 'When did you die?' (IV.vii.49), then asking himself, 'Where have I been? Where am I?' (IV.vii.52). Realizing that he is still alive, he wishes to 'die with pity' for having been only 'mightily abused' (IV.vii.53) by a ghostly vision of Cordelia. The weight of reality sinks in slowly, and the heart absorbs it warily, being long deprived of any hope of happiness. Cordelia then speaks to reassure him: 'O, look upon me, sir, / And hold your hands in benediction o'er me: / No, sir, you must not kneel' (IV.vii.57–9). The last line, in a tellingly low-key manner, brings out the most touching moment of this scene. Lear's kneeling down, a striking pose for a king and a father, conjures up all the memory of the once majestic and rash figure and the later horrible sufferings he has undergone which lead him to his present repentance and humility, and thus brings the scene in one action right to the climax of its emotional intensity.

Then Lear speaks:

Pray, do not mock me.
I am a very foolish fond old man,
Fourscore and upward, not an hour more nor less;
And, to deal plainly,
I fear I am not in my perfect mind.
Methinks I should know you, and know this man;
Yet I am doubtful; for I am mainly ignorant
What place this is; and all the skill I have
Remembers not these garments; nor I know not
Where I did lodge last night. Do not laugh at me;
For, as I am a man, I think this lady
To be my child Cordelia. (IV.vii.60–71)

It is Lear's first speech after regaining sanity, and it is also the first, and last,
utterance in the whole play where he '[deals] plainly' with both the self and the
other. The self-portrayal is made in a temperate tone, and the uncertainty of his
mental state as well as the ignorance of the external world are also honestly
admitted. Only after thus preparing himself is Lear able to achieve the recogni-
tion of Cordelia, which is still preceded first by a repeated request of 'do not
laugh at me', and then by the condition 'as I am a man', indicating the neces-
sary realization of his human limitations before the reunion with Cordelia can
take place, before it is eventually accomplished when 'this lady' becomes 'my
child Cordelia'. Cordelia, who once could only 'love' yet 'be silent' (I.i.60), now
answers, 'And so I am, I am' (IV.vii.71), the repetition conveying eagerness, and
the simplicity of 'I am' reaching out from the essence of her self with love to
reunite with Lear. After the recognition immediately follows contrition: 'I know
you do not love me; for your sisters / Have, as I do remember, done me wrong. /
You have some cause, they have not' (IV.vii.74–6). To Lear's confession Cordelia
returns, 'No cause, no cause' (IV.vii.77), again a simple repetition charged with
emotion, powerfully expressing her forgiving and loving heart. The reconcili-
ation scene is thus concluded by Lear's speech which also becomes plain and
honest: 'You must bear with me: / Pray you now, forget and forgive. I am old
and foolish' (IV.vii.84–5).

The emotional intensity of this scene is conveyed by its simplicity and tender-
ness, which is quite different from any of the other scenes in the play, which are
composed of far more violent forces. Its isolated serene beauty seems ominously
vulnerable in the dark surroundings of the play, just as Cordelia is a figure too
good for this world. Yet this is exactly what makes this scene crucial, for without
this scene, the audience would be deprived of their only experience of emo-
tional fulfilment, and might be suffocated by the enveloping darkness of the

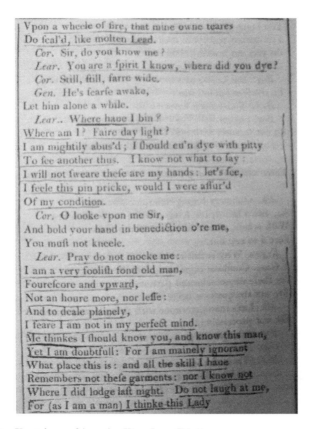

FIGURE 2.8 Keats's markings in *King Lear*, IV.vii.

preceding scenes. If the tragic intensity of the play cannot be achieved without those 'disagreeables', then this scene is equally indispensable, 'For shade to shade will come too drowsily, / And drown the wakeful anguish of the soul' ('Ode on Melancholy' 9–10). Nor would the catastrophe achieve such a thoroughly tragic effect. Unsurprisingly, Keats's markings of this scene start from Cordelia's speech (IV.vii.14–7) before Lear wakes up, and after that waking, run almost continuously to the very end (see Figure 2.8).[9] As the scene in the play crystallizing what 'Beauty & Truth' really is, this must have been a key scene for Keats, enabling him to realize that intensity has to be composed of both the ugly and the beautiful wrought to an extreme.

Preceded by such a scene, the play draws to its tragic end. This final plunge from ultimate fulfilment to total devastation intensifies the violent dramatic movement throughout the whole play, and by the very nature of its conclusion, refuses to resolve the tension. *Lear*'s tragic intensity is thus accomplished by keeping the opposites irreconcilable, and by perpetuating the dialogic energy generated from the sustained tension. The impact of *Lear*'s intensity on Keats is obviously profound, for the paradoxical and irreconcilable relationship between opposites becomes a perennial Keatsian theme, especially prominent in his mature poetry, which is the poetic expression of this aspect of negative capability.

'The Camelion Poet' and the 'Bye-Writing'

This 'close relationship' between contrarieties, then, lies at the heart of Keats's term 'intensity'. The term, we remember, is approached from its opposite exemplar, West's painting, on which Keats comments: 'there is nothing to be intense upon; no woman one feels mad to kiss; no face swelling into reality'. Brief as it is, the comment indicates another essential attribute 'intensity' entails, artistic truthfulness, or in the case of *Lear*, dramatic truthfulness. The stress on truthful or effective artistic mimesis indicates Keats's awareness of an artist's essential quality of dramatic imagination, which is picked up by him again when he says that a poet should taste 'different tons and hogsheads of wine in a vast cellar' and still remain sober, yet can at the same time convey diverse experiences with vivid life. The thought takes on a very clear shape when he changes the figure of the poet with that of the self-effacing 'camelion'. If intensity is the end, and the end is achieved by the means of a negatively capable mind, then the mind also needs to be sympathetic as well as disinterested. The dramatic world of *Lear* is such 'a vast cellar', composed of a multitude of characters, yet diverse as they are, they all 'swell into reality', for the 'camelion poet' has the metamorphic capability of 'continually' 'filling some other Body'.

This is fully illustrated by a moment in the play that Keats has noticed, though it is an apparently insignificant moment. Keats marked the conversation when Regan arrives at Gloucester's castle in Act II as the following (see Figure 2.9):

Reg. Was he not companion with the riotous Knights
That tended vpon my Father?
Glo. I know not Madam, 'tis too bad, too bad.
Baft. Yes Madam, he was of that confort. (II.i.95–8)

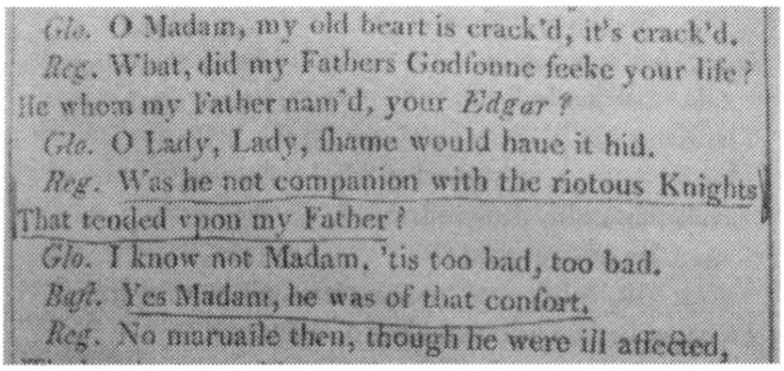
Glo. O Madam, my old heart is crack'd, it's crack'd.
Reg. What, did my Fathers Godſonne ſeeke your life?
He whom my Father nam'd, your *Edgar*?
Glo. O Lady, Lady, ſhame would haue it hid.
Reg. Was he not companion with the riotous Knights
That tended vpon my Father?
Glo. I know not Madam, 'tis too bad, too bad.
Baſt. Yes Madam, he was of that conſort.
Reg. No maruaile then, though he were ill affected,

FIGURE 2.9 Keats's markings in *King Lear*: 'bye-writing' and wrote in the margin (see Figure 2.10): 'This bye-writing is more marvellous than the whole ripped up contents of Pernambuca – or any buca whatever – on the earth or in the waters under the earth – '. It is indeed a 'bye-writing', an inconspicuous, fine touch among the much more violent tides of the play. The fact that Keats could pay attention to such a detail is very telling about his reading of *Lear*. What Keats finds 'marvellous', presumably, is how each character 'swells into reality' in this brief exchange. Losing no time to fabricate a crime for Edgar, Regan shows her unscrupulous, quick mind that works towards the sole end of securing her own interest. While Gloucester is caught up by his own 'cracked' 'old heart' (II.i.91) and so replies in distraction, Edmund matches Regan's dexterity by promptly seizing the chance to ensure his own advancement in confirming the slander. In the rushing flow of events, the characters betray their deepest natures in their instinctive reactions to the critical moments, and by capturing such tiny but revealing moments, Shakespeare leads his audience into the very quick of his characters. Without the capability of casting himself into the beings of his characters, the poet could not follow the vivid pulse of their lives in the ebb and flow of experience, and such a 'bye-writing' would be impossible. And the metamorphosis of 'the camelion poet' has to be thorough enough to infiltrate all the dramatic characters with life, be it 'an Iago' or 'an Imogen'. On the other hand, it also requires the poet reader to have a dramatically receptive mind to be able to discern such 'bye-writing'.

Interestingly enough, the 'bye-writing' that Keats finds 'marvellous' sketches two Iago-like characters, and in a certain sense, it is exactly in making the 'Iago[s]' 'swell into reality' that the ingenuity of a camelion poet is more clearly shown, for it takes tremendous audacity to take the plunge into the heart of darkness. The example here briskly outlines the common unscrupulous self-interestedness of Regan and Edmund, a dominant trait of both of them, which is also shared by Goneril. Yet these ungrateful children are presented throughout the play as a diverse lot, with not only Edmund standing apart from the sisters, but the sisters themselves clearly distinguished from each other. So is it difficult to group any characters in the play into a type, though there are naturally many parallels and antitheses, with the play operating on double plots, both of which are built upon conflicts of a similar nature. Lear as a human being is as different from Gloucester as fire from water, the one being chiefly driven by furious energy and the other often subject to corrosive despondence. While Lear has gone through all the drastic changes in desperate resistance and defiance, Gloucester has responded to the shocks suffered in his life with fatalism and despair. No more is Cordelia close to Edgar, with one characterized by reticence, the other constantly articulating his thoughts, even when he can only do so by making asides to the audience. It is in how each character, and especially each Iago-like character, is animated with an individual life that the poet's dramatic imagination is demonstrated most powerfully.

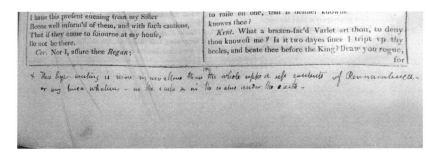

FIGURE 2.10   Keats's marginalia in *King Lear*: 'bye-writing'

Edmund, the Iago in *Lear*, is one of the first characters introduced to the audience. As soon as the play opens, he is brought forth onto the stage in the midst of his father's claims about the 'brazed' shame 'to acknowledge him' (I.i.9), the flippant jests about the 'good sport at his making' (I.i.21–2), and an apparently casual decision to dispatch him, 'he hath been out nine years, and away he shall again' (I.i.30–1). Meanwhile, he is presented as a young man who looks 'proper' (I.i.17), and speaks to Kent in humbleness: 'My services to your lordship' (I.i.27); 'I shall study deserving' (I.i.29). Inevitably, '[o]ur eyes have been questioning him' (I:50), as Coleridge says, wondering what lies behind the humble attitude of this 'proper' young man who has grown up in humili- ation. It is in these subtle 'bye-writings' that his monologue opening the second scene is prepared with pent-up energy, thus becoming the signature speech by which the audience will chiefly remember him. The 'services' he has just pledged to Kent are now 'bound' to the 'law' of 'nature' (I.ii.1), just as the 'deserving' he said he should 'study' is later to be repeated in irony when he believes that his betrayal of his father to Cornwall 'seems a fair deserving' (III.iii.20). For Edmund, the constant grudge is that he has been deprived of his 'fair deserving', for the gaining of which he can pledge any 'services', as he declares in this monologue:

Wherefore should I
Stand in the plague of custom, and permit
The curiosity of nations to deprive me,
For that I am some twelve or fourteen moonshines
Lag of a brother? Why bastard? wherefore base?
When my dimensions are as well compact,
My mind as generous and my shape as true,
As honest madam's issue? Why brand they us
With base? with baseness? bastardy? base, base?

Who, in the lusty stealth of nature, take
More composition and fierce quality
Than doth, within a dull, stale, tired bed,
Go to the creating a whole tribe of fops,
Got 'tween asleep and wake? Well, then,
Legitimate Edgar, I must have your land.
Our father's love is to the bastard Edmund
As to the legitimate. Fine word – 'legitimate'!
Well, my legitimate, if this letter speed,
And my invention thrive, Edmund the base
Shall top the legitimate. I grow; I prosper.
Now, gods, stand up for bastards! (I.ii.2–22)

It is a caustic and disdainful voice mixed with devilish charm and insatiable, vigorous desire, uttered by one whose identity is determined by the several words that he turns over again and again in his speech until every word becomes slippery by his distortion. 'Nature' is his 'natural' identity, used to justify a naturalistic theory that is to be practiced without any scruple: 'All with me's meet that I can fashion fit' (I.ii.168). Anything will serve so long as he can turn from the 'base' to the 'top' of the wheel of fortune, even if it has to, ironically, turn against nature. Similarly, 'base' is at once his 'bastardy', his natural illegitimacy, and his 'baseness', his inferior social status which deprives him of land, both of which impose upon him a low moral stature. It almost seems that his base social status should be responsible for the base man he turns out to be. By his insistent furious questionings, Edmund manages to bring the audience face to face with the injustice he has received as immediately as Shylock, and his questions may very well take the form of 'Hath not a [bastard] eyes? Hath not a [bastard] hands, organs, dimensions, senses, affections, passions? . . . . And if you wrong us shall we not revenge?' (*Merchant* III.i.49–56). The concluding '*I* grow; *I* prosper' therefore pounds on our ears with an ego that has long been suppressed and poses threatening energy when it is about to assert itself, as it soon does.

It is this revelation of his inner world that brings him closer to the audience, and occasionally lends him to pity and forgiveness, even though his conspiracy with the sisters leads to the irredeemable consequences of his father's blinding and Cordelia's death. In his entangled relationship with the two sisters, for instance, he is the one going along while Goneril and Regan are the ones making the initial advances. He sounds almost innocent when he asks himself, 'Which of them shall I take?/Both? one? or neither?' (V.i.57–8), and his dismissal of it, 'my state/Stands on me to defend, not to debate' (V.i.68–9), betrays an inveterate habit of self-defensiveness in the face of moral challenge. It is almost pathetic when, with his last breath, at the sight of the two sisters' dead bodies, he says, '[y]et Edmund was beloved' (V.iii.238). Because of his more mixed psychology revealed in these sporadic moments, his final repentance does not feel abrupt, which is yet qualified by his characteristic sarcasm: 'Some good I mean to do, / Despite of mine own nature' (V.iii.242–3). His last word calls back his monologue, reminding us that after all, his 'nature' is not completely inherent, but 'plagued' by his 'natural' status all along.

As Hazlitt remarks, the character of Edmund is depicted with 'its careless, light-hearted villainy, contrasted with the sullen, rancorous malignity of Regan and Goneril' (IV:259), who are between themselves carefully distinguished, though together they are differentiated from Edmund. Their very first performances in the love contest are respectively characteristic, both false but the falsity achieved by distinct means. Goneril is the first who speaks:

Sir, I love you more than words can wield the matter;
Dearer than eye-sight, space, and liberty;
Beyond what can be valued, rich or rare;
No less than life, with grace, health, beauty, honor;
As much as child e'er loved, or father found;
A love that makes breath poor, and speech unable;
Beyond all manner of so much I love you. (I.i.53–9)

Regan follows:

Sir, I am made
Of the self-same metal that my sister is,
And prize me at her worth. In my true heart
I find she names my very deed of love;
Only she comes too short, that I profess
Myself an enemy to all other joys,
Which the most precious square of sense possesses,
And find I am alone felicitate
In your dear highness' love. (I.i.67–75)

Both speeches excel in exaggeration, appealing by flattering blatantly, but Goneril adopts a grandiose style of insubstantiality, whereas Regan goes straight to the point, having no patience with tortuous rhetoric. If Goneril still *suggests* by resorting to comparatives, then Regan straightforwardly *tells* by employing the superlative. With her fully armoured spirit of competition, Regan does not hesitate to exploit her sister's preceding performance, and after taking what she can, does not forget to downgrade her. This is not to say that Regan is the stronger of the two: she is simply the cruder. If there is still some truth in Regan's unrestrained grabbing stance, then Goneril's speech is deliberately false, and in its craftiness, the hollowness betrays deeper malice. Her comparison of her love as 'dearer than eye-sight' also turns us cold in retrospect, for it is Goneril who, learning about Gloucester's 'betrayal', wastes no time to suggest, 'Pluck out his eyes' (III.vii.5), while her sister only comes up with an uninventive 'Hang him instantly' (III.vii.4).

Similarly, their conspiracy at the end of the opening scene reveals much about their individual differences. When Cordelia comes to bid farewell, Regan simply cuts her short curtly, 'Prescribe not us our duties' (I.i.277), while Goneril counters less directly but with more force: 'Let your study / Be to content your lord, who hath received you / At fortune's alms. You have obedience scanted, / And well are worth the want that you have wanted' (I.i.277–80). It is rather typical of Goneril not to bark but to bite, and bite where it hurts. Then when the stage is left to themselves, it is Goneril who initiates the conference, yet she carefully avoids committing herself: 'You see how full of changes his age is . . .: he always loved our sister most; and with what poor judgment he hath now cast her off appears too grossly' (I.i.287–90). Regan's reply, in comparison, is more forthright, ''Tis the infirmity of his age; yet he hath ever but slenderly known himself' (I.i.291–2). Only then does Goneril continue with a tone that suddenly becomes more candidly acrid and venomous: 'The best and soundest of his time hath been but rash; then must we look to receive from his age, not alone the imperfections of long-engraffed condition, but therewithal the unruly waywardness that infirm and choleric years bring with them' (I.i.293–7). Thus prompted, Regan takes the hint, 'Such unconstant starts are we like to have from him as this of Kent's banishment' (I.i.298–9). Then Goneril finally gets to the point, 'let's hit together: if our father carry authority with such dispositions as he bears, this last surrender of his will but offend us' (I.i.301–3), to which Regan replies, 'We shall further think on 't' (I.i.304). Regan's reaction seems too lethargic in comparison with Goneril's rejoinder: 'We must do something, and i' the heat' (I.i.305).

As mentioned above, this is the conversation that Keats underlines and annotates with the comment, 'How finely is the brief of Lear's character sketched in this conference'. 'Finely' 'sketched' here are not only 'the brief of Lear's character', but those of the two sisters as well. From their shockingly swift change from the fervid profession of loyalty to the impassive disclosure of enmity, the audience get the first glimpse of the menacing malignity of the two sisters, and in both episodes, they are each portrayed with unmistakably distinctive traits in their respective ways of being malicious. Goneril usually takes the lead, while Regan more often than not follows, and the same pattern is found in their later amorous relationship with Edmund and 'punishment' of Gloucester. Even in their respective matrimony, Goneril 'is the better soldier' (IV.v.4) mocking her husband for being a '[m]ilk-livered man' (IV.ii.52), while Regan's husband is 'the hot duke' (II.iv.98). After all, it is Goneril who poisons Regan instead of otherwise. On the other hand, however, by no means will Regan wince when she does act, and in fact, having started by following Goneril, she often surpasses her, advancing with an unalloyed and thus a more brutal animalistic nature. Goneril is the more treacherous one, who plots ahead, acts promptly, and strikes with more deadly force, constantly driven by a sense of threat, as she later reveals to her husband, 'Let me still take away the harms I fear, / Not fear still to be taken' (I.iv.307–8). She is the one who habitually speaks tortuously, while Regan's speech is usually shamelessly blunt. When Goneril makes the first challenge to her father, she speaks with deliberate involvedness, and by accusing Lear of encouraging his riotous knights, she cunningly justifies her own malignancy: 'the fault / Would not 'scape censure, nor the redresses sleep, / Which, in the tender of a wholesome weal, / Might in their working do you that offense, / Which else were shame, that then necessity / Will call discreet proceeding' (I.iv.183–8). Such a speech would never be uttered by Regan, who, in confronting Lear, attacks straightforwardly: 'O, sir, you are old; / Nature in you stands on the very verge / Of her confine. You should be ruled and led / By some discretion, that discerns your state / Better than you yourself' (II.iv.139–43). The same coarseness is found again in 'I pray you, father, being weak, seem so' (II.iv.196). It is also Regan who cuts Lear short with the impatient dismissal, 'Good sir, to the purpose' (II.iv.175), and again when Lear pleads pitiably 'I gave you all – ' (II.iv.245) with unblinking cruelty, 'And in good time you gave it' (II.iv.245). Nevertheless, when the conflict reaches towards the climax, with Lear being pushed back and forth between them in the argument about the number of knights, it is Goneril who makes the final, decisive move to turn the reduction into complete deprivation, 'What need you five-and-twenty, ten, or five . . .?' (II.iv.256), while Regan catches up by securing the victory with her typical thoroughness, 'What need one?' (II.iv.258).

It is by depicting the sisters, abominable as they are, with such meticulous particularity, that Shakespeare demonstrates to what extent the metamorphosis of a poet should reach. Yet the poet's dramatic disinterestedness should be distinguished from amorality. By making Goneril and Regan 'swell into reality', Shakespeare manages to make the audience vividly experience how repulsive monstrosity can be, and he goes out of his way to ensure such an effect. Unlike Edmund, into whose deeper being we are allowed some glimpses, through his monologues and other subtle touches, Goneril and Regan are the only major characters in the play who have not communicated directly to the audience. They remain inscrutable in their monstrosity, having never revealed any deeper motives to account for their deeds, nor manifesting the tiniest bit of compunction. Shakespeare has not left any chance for the audience to be reconciled with them. Keats's very rare markings of the sisters' speeches seem to indicate a strong antipathy to them as well, for even Edmund attracts quite a proportion of the underlinings, at least in his signature speech.

Not only are the villains of the play given particularity, but the minor characters depicted with care. Kent's adamant loyalty is encapsulated in his refusal to 'go out of' his plain 'dialect' (II.ii.101), and his integrity gives him the strength to be 'unmannerly' (I.i.145) to both Lear himself and his enemies, be it the sycophantic Oswald or the 'fiery'-tempered duke. But the more ingenious creation is Lear's Fool, in whom Keats shows a particularly keen interest in both his reading of the play itself and that of Hazlitt's commentary. If there is an odd one among the characters of the play, then it is the Fool, and out he goes well before the play ends.

Both his entrance and exit are unconventional. He disappears after Act III Scene vi with no explanation whatsoever, but before he turns up, his signifi- cance has already been given some crucial hints. The first one is provided by Goneril, whose question to Oswald, 'Did my father strike my gentleman for chiding of his fool?' (I.iii.1), indicates the special favour this jester enjoys from Lear. The impression is confirmed by Lear's impatient search for him in the following scene, 'Where's my fool' (I.iv.38,42,61), this being his sole interest despite the interruption of the disguised Kent and Oswald's offence. The knight's answer to Lear's repeated demands comes more unexpectedly, 'Since my young lady's going into France, sir, the fool hath much pined away' (I.iv.62–3). Such an unusual introduction forewarns that this is not a simple jesting courtier whose dramatic duty is merely to provide intermittent comic relief, but a complex character whose state of mind is at odds with the role he has to play. His connection with Cordelia is also stressed from the outset, tied up with his special relationship with Lear. The inner tension of this character must have intrigued Keats, who well remembers this first description of him, as we shall see.

The Fool finally enters, but as soon as he does, he insists on giving away his coxcomb, thus starting his performance by indicating his wish to stop playing. Moreover, he repeatedly insinuates that Lear should take over his role, asking Lear to 'beg another [coxcomb] of thy daughters' (I.iv.93), and when Lear calls him 'A bitter fool!' (I.iv.117), he turns it against Lear himself: 'The sweet and bitter fool / Will presently appear; / The one in motley here, / The other found out there' (I.iv.125–8). When Lear threatens by feigned anger, 'Dost thou call me fool, boy?' (I.iv.129), he retorts more sharply, 'All thy other titles thou hast given away; that thou wast born with' (I.iv.130–1). Lear, on the other hand, is found to be unusually lenient to the Fool, fondly calling him 'my boy', ready to take his stinging jokes, and even willing to serve as his butt sometimes. Blessed with his role, the Fool enjoys a privileged freedom of speech, just as kingship has once endowed Lear's speech with authority, but he asserts his freedom in deliberate elusiveness. He can be true without being literal, and incisive with- out being directly critical. Besides, already beginning to feel the consequences of his folly by now, Lear has to bear his sharp tongue, and the Fool is the only truth he is left with.

'Truth's a dog must to kennel; he must be whipped out' (I.iv.95): the Fool declares his truthfulness together with his cynicism. The truth he insists on telling is unpleasant: Lear is the real fool, who 'has banished two on's daugh- ters, and did the third a blessing against his will' (I.iv.87–8). And it is not enough just to tell it. He has to drive it home by repeating it in every possible way: 'If I gave them all my living, I'd keep my coxcombs myself' (I.iv.92–3), and in a different figure, '[t]hou hadst little wit in thy bald crown, when thou gavest thy golden one away' (I.iv.141–2), and again, 'thou hast pared thy wit o' both sides, and left nothing i' the middle' (I.iv.163–4), and yet more variations, 'thou art an O without a figure' (I.iv.168), 'I am a fool, thou art nothing' (I.iv.169). The incessant blame sounds almost obsessive, and the reason for this obsession is soon revealed in his reply to Lear's question, 'When were you wont to be so full of songs' (I.iv.148):

> I have used it, nuncle, ever since thou madest thy daughters
> thy mothers; for when thou gavest them the rod, and put'st
> down thine own breeches,
>> *Singing*
>>> Then they for sudden joy did weep,
>>> And I for sorrow sung,
>>> That such a king should play bo-peep,
>>> And go the fools among. (I.iv.149–55)

Then he stops, 'Prithee, nuncle, keep a schoolmaster that can teach thy fool to lie. I would fain learn to lie' (I.iv.156–7). So he is telling a deeper truth, – about how he is affected by Lear's foolishness. The sorrow he reveals, coherent with his having 'pined away', gives access to his inner being underneath his apparent harshness and thus softens the vindictive edge of his reproach. As a Fool, the only way to express sorrow is to put it in the disguise of playfulness. The sorrow mars his career, but play he must, so he gives his jokes at the price of bitterness. In a sense, he is caught in the same plight as Cordelia in the opening scene, who simply cannot 'heave [his] heart into [his] mouth' (I.i.90–1). Hence the wish to abandon his role, as he replies bitterly to Lear's warning to whip him if he lies:

> I marvel what kin thou and thy daughters are. They'll
> have me whipped for speaking true, thou'lt have me whipped
> for lying; and sometimes I am whipped for holding my peace.
> I had rather be any kind o' thing than a fool ... (I.iv.159–162)

In this light, it is easy to understand why Keats found Hazlitt's comment on the Fool inadequate, which goes:

> The contrast [between Lear's anguish and his two daughters' cruelty] would be too painful, the shock too great, but for the intervention of the Fool, whose well-timed levity comes in to break the continuity of feeling when it can no longer be borne, and to bring into play again the fibres of the heart just as they are growing rigid from over-strained excitement.

Keats underlined the above and annotated:

> This is almost the last observation from Mr Hazlitt. And is it really thus? Or as it has appeared to me? Does not the Fool by his very levity – nay it is not levity – give a finishing touch to the pathos; making what without him would be within our heart-reach really unfathomable. The Fool's words are merely the simplest translation of Poetry high as Lears – 'Since my young Ladies going into France/Sir, the Fool hath much pined away'. (Hilton 63)

Yet in just a few lines' space, he found that Hazlitt expresses a similar opinion:

> In another point of view it is indispensable . . . it carries the pathos to the highest pitch of which it is capable, by shewing the pitiable weakness of the old king's conduct and its irretrievable consequences in the most familiar point of view. (Hilton 63)[10]

Underlining 'carries the pathos to the highest pitch' and putting a cross at its side, Keats noted in the margin: 'Aye – this is it – most likely H. is right throughout. Yet is there not a little contradiction?' (Hilton 63). This brief divergence Keats had from the critic he always admired suggests his unusual sensitivity about the paradoxical effect of contrast and the complexity of characterization, which is demonstrated by his deep impression of the Fool's 'pining away' and his reading the Fool in association with Lear, as shown by his marking the Fool's comparison of the two sisters, 'as a <u>Crabbe's</u> like an <u>Apple</u>' (Keats's underline, I.v.15), with an annotation of Lear's later line, 'Thy fifty yet doth double five and twenty' (II.iv.254), a bitter recognition of the Fool's forewarning. The Fool, for all his apparent comic 'levity', paradoxically intensifies the pathos because of the contrast between his sharp folk wisdom and Lear's blinding and indomitable self-will, and because of the inherent tension within himself, between what his role obliges him to act and how he internally feels. His speech, as Lear's, is 'high' poetry, because it closely follows the heart, yet expresses it in the most discordant forms imaginable, in the same way that 'pining away' is a powerful touch for its very incongruity with the subject it describes.

It is also on this account that as the play progresses, it becomes inevitable for him to renounce his role and, as he has prophesied, to pass it on to Lear. When Lear begins to go through his 'mighty grapple', the Fool 'labors' increasingly hard to 'out-jest / His heart-struck injuries' (III.i.16–7), whereas Lear becomes ever more proficient in speaking and acting wildly to take his place. After Lear receives the first blow from Goneril, the Fool is found to fail his duty to distract Lear from his fury and shock, instead applauding Lear's poor effort at joking, 'Thou wouldst make a good fool' (I.v.32). As Lear's mind becomes more impenetrable, he also has to adopt a less elusive speech in order to get it across to Lear, as the already evident comparison of Regan with Goneril, 'she's as like this as a crab's like an apple' (I.v.12), is replaced by a yet plainer message, 'She will taste as like this as a crab does to a crab' (I.v.15). Though he still chides Lear, 'If thou wert my fool, nuncle, I'd have thee beaten for being old before thy time' (I.v.34–5), for, 'Thou shouldst not have been old till thou hadst been wise' (I.v.37), tenderness replaces his former sarcasm. Their exchange of roles has imperceptibly begun, and becomes more evident when the play proceeds to the storm scenes. While it is the Fool who has up to this point stood in the lime-light by displaying his wit in jests and satire to Lear, now it is Lear who dom-inates the stage with his raging speeches and the Fool has to struggle to find his turn to speak. After Tom joins Lear with his obsessive songs and speeches about the fiends, the Fool is only left with a cynical comment as a sober onlooker, 'This cold night will turn us all to fools and madmen' (III.iv.75). The time has come for him to quit.

His last appearance is in the scene of the illusory trial, at the end of which Lear says in exhaustion, 'Make no noise, make no noise; draw the curtains. So, so, so. We'll go to supper i' the morning' (III.vi.76–7), which is paralleled by the Fool with 'And I'll go to bed at noon' (III.vi.78). This is the last line the Fool delivers before he leaves the stage for good, which symbolizes an untimely con-clusion, and Lear's 'curtains' seem to be drawn for him. When his performance can no longer distract Lear, who has already been distracted in his own mind by much deeper pain, he is no longer needed as a jester by Lear, a king no more. When Lear returns to the stage the next time, he speaks with sharper wit and more piercing cynicism than the Fool and begins to serve as his own Fool, so to speak. Moreover, it is only appropriate that the Fool, who has appeared onstage only after Cordelia has left, should leave the stage when Cordelia is soon to return. He has been, for all his censure and bitterness, entertained and needed by Lear in Cordelia's absence. In a sense, the Fool, as Lear's only solace, is a sur-rogate for Cordelia, though a grotesque surrogate. And at the very end of the play, it is 'my poor fool' (V.iii.304) that Lear calls the dead Cordelia.

'The Vale of Soul-Making'

With the characters, even the antagonistic and the minor ones, 'swelling into reality', the dramatic world of *Lear* projects a vision of the actual complex and diverse human experience, which alone has the power to convey the 'deep, eternal theme' of great poetry. Within this tragic dramatic world, Lear, more than any other character, has to experience a trial of his being by going through the most violent vicissitudes, thus epitomizing the tragedy of human existence in himself. If the play approximates the real 'world of Pains and troubles', then it is Lear's heart that is forced to 'feel and suffer in a thousand diverse ways' most relentlessly, and this is suggested by Keats's way of reading the play as well. I do not intend to over-read Keats's markings, which, like markings by anybody, are likely to be as random as they are telling, but if anything at all can be made out from them, then it is too obvious to escape notice that they are predominantly of Lear's speeches.[11] Keats's overwhelming attention to Lear has never wavered from the opening to the end, and he has not missed any of the 'thousand diverse ways' in which Lear's heart has had to 'feel and suffer'.

Once 'every inch a king', Lear is the one who, with his very being rooted in his sovereignty over the world, witnesses that world falling apart piece by piece in front of his eyes. The disparity between his opening status and subsequent state becomes so shocking that his very self-identity is at stake, 'Who is it that can tell me who I am?' (I.iv.205). What the human heart can endure is pressed to its uttermost limit when Lear has to undergo the atrocious agony of being afflicted by his own flesh and blood, by whom he is reduced to 'a poor old man, / As full of grief as age; wretched in both' (II.iv.267–8). He is finally blessed with his only joy in the midst of all these pains, only to be deprived of it and to be tortured by the impossible thought that if Cordelia comes back to life, 'It is a chance which does redeem all sorrows / That ever I have felt' (V.iii.265–6). Yet it is in this process of extreme physical and emotional suffering that he has to '[e]xpose [himself] to feel what wretches feel' (III.iv.35), and confront the stark human reality itself that 'unaccommodated man is no more but such a poor, bare, forked animal'. And it is by going through such a shocking disparity between his self and the greater Other that he is delivered from his wilful blindness to the honest recognition that 'I am a man', making it possible for him to reconcile himself with Cordelia and ask for her forgiveness. Moreover, throughout his tortuous experience, he adamantly refuses to succumb to the crushing reality, and in his desperate defiance of the fate that befalls him, the inherent majesty he exemplifies at the same time demonstrates the indomitable majesty of human will. It is in Lear's life, which 'he hath endured so long' (V.iii.315), that the painful dramatic world becomes 'the art of necessities', and by the tragic intensity his life conveys to the audience, 'the vale of tears' is most powerfully turned into 'the vale of soul-making'.

If the world is inevitably 'a vale of tears', to make a truthful artistic representation of it becomes in itself a soul-making process for the artist. Keats was brought back to the play time and again because of the tragic resources it offered to the soul to be made, and with that fortified soul having gained by the dramatic experience, he could create 'vales of soul-making' in his own poetry. If the 'poor Tom' in Keats's here and now becomes the 'youth' who 'grows pale, and spectre-thin, and dies', is not the world 'where palsy shakes a few, sad, last gray hairs' also that of Lear, both of which become part of his own immortal song of the 'deep, eternal theme'? Only after going through such a soul-making process, does the poet end his journey in purgatory and reach paradise, just as Apollo in *Hyperion* has to 'die into life' before becoming deified. And by this soul-searing experience, the poet is endowed with negative capability; he can now go back to the darkness fearlessly with all his relish in light, with a mind that reaches out for real human experience which is impossible to be reduced or resolved, and that opens itself to the vastness of humanity, in which every mind is a labyrinth.

Chapter 3

Negative Capability and Keats's Poetry

Keats's critical insight into his presider's 'enormous' negative capability did not automatically turn into a poetic quality of his own. The letter was written by the end of 1817, but his 'Great Year'[1] did not come until the autumn of 1818, when his poems began to exemplify a matured mind of negative capability, marked by the deliberate refusal of resolution, the inclusion of both sides of the opposition and the exploration of their paradoxical interdependence and irreconcilable conflict, and an active shift of point of view that gives his poetry a dramatic scope. In essence, they became increasingly 'the poetry of experience'.[2] As Keats writes, 'axioms in philosophy are not axioms until they are proved upon our pulses'. His greatest poems, instead of reaching after the conclusion whether 'axioms in philosophy' are axioms or not, are all firmly oriented to the experience of proving axioms upon our pulses.

It is only natural that Keats the critic led the poet on the way to negative capability, for a critical mind usually visualizes a further horizon than that to which the creative hand reaches. It was the critic within Keats that brought him to constantly strive for greater poetry than that he was writing for the time being, thus giving it a fluidity with an ever present 'forwardness' (*KL* II:109). The wonder that he could be 'among the English Poets' (*KL* I:394) within about three years could not have been accomplished without his keen critical awareness characterized by negative capability in the first place. Both the scale and the speed of his metamorphosis exemplify the unsettledness of his critical mind, which evolved into an artistry in his poetry by its constant 'watchfulness' (*KL* I:374) against certitude and closure.

'A Vast Idea': Early Poetry

'Sleep and Poetry', the last poem in Keats's first published collection, makes a proper conclusion to his early poetry. It is the first poem in which Keats fully asserts his poetic voice, formulating his ideas about poetry, expressing his attitude towards poets of past and present, and in the midst defining his own direction. It also contains many central concerns that are to persist in a more complex shape later in his career, and the most marked one is the conflict revealed in the famous declaration of his poetic aim: though 'the realm' (101) of 'Flora' and 'old Pan' (102) is ever temptingly enchanting, the poet claims, 'I must pass them for a nobler life, / Where I may find the agonies, the strife / Of human hearts' (123–5).[3] Throughout the poem, these two ideals of poetry as romance and tragedy strangely coexist at odds with one another, and they remained as an antithesis he had to vacillate between, as he did at the conclusion of *Endymion*. It was only later that the conflict itself became a domain of his poetry, building up tension, presenting debates, but offering no ready-made resolutions.

The two chief symbols in the title already indicate this contradiction: while 'sleep' suggests an impulse to be delivered out of the world, 'poetry' signifies a revelatory power and truthful insight into the world. This opposition is to run all the way through to *The Fall of Hyperion*, where Moneta clearly states that 'The poet and the dreamer are distinct, / Diverse, sheer opposite, antipodes' (I:199–200). On the other hand, the pair is also intimately related. Sleep, in a state of slumberous indolence, accumulates creative energy, and it also suggests a passive receptiveness open to poetic vision. Their connection is to become more intricate along with the development of Keats's poetry. Endymion is visited by his Goddess in sleep, and Madeline dreams of Porphyro, but it is also in sleep that Isabella sees the ghost of Lorenzo, and the knight in 'La Belle Dame sans Merci' has the nightmare of her 'death pale' (38) victims. On the other hand, sleep itself is to become a consistent inspiration for his poetry, welcomed as the 'soft embalmer' (1) in the sonnet 'To Sleep' or 'the drowsy hour' that is 'ripe' (15) in 'Ode on Indolence', though it can also be cursed as painful 'drowsy numbness' ('Ode to a Nightingale' 1) that overwhelms poetic intensity, or '[drowns] the wakeful anguish of the soul'.

Not only the title, but the settings in 'Sleep and Poetry' suggest the poet's contradictory impulses to leave the world and to plunge into its miseries. The poem presents a characteristic early Keatsian setting, a shady world at once ethereal and sensuous, that combines the Arcadian world with Spenserian Romance. On the other hand, the poet is also eager to 'seize' 'the events of this wide world' (81), convinced that 'the great end / Of poesy' is to 'sooth the cares' of men (245–7). This conviction is to recur in *The Fall of Hyperion*, where a poet is believed to be a 'physician to all men' (I:190). However, throughout his poetic career, the fever and pain of mortality have never been fully reconciled, and the contention between the faith in and scepticism about poetry and art to heal human sufferings is to dominate his poetry.

The opposition of the two poetic ideals is further revealed in his admiration for poetic models of very different natures, and the hybridity of his genealogy only betrays his own conflicting inclinations. At the end of his overview of poetic history, he concludes, 'they shall be accounted poet kings / Who simply tell the most heart-easing things' (267–8). One of his 'poet kings' was of course

Leigh Hunt. Hunt's stylistic influence on the early Keats has been too much discussed to be repeated here. Most disastrously, it was from Hunt that Keats began to adopt a loose, diffusive style and a cloying sweetness, which are the very opposites of intensity and disagreeables. The 'heart-easing' ideal of poetry poses a disappointing contrast to the 'soul-making' power of great art that he still had to go through many trials to realize.

At the same time, a very non-Huntian image emerges with an intensity and pregnancy of meanings: 'A drainless shower / Of light is poesy; 'tis the supreme of power; / Tis might half slumb'ring on its own right arm' (235–7). The image has deservedly caught much attention. Hazlitt would be the first critic to notice it, misquoting it as 'Like strength reposing on his own right arm' (VI:189) in his *Lectures on the Dramatic Literature of the Age of Elizabeth* without acknowledging the source, but the very fact that these lines came to his mind seemingly spontaneously suggests the deep impression they made on him. More recently, Hirst points out, after many other critics, that 'the image is an embodiment of negative capability', for '[t]he indomitable and dozing figure combines omnipotence with an attitude of indeterminateness, of acquiescence in half-knowledge and mysteries which precludes all irritable reaching after fact and reason' (60). It is also remarkable that the image sounds like an offhand remark, and its unintentional nature fits in with the truth Keats momentarily intuited about great poetry that was to be contemplated by him only later: 'Poetry should be great & unobtrusive, a thing which enters into one's soul, and does not startle it or amaze it with itself but with its subject', which is the quality that distinguishes the modern poets 'with a palpable design' from the ancient bards' disinterested magnitude. Also significantly, the intuition is not expressed as an abstraction, but finds a perfect embodiment in a classical pose, a pose on the verge, caught in a fragile balance of motion and stasis, half way between sleep and wakefulness. Already, in his early poetry, Keats has shown a markedly sensuous and tangible imagination, which will gradually mature into a dramatic quality in his poetry. Also manifested is his sensitivity to images of inherent tension, which will develop into intensity when his negatively capable genius to entertain both sides of an opposition further revealed itself.

At the end of 'Sleep and Poetry', Keats reasserts his embrace of this wide world of humanity:

> . . . though I do not know
> The shiftings of the mighty winds that blow
> Hither and thither all the changing thoughts
> Of man: though no great minist'ring reason sorts
> Out the dark mysteries of human souls
> To clear conceiving: yet there ever rolls
> A vast idea before me . . .
> . . . thence too I've seen
> The end and aim of Poesy. (285–93)

Significantly, envisioning the 'vast idea' of poetry, he also recognizes that the human mind is ever 'changing', full of 'dark mysteries', defying one 'great minist'ring reason' and 'clear conceiving', all forecasting a negatively capable mind allowing for the multitude of possibilities in the human world. His first long poem is concluded in an expectation of further exploration of 'dark mysteries', though the first spot on which he landed was still in the realm of Romance.

'A Symbol of Immensity': *Endymion*

'I stood tip-toe upon a little hill', the second longest poem in his 1817 collection, was at first referred to by Keats as 'Endymion' (*KL* I:121). With it finished, he was ready to embark on *Endymion* proper, which, ideally, would bring together the human and the natural world, the mortal and the divine, reality and fantasy, making a happy marriage of his two conflicting ideals of poetry. As a new-fledged poet, he was anxious to decree for himself an ordeal that he thought any great poet should go through; as he asked, 'Did our great Poets ever write short Pieces?'(*KL* I:170). Written from April to November in 1817, *Endymion* turned out not to be the poem making him a laureate, though he claimed in the spring, 'I put on no Laurels till I shall have finished Endymion' (*KL* I:170). But it witnesses the formation of the idea of negative capability, 'fermented' by his reading of Shakespeare and his apprenticeship itself. Despite the severe criticism it has received ever since its publication, one cannot take Matthew Arnold's advice that 'the poem as a whole' could 'be suppressed and lost' (*KPA* 118), for it marks the most important transition in Keats's poetic career.

A revision Keats made in December 1817 gives us some suggestion of his transformation in the process of writing *Endymion*. The following lines were added to Endymion's long speech to Peona in Book I when he defends love as happiness of the highest degree: 'Wherein lies happiness? In that which becks / Our ready minds to fellowship divine, / A fellowship with essence; till we shine, / Full alchemiz'd, and free of space. Behold / The clear religion of heaven!' (I:777–81). Keats explains to Taylor, his publisher, about this revision in his famous 'Pleasure Thermometer' letter dated 30 January 1818:

> You must indulge me by putting this in for setting aside the badness of the other, such a preface is necessary to the Subject. The whole thing must I think have appeared to you, who are a consequitive Man, as a thing almost of mere words – but I assure you that when I wrote it, it was a regular stepping of the Imagination towards a Truth. (*KL* I:218)

The word 'consequitive', we remember, had been used by Keats in his letter to Bailey written a few days before completing *Endymion*, 'I have never yet been able to perceive how any thing can be known for truth by consequitive reasoning.'

In both usages, a 'consequitive' mind poses an antithesis to a negatively capable mind, and both the letters and the revision itself suggest his constant contemplation around that time of the idea that truth is approached from a 'ready' mind's imaginative openness instead of any 'consequitive' 'reaching after fact & reason', and the truth he felt he was approaching now is on the 'subject' of 'a fellowship with essence', the non-egotistical quality of both a human being and an artist.

He continues his justification of the revision:

> My having written that <Passage> Argument will perhaps be of the greatest Service to me of any thing I ever did – It set before me at once the gradations of Happiness even like a kind of Pleasure Thermometer – and is my first Step towards the chief Attempt in the Drama – the playing of different Natures with Joy and Sorrow. (*KL* I:218–19)

This letter was written only a few days after his re-reading of *Lear,* which was preceded by the *Lear* sonnet, and about a month after he wrote the negative capability letter. As expressed in the *Lear* sonnet, here again is indicated the turn from Romance to Drama, or poetry of greater weight and complexity. It is this preface on 'a fellowship with essence' that gives rise to his dramatic inspiration, for being able to cast the self into diverse others is the essence of dramatic art. At the same time, dramatic creativity is also associated with the capability of embracing the contradictory yet interdependent 'Joy and Sorrow', by which only can 'intensity' be achieved. This 'preface' may be seen as a clarification of his thoughts for these months while *Endymion* was being composed.

Following this 'preface', Endymion gives a fuller expression of the 'gradations of Happiness', believing 'there are / Richer entanglements, enthralments far / More self-destroying, leading, by degrees, / To the chief intensity: the crown of these / Is made of love and friendship' (I:797–801). The word 'intensity', though not employed in the artistic sense as in his reference to 'the excellence' of *Lear,* is tied up with the 'self-destroying' 'entanglements' with the other, which is essential to produce great art as well, as he would come to realize after the composition of *Endymion.* This long speech of Endymion's, therefore, as the apology for the whole Romance, also lays out the ground for the later, more lucid thoughts centring on negative capability.

But this is all viewed from hindsight. From the time he composed the 'subject' to the time he added this 'preface', 'there is a space of life between', as Keats himself observes in the preface to *Endymion.* To arrive at the point where he felt he was gradually approaching 'a Truth', Keats had to explore the creative experience itself, as his romantic hero did by first going through the pilgrimage.

The whole poem starts out, with its opening line of 'A thing of beauty is a joy for ever', as a natural continuation of the early poetry, but there is a notably different image: 'such too is the grandeur of the dooms / We have imagined for the mighty dead' (I:20–1). Contrary to other images of beauty that are placid and undisturbing, this brings forth tension and carries weight. The exposure to other influences than Hunt is revealed in the phrase 'the mighty dead', borrowed from Hazlitt, and the image also calls to mind a sonnet Keats wrote about a month before, which, like the sonnet on Chapman's Homer, acquires an unprecedentedly powerful voice inspired by its majestic subject, 'On Seeing the Elgin Marbles'. The sonnet unfolds a theme that would become perennially Keatsian, the opposition between history and time, human transience and artistic permanence. With the 'Grecian grandeur' (12) confronting the human viewer, this conflict turns into an interior drama within the human viewer himself, bringing forth 'an undescribable feud' (10), which remains unresolved to the end, being left as the ambivalent 'shadow of a magnitude' (14), at once suggesting artistic triumph and artistic ruin. A similar confrontation was to recur in about two years' time, between a human spectator and another piece of artifice of 'Grecian grandeur'. But to come back to the year of 1817, the indelible impression left by the 'Grecian grandeur' emerged in *Endymion* as well, which was started about a month after Keats visited the Elgin Marbles. Like the Shakespearean tragedy that began to 'haunt' him then, the Elgin Marbles were also an artistic feat that drew him towards a more sublime and majestic plane of art and poetry than his early models. Here at the start of *Endymion*, this image conspicuously outgrowing the others in the catalogue of 'beauty' suggests the subtle change, which is exemplified more fully in the hymn to Pan in Book I.

The anticipation of the great odes by the hymn has been commonly recognized; it 'may be called the first of Keats's great odes' (1967, 48) according to Douglas Bush. It opens with a scene that is markedly different from the bowery Arcadian setting pervading the early poetry:

O thou, whose mighty palace roof doth hang
From jagged trunks, and overshadoweth
Eternal whispers, glooms, the birth, life, death
Of unseen flowers in heavy peacefulness;
Who lov'st to see the hamadryads dress
Their ruffled locks where meeting hazels darken;
And through whole solemn hours dost sit, and hearken
The dreary melody of bedded reeds –
In desolate places, where dank moisture breeds
The pipy hemlock to strange overgrowth;
Bethinking thee, how melancholy loth

Thou wast to lose fair Syrinx – do thou now,
By thy love's milky brow!
By all the trembling mazes that she ran,
Hear us, great Pan! (I:232–46)

It is a vigorously majestic voice, presenting a scene of the sublime rather than the beautiful, composed of disagreeable shapes (jagged, ruffled), disturbing sights (flowers in heavy peacefulness, strangely overgrowing hemlock), unpleasant feel and sound (dank moisture, dreary melody), in oppressing 'darkening' 'glooms', all of which project a 'solemn' and 'desolate' mood in which Pan emerges as an immortal caught in a loss that is entirely human. The sublimity is thus not only aesthetic but psychological, achieving an emotional intensity that is at the same time restrained by keeping the usually too luxuriant imagination to a compactness of images. Pan has evolved from the god of nature free from human cares in 'Sleep and Poetry' to the god of experience, and the experience is that of love, the most intense form of 'fellowship' with the other, for which the shepherds are invoking him now. The invocation implies a similar fellowship of Pan with the world they reside in, for the humanized lover of Syrinx is at the same time the benign god of the natural world of diverse beings and the human realm. So his ultimate role is 'Dread opener of the mysterious doors / Leading to universal knowledge' (I:288–9), a bearer of the 'burden of the Mystery', whose 'universal knowledge' is gained from his magnanimous affinity with all beings. The apostrophe thus concludes in hailing him to 'Be still a symbol of immensity; / A firmament reflected in a sea; / An element filling the space between; / An unknown' (I:299–302).

Pan's all-pervasive 'immensity' epitomizes the fusion of immortality and humanity by its embrace of diversity, ever leading to universal truth yet ever promising more mystery, ultimately an 'unknown' infinity. The hymn to Pan is thus a celebration of a vast, negatively capable mind, which is being approached by the poet himself while composing it.

If Pan is the god embodying negative capability, then Endymion can be likened to the poet himself in search of it. When Endymion appears in the festivity as the love-stricken hero, he is at the same time paralleled with the melancholy Pan as the immortal lover and set against the god's all-embracing magnanimousness with his self-indulgent sorrows. The 'self-destroying' happiness is yet to be gained from the trial of experience, which begins from his search for his beloved in all spheres, from down in the earth and the sea to up in the air. In Book II, in his pilgrimage at the abysm of the earth, Endymion has caught a glimpse of Diana and lost it, and thus

. . . long he travers'd to and fro, to acquaint
Himself with every mystery, and awe;
Till, weary, he sat down before the maw

Of a wide outlet, fathomless and dim,
To wild uncertainty and shadows grim.
There, when new wonders ceas'd to float before,
And thoughts of self came on, how crude and sore
The journey homeward to habitual self! (II: 269–76)

Without trying to make the Romance a systematic allegory, one can still read
the passage in the light of negative capability. If the pilgrimage is a search for
truth, and the glimpse of Diana is very much 'a fine isolated verisimilitude
caught from the Penatralium of mystery', then one must go through the expos-
ure to the 'fathomless' 'wild uncertainty', whereas 'the journey homeward to
habitual self' is an inevitable obstacle that has to be faced on the way. This occu-
pation with the self can only be overcome by the ardent pursuit of the ideal
other. So from there Endymion is led to the chamber of Adonis, his alter ego as
the mortal beloved of Venus revived every summer, and by rejoicing in the
reunion of Adonis and Venus, Endymion is also experiencing the 'happiness'
brought by the feeling of 'fellowship' with Adonis, before he himself is brought
to 'a jasmine bower' (II:670) to finally consummate his love for his Goddess.
When Endymion meets Glaucus in Book III, the intensity of the sympathetic
'fellowship' reaches a climax which is powerful enough to turn him into the
very saviour who will deliver Glaucus out of his long suffering.

Glaucus is found in a submarine world of debris and ruin, who, though worn
with age, wears an 'awful' (III:194) look:

A cloak of blue wrapp'd up his aged bones,
O'erwrought with symbols by the deepest groans
Of ambitious magic: every ocean-form
Was woven in with black distinctness; storm,
And calm, and whispering, and hideous roar,
Quicksand and whirlpool, and deserted shore
Were emblem'd in the woof; with every shape
That skims, or dives, or sleeps, 'twixt cape and cape. (III:197–204)

The cloak, reminiscent of the multitudinous scope of Achilles's shield, is one of
plenitude as well, composed of both 'storm' and 'calm', 'whispering' and 'roar'.
Confronted with the old man in this hieroglyphic robe, Endymion must solve
the mystery as decreed in the scroll that Glaucus presents to him: 'If he utterly /
Scans all the depths of magic, and expounds / The meanings of all motions,
shapes, and sounds; / If he explores all forms and substances / Straight home-
ward to their symbol-essences; He shall not die' (III:696–701). Glaucus must
fulfil his mission first by putting together the bodies of 'all lovers tempest-tost'
(III:703), the very deed itself deciphering 'all forms and substances'. The 'symbol-
essences' thus correspond with the 'fellowship with essence', which defines the

connection of Glaucus with the sea-drowned lovers as well as with Endymion, and the scroll itself was handed to Glaucus by an old man whom he tried to save out of sympathy. Endymion is 'the youth elect' (III:710) to deliver Glaucus, for he, as the ardent lover, possesses in his nature a 'fellowship' with Glaucus, whose predicament was brought by love. What he needs to perform, like that which Glaucus has performed for the drowned lovers, is to fulfil the 'fellowship', and by reviving Glaucus at the same time solves the mystery presented to him by Glaucus's sublime cloak. Moreover, in redeeming the love and youth of Glaucus, Endymion also comes closer to his own love, the most intense form of 'fellowship'. The whole episode thus epitomizes the opening apology for love as the highest 'self-destroying' happiness, by which Endymion also approaches the goal of his pilgrimage.

When the last book opens, however, a weary voice is heard: 'on/ I move to the end in lowliness of heart' (IV:28–9). It is not surprising that Keats should have felt exhausted, having persevered through three-fourths of this 'self-imposed marathon' (W. J. Bate 1964: 170). The weariness also manifests itself in the trials of different metrical forms Keats began to make in the last book, most notably in the Indian maid's song to Sorrow. The light-footed tone of the song forecasts many light, comical or even bawdy verses he would write in early 1818 after finishing *Endymion*, which may have been a natural relief after this long labour. The song indicates Keats's 'first attempt' at the drama of emotion or, as he puts it, 'the playing of different Natures with Joy and Sorrow': 'Come then, Sorrow! / Sweetest Sorrow! / Like an own babe I nurse thee on my breast: / I thought to leave thee / And deceive thee, / But now of all the world I love thee best' (IV:279–84). This joyous celebration of Sorrow can be seen as an early version of 'Ode on Melancholy', and it indicates the beginning of Keats's realization of pain as a necessary component of human life and his later acceptance of the world of suffering as the schooling process for the soul to be made. The realization grew with this long poem of experience, in which it already manifests itself in an earlier passage in Book II:

> . . . this is human life: the war, the deeds,
> The disappointment, the anxiety,
> Imagination's struggles, far and nigh,
> All human; bearing in themselves this good,
> That they are still the air, the subtle food,
> To make us feel existence, and to shew
> How quiet death is. (II:153–9)

The paradoxical truth about human life achieved here underlies the pervasive theme of the great odes that were to come, that pain is at the same time the very substance that intensifies human existence. It is this insight that prepares the way for a camelion poet, inspired by both 'Muses bright and Muses pale'

('Welcome joy, and welcome sorrow' 24), to 'welcome joy, and welcome sorrow'. This inclination to the 'disagreeable' side of life shows itself more prominently when Endymion approaches the end of his journey, as he arrives at the Cave of Quietude.[4] Instead of being disheartened by its abysmal darkness, he hails it as 'Happy gloom!' (IV:537). The celebration derives from the realization of the paradoxical coexistence of bliss and agony, and symbolically, only after passing this final stage of the ordeal, is Endymion sent back to the earth, ready to conclude his pilgrimage.

Despite all the rush towards the end and the curious turns and twists in the last book as the final efforts of 'invention' to fill the 'bare circumstance', the incarnation of Cynthia in the earthly Indian maid does not seem a whim. It is consistent with Keats's faith in 'the holiness of the Heart's affections and the truth of Imagination', and in Adam's dream that, when he awoke, he found true. After all, the happy ending of Endymion is achieved by casting himself into an intense 'fellowship' with all the realms of the actual world, the Indian maid included, rather than a dogmatic search for an abstract ideal. Besides, the emotional confusion of Endymion in the last book only reveals more clearly that the poet himself was undergoing 'a gradual ripening of the intellectual powers'. The poem itself, therefore, for all the ideas fermenting within it, only remains 'a trial of . . . Imagination'. As Keats would realize later, 'the foundations are too sandy' (*KPS* 102). But the great 'service' the Romance, by its very desultoriness, did for Keats was to bring home to him the value of artistic intensity. As he would later advise Shelley: 'curb your magnanimity and be more of an artist, and "load every rift" of your subject with ore'. No other experience could have conveyed it to him more forcefully, as he adds self-mockingly to Shelley: 'is not this extraordina[r]y talk for the writer of Endymion?' (*KL* II:323).

'Knowledge Enormous': From *Endymion* to *Hyperion*

Already revealed at the very end of the preface to *Endymion*, Keats's mind was set on another big project after *Endymion* was finished: 'I hope I have not in too late a day touched the beautiful mythology of Greece, and dulled its brightness: for I wish to try once more, before I bid it farewel' (*KPS* 103). Hints in *Endymion* suggest that even during its composition, Keats had started to conceive of *Hyperion*, and he mentioned to Haydon his plan for the epic early on 23 January 1818:

> [I]n Endymion I think you may have many bits of the deep and sentimental cast – the nature of *Hyperion* will lead me to treat it in a more naked and grecian Manner – and the march of passion and endeavour will be undeviating – (*KL* I:207)

It was, however, not until that autumn that he finally began *Hyperion*. Of course it took time to prepare himself for the 'naked and grecian Manner', to acquire intensity and to get rid of the loose, extravagant style in *Endymion*, but he was dealing with problems more fundamental than stylistic ones during this time. With the conception of negative capability formed in the writing of *Endymion*, Keats was able to see that its 'sentimental cast' derived from its 'sandy' 'foundation' in experience. For *Hyperion*, an epic tragedy, he would expose himself to actual experience, especially 'the strife' and 'agonies' in it, to convey the 'undeviating' 'passion', or tragic intensity. In the process, however, experience turned out to be full of uncertainties, mysteries and doubts that could be perplexing and painful, and he found himself not capable of resting with them in equanimity but had grappled desperately with them. What he did was not reach after fact and reason, but search for some kind of philosophy to make sense of human sufferings and on that basis, to accept them. As he wrote to Reynolds on 3 May, 'An extensive knowlege is needful to thinking people – it takes away the heat and fever; and helps, by widening speculation, to ease the Burden of the Mystery' (*KL* I:277). From *Endymion* to *Hyperion*, Keats was trying to reconcile experience with knowledge, or what he calls 'philosophy', and, in a broader sense, seeking ways to transform experiential suffering into tragic poetry. It was therefore very much a process for his newly conceived idea of negative capability to undergo 'fierce dispute / Betwixt damnation and impassion'd clay'. Before he could come to terms with human experience himself, he could not very well start *Hyperion*, since he had already learned from *Endymion* that 'if Poetry comes not as naturally as the Leaves to a tree it had better not come at all'.

All these struggles are most acutely expressed in the verse letter Keats wrote to Reynolds on 25 March, which, as Sperry observes, 'illuminates more clearly than any single work the major problems with which Keats wrestled in passing from *Endymion* to . . . *Hyperion*', which he calls 'a period of crisis' (131), and the crisis applies to negative capability as well. A month back, Keats could tell Reynolds, 'let us open our leaves like a flower and be passive and receptive', and claim that the thrush had told him, 'fret not after knowledge' (*KL* I:233), but now the mind is overwhelmed by 'the Burden of the Mystery':

> . . . in the world
> We jostle . . .
> . . . and to philosophize
> I dare not yet! – Oh never will the prize,
> High reason, and the lore of good and ill,
> Be my award. Things cannot to the will
> Be settled, but they tease us out of thought. (71–7)

The 'unsettledness' in actual experience becomes disturbing and menacing, and he cannot help reaching after 'high reason', a kind of philosophy, or 'lore', equivalent of knowledge, but is not equipped with a vision that illuminates the meaning of existence: 'Or is it that imagination brought / Beyond its proper bound, yet still confined, – / Lost in a sort of purgatory blind, / Cannot refer to any standard law / Of either earth or heaven?' (78–82). Imagination, for all its power to turn Adam's dream into reality, is also capable of conjuring up night-marish sights. The purgatorial blindness is experienced by the human mind always reaching out by its imagination which, however, possesses only a limited vision. As he would tell Fanny Brawne two years later in his sickness, 'My Mind has been the most discontented and restless one that ever was put into a body too small for it' (*KL* II:275). Disturbed by the thought of these irreconcilable conflicts in human existence, the poet extends his doubts to the natural world. The sea which used to enchant him now unfolds a heinous scene: 'but I saw / Too far into the sea; where every maw / The greater on the less feeds evermore: – / But I saw too distinct into the core / Of an eternal fierce destruction' (93–7). As Finney points out, Nature here has passed into 'the Darwinian era' when it becomes 'red in tooth and claw' as it does in Tennyson (I:391). This foresight could have been the product of a purely abstract existential crisis, but, more likely, it was provoked by the more immediate 'destruction' that Keats found inconsolably cruel in human experience, as he unwittingly betrays when he concludes the poem with an attempt at cheerfulness: 'Do you get health – and Tom the same – I'll dance, / And from detested moods in new romance / Take refuge' (110–12).

The poem was written in Teignmouth, when Tom, for all his 'exquisite love of Life', was going 'to the Grave' (*KL* I:293). The immediacy of his brother's waning life spoke more eloquently than any natural scenes about the cruelty of mortality. As he admits when talking about Tom's situation, 'I am not old enough or magnanimous enough to anihilate self' (*KL* I:292). The metaphys-ical principle of disinterestedness appeared too remote to relieve the acute pain in experience. When the mind was subjected to uncertainties, mysteries and doubts about the meaning of existence itself, negative capability could only throw one deeper into the abyss. Thus did he 'take refuge' in a romance, despite his repeated resolutions to leave it behind, for before he could deliver himself from the crisis by some 'philosophy', he could not start *Hyperion*, what he calls the 'abstr[a]ct' (*KL* II:132) poem, in which he had to offer some kind of 'speculations' about human experience.

But the 'new romance' is overshadowed by the macabreness described in his critical moments. 'Isabella' is clearly post-*Endymion*, shown in the poet's con-scious introduction of the 'disagreeables' into the romance. Indeed the poem reads like a Jacobean tragedy. The climax of the story is handled by fusing together violence and pity, horror and tenderness, when Isabella digs 'the murderous spot' (365) for Lorenzo's corpse, and when she brings home the skull and cleans it 'with tears' (406). For all its improvements from *Endymion*, 'Isabella' still fell short of Keats's own standard, as he would comment a year later: 'Isabella is what I should call were I a reviewer "A weak-sided Poem" with an amusing sober-sadness about it', because 'in my dramatic capacity I enter fully into the feeling: but in Propria Persona I should be apt to quiz it myself' (*KL* II:174). The romance does suggest the conspicuous dramatic attempt Keats has made, especially in his portrayal of Isabella's two brothers that is not found in Boccaccio, where they are assigned the social status of the owners of 'torched mines and noisy factories' (108), and thus possess the nature to only 'pinch and peel' (120), giving rise to Bernard Shaw's radical Marxist reading of 'Isabella'.[5] Keats thus provides the motive for their murder of Lorenzo, that as their social inferior, Lorenzo gets in the way of their plan to marry their sister to 'some high noble and his olive-trees' (168). Their internal world is also tended to, so that after the murder, they are haunted as Macbeth by the spectre of 'their murder'd man' (209) and the nightmare of 'their sister in her snowy shroud' (264). But, as Keats suggested, the dramatic attempts were made by his poetic persona, the one who tried to take 'refuge' in the romance, while his true self was struggling elsewhere. 'Isabella' thus, according to Keats himself, 'is too smokeable', for 'for '[t]here is too much inexperience of live, and simplicity of knowledge in it' (*KL* II:174).

'Experience' and 'knowledge', these were his chief concerns during this time. He wrote to Taylor on 24 April, 'I have been hovering for some time between an exquisite sense of the luxurious and a love for Philosophy – were I calculated for the former I should be glad – but as I am not I shall turn all my soul to the latter' (*KL* I:271). It was during this time that he was thinking of asking Hazlitt about 'the best metaphysical road [he] can take' in the future. Even the walking tour to the Lake District and Scotland in the summer was taken in the hope that 'it would give [him] more experience', in addition to the purpose that the expedition would 'load [him] with grander Mountains' (*KL* I:342) to prepare for the epic setting in *Hyperion*. For all the change of the scene, the epistemic pain acutely experienced in Teignmouth was still on his mind. In the sonnet composed on the top of Ben Nevis, 'Read me a lesson, Muse, and speak it loud', the pervasive mist, emblematic of boundless 'uncertainties, Mysteries, doubts', dramatizes a moment when negative capability is experienced as an agnostic state of blindness. All these thoughts in his critical period finally evolved into *Hyperion*, an epic attempt to philosophize about human experience subjected to constant process and change.

The 'philosophy' of *Hyperion* is easily identified with the long speech of Oceanus, the 'Sophist' (II:168) of the Titans, which takes the central place in Book II explicating the inevitability of natural process. But the epic is not about passive acceptance, and the hero of *Hyperion* is not Oceanus but Apollo, as Keats made clear when he planned for *Hyperion* as a different Greek project from *Endymion*: 'the Hero of the written tale being mortal is led on, like Buonaparte, by circumstance; whereas the Apollo in Hyperion being a fore-seeing God will shape his actions like one' (*KL* I:207). What Keats attempts to 'philosophize' in

Hyperion is laid on Apollo, who becomes the god of poetry by his knowledge of sufferings gained from sympathetic imagination. Ironically, it is precisely the part on Apollo that was left unfinished. The epic thus turns out to be a drama rather than a philosophy of agony, and Apollo's symbolic role is consequently open to question. It is as if *Hyperion* started out reaching after 'knowledge enormous', but ended up in uncertainties and doubts. By the incomplete philosophy in Apollo's fragment, however, negative capability is kept intact after all the struggles with it as a perilous mental state in need of philosophical reference points.

The opening that has amazed generations of readers with the miracle of the sudden emergence of a great poet unfolds the epic together with the fertile, final year of Keats's short poetic career:

> Deep in the shady sadness of a vale
> Far sunken from the healthy breath of morn,
> Far from the fiery noon, and eve's one star,
> Sat gray-hair'd Saturn, quiet as a stone,
> Still as the silence round about his lair. (I:1–5)

The sublime blank verse with heavy alliteration vocally brings out the sad, still Saturn, who has fallen into an abysm that is neither temporal, being 'far from' 'morn', 'noon' or 'eve', nor timeless, the grey hair being the cruel reminder of age. The physical motionlessness embodies his mental paralysis after the fall. Saturn, as the king of the fallen immortals, is caught between mortality and divinity. In this new, strange state of being, the self becomes dislocated, as Saturn then relates to Thea, 'I am gone / Away from my own bosom: I have left / My strong identity, my real self, / Somewhere between the throne, and where I sit / Here on this spot of earth' (I:112–16). The violence of the shock fallen from the heavenly throne to this earthly spot is proportionate with the 'strong identity' he possesses, deprived of which he is left completely petrified. As many critics have noted, the trace of Milton's Satan is evident, and it also calls back the identity crisis Lear experiences after abandoning the crown and being deprived of sovereignty. Like Lear, who immediately turns his shocked self into the third-person other by asking 'Doth Lear walk thus? speak thus? Where are his eyes?' (I. iv. 202), Saturn also feels a keen sense of self-estrangement: 'tell me if this feeble shape / Is Saturn's; tell me, if thou hear'st the voice / Of Saturn' (I:98–100). Because of his fast clinging to the self, the only resort Saturn can take to deal with the loss is to seek for restoration, and the mighty agony caused by his 'strong identity' defines the emotional tone of all the other fallen Titans, except Oceanus.

In contrast to the other Titans who parallel Saturn in their unbending identities which have thrown them deeper into their agonies, Oceanus embodies disinterestedness when dealing with one's personal pain. Therefore he admonishes the Titans to 'be content to stoop' (II:178) and 'take that comfort in its truth' (II:180), and reproaches Saturn for being 'blind from sheer supremacy' (II:185), who thus cannot see the 'eternal truth' (II:187) as he does. As the 'sage' (II:168) of the Titans, his wisdom is encapsulated by his famous lines of 'to bear all naked truths,/ And to envisage circumstance, all calm,/ That is the top of sovereignty' (II:203–5). Unlike the other Titans who 'nurse' their 'agonies' (II:174), Oceanus's calmness derives from a disinterested perspective which enables him to 'envisage' the 'circumstance' of their fall as inevitable, and thus to 'bear' its 'naked truth'. He asks rhetorically:

> . . . doth the dull soil
> Quarrel with the proud forests it hath fed,
> And feedeth still, more comely than itself?
> Can it deny the chiefdom of green groves?
> Or shall the tree be envious of the dove
> Because it cooeth, and hath snowy wings
> To wander wherewithal and find its joys?
> We are such forest-trees, and our fair boughs
> Have bred forth, not pale solitary doves,
> But eagles golden-feather'd, who do tower
> Above us in their beauty, and must reign
> In right thereof; for 'tis the eternal law
> That first in beauty should be first in might: (II:217–29)

By disinterestedness, Oceanus recognizes the greater purpose of the universe and willingly submits to his own agony. But here one needs to be wary. Though consistent with Keats's objections to egotism, Oceanus's 'philosophy' should not be taken as the final words of Keats. Oceanus's optimistic outlook of the evolution in the universe flashes back ironically to the 'eternal fierce destruction' in the epistle to Reynolds that presents the same evolutionary process in a very different light. On the other hand, the contradiction itself reveals the inherent paradoxes of the natural law which prescribes both rise and fall, birth and death, in which the cruelty of mortality is interdependent with the renewal of life. Oceanus's 'philosophy' therefore is more likely one line of argument Keats took in contention with other lines in his 'speculations' about human existence.

This inevitable process of evolution is epitomized in the succession of Hyperion by Apollo, who represents the most beautiful of the Olympians, as Hyperion is the mightiest of Titans, being the last dethroned. And it is in Hyperion that the drama of this epic is most fully played out; he is the only character undergoing the process of dethronement, thus exemplifying a more complex range of emotions than the already fallen Titans. Being both 'earth-born' (I:309) and 'sky-engendered' (I:310), he holds tension within himself as a god mixed with humanity. Hyperion enters the scene as an immortal preyed upon by human weakness: 'as among us mortals omens drear / Fright and perplex, so also shuddered he' (I:169–70). Juxtaposed with the calm Oceanus in his fear, Hyperion also differentiates himself from the other Titans in his bending 'his spirit to the sorrow of the time' 'by hard compulsion', despite his nature that is 'unus'd to bend' (I:301, 300). Perfectly exemplifying what Keats writes in the letter, that 'a mighty providence subdues the mightiest Minds to the service of the time being' (*KL* I:282), Hyperion reaches 'the top of sovereignty' by his submission, but his 'hard compulsion' also forecasts his loss of the actual throne, to be superseded by Apollo who is to go through a similar convulsion. When Hyperion comes to the Titans in Book II, lighting up the abysm they are in, he is at once their ally, by exerting the last power of the Titans, and their most cruel traitor by exposing the 'naked' truth of their fall into a glaring sight. In their 'misery his brilliance had betray'd' (II:369), Hyperion sees his own sad fate, which makes him part of their darkness exposed by his own light, becoming himself 'a vast shade / In midst of his own brightness' (II:372–3). In these paradoxes and conflicts that Hyperion manifests, he dramatizes the fear of change in his foresight, the struggles for acceptance in his attempts at submission, and the agony of loss not consoled but aggravated by his clear vision of its inevitability.

But the epic is not meant to be a drama of Hyperion. Apollo finally appears in the last book, entering the scene in 'bright tears' (III:42). As sorrow is native to him, so is he born with a golden lyre, as related by Mnemosyne:

> Thou hast dream'd of me; and awaking up
> Didst find a lyre all golden by thy side,
> Whose strings touch'd by thy fingers, all the vast
> Unwearied ear of the whole universe
> Listen'd in pain and pleasure at the birth
> Of such new tuneful wonder. Is't not strange
> That thou shouldst weep, so gifted? (III:62–8)

Dreaming of the mother goddess of the Muses and awaking to find the golden lyre, Apollo comes to the world as the very incarnation of imagination which will turn him into the god of poetry. Significantly, his golden melody delivers both 'pain and pleasure' to the universe, just as he is caught by grief even when he is endowed with the pre-eminent gift. In contrast with Hyperion, who is haunted by the fear for an unknown fate, Apollo is tortured by 'fearless' and 'aching ignorance' (III:107) and cannot help pursuing the source of his sorrow: 'I strive to search wherefore I am so sad' (III:88). With his powerful sympathetic imagination, he reads in the face of the goddess of memory the history of the fallen gods, whose agony is intuitively envisioned by him and taken on as his own burden. Mnemosyne's countenance recording the experience of the universe becomes the very threshold Apollo has to cross before achieving divinity: 'Knowledge enormous makes a God of me. / Names, deeds, gray legends, dire events, rebellions, / Majesties, sovran voices, agonies, / Creations and destroyings, all at once / Pour into the wide hollows of my brain, / And deify me' (III:113–18). The deifying 'knowledge', paradoxically, is the knowledge of the world, the world of magnitude and diversity. It is the knowledge of experience, especially painful experience, as that undergone by the Titans, whose 'agonies' are but part of the universal process composed of interdependent 'creations and destroyings' that constantly regenerate the world. Only by acquiring this knowledge perceived from a sympathetic imagination of the painful experience of those he is to supersede, can Apollo take Hyperion's place and transfigure himself into the god of immortal poetry who will convey such 'knowledge enormous'. Before finally passing into Godhood, Apollo is yet to suffer from physical agony 'like the struggle at the gate of death' (III:126). Only after experiencing mortality does Apollo eventually gain divinity and 'die into life' (III:130).

Here the fragment ends, and since the epic was suspended when Tom died on 1 December, it was never resumed with the same swing of power, until in a year's time, it was reconstructed into a vision of *The Fall of Hyperion*, in which the poet himself has to undergo a 'struggle at the gate of death' before he can 'see as a God sees' (I:304). Of course, the second *Hyperion* is again unfinished, but it is not given up for exactly the same reasons. Back in May, when Keats told Reynolds that knowledge would 'ease the Burden of the Mystery', he wrote in the same letter:

> The difference of high Sensations with and without knowledge appears to me this – in the latter case we are falling continually ten thousand fathoms deep and being blown up again without wings and with all [the] horror of a <Case> bare shoulderd Creature – in the former case, our shoulders are fledge<d>, and we go thro' the same <Fir> air and space without fear. (*KL* I:277)

But when he continues, he hesitates, 'it is impossible to know how far knowlege will console <as> us for the death of a friend and the ill "that flesh is heir to<o>"' (*KL* I:277–8). And death indeed happened, in face of which, the 'knowledge enormous' that he had hoped for Apollo to embody turned out to fail to attach wings to his bare shoulders, but only revealed to him again that a human being is 'no more than a poor, bare, forked animal'. When he was not convinced of his philosophizing project, he left it as 'half knowledge' and chose to remain in uncertainties. After all, as he puts it, 'The Genius of Poetry must work out its own salvation in a man' (*KL* I:374).

'Phantoms' in the Romances

The two *Hyperions* roughly mark out the starting and ending points of this 'Great Year', in which the next accomplishment is again a romance. Douglas Bush claims 'The Eve of St. Agnes' to be 'by far the most beautiful short narrative of its age, or perhaps of any age of English poetry' (1967: 111), and one should not forget that its beauty is sharply delineated by its contrasting cold and dark background, just as the romantic love is constantly threatened by its realistic and hostile surrounding. It is a romance haunted by phantoms of doubts if not disbelief, surreptitiously reminding its readers that it is composed of only 'shadows haunting fairily / The brain' (39–40).

Keats was all too deliberate in conveying this effect, as is most evidently exemplified in its ending:

And they are gone: ay, ages long ago
These lovers fled away into the storm.
That night the Baron dreamt of many a woe,
And all his warrior-guests, with shade and form
Of witch, and demon, and large coffin-worm,
Were long be-nightmar'd. Angela the old
Died palsy-twitch'd, with meagre face deform;
The Beadsman, after thousand aves told,
For aye unsought for slept among his ashes cold. (370–8)

What brought Keats to conclude with such an anti-Romantic ending is related by Woodhouse: 'He says he likes that the poem should leave off with this Change of Sentiment – it was what he aimed at, & was glad to find from my objections to it that he had succeeded' (*KL* II:163). Indeed, this sudden shift in both the narrative tone and the temporal scale not only changes the 'Sentiment' but also turns the poem into a problem Romance. The abrupt distancing of the narrated time scale announces the death of the lovers, and even when the next line returns to the temporal framework of the narrative, the ominous tone in the lovers' disappearance into the storm is too clear to miss, which is yet reinforced by the following gothic, nightmarish images, and culminates in the concluding image of death. With the last note falling on the 'ashes cold', the ending tolls the readers back to the opening scene of coldness and stillness, thus conveying a keen sense of disillusionment, as if the whole poem is but an elaborate beautiful dream:

St. Agnes' Eve – Ah, bitter chill it was!
The owl, for all his feathers, was a-cold;
The hare limp'd trembling through the frozen grass,
And silent was the flock in woolly fold:
Numb were the Beadsman's fingers, while he told

His rosary, and while his frosted breath,
Like pious incense from a censer old,
Seem'd taking flight for heaven, without a death,
Past the sweet Virgin's picture, while his prayer he saith. (1–9)

The opening scene sets the narrative on a dramatic track for it to unfold itself, with the authorial presence hidden behind the scene, unlike 'Isabella' where the narrator every now and then intrudes. The whole poem is not only dramatic but has a cinematographic quality, with its pictorial detail in fine grain and motion followed in precise gradations. With the camera following the Beadsman, the tale moves out of its initial cold, still sepulchral world and opens to chambers of life and warmth where sound and light pour in to enliven the whole scene: 'At length burst in the argent revelry, / With plume, tiara, and all rich array, / Numerous as shadows haunting fairily / The brain, new stuff'd, in youth, with triumphs gay / Of old romance' (37–41). The brilliant and rich colouring, however, becomes phantasmal when it is compared to the 'numerous' 'shadows' 'haunting' the mind, as 'youth' is undercut by its 'triumphs' only in the remote 'old romance'. Only after such a prologue betraying a not altogether willing suspension of disbelief, does Madeline finally enter.

Porphyro's entrance is no less ominous. 'With heart on fire' (75), he is countered by the 'hot blood' (86) of the 'blood-thirsty race' inside (99). The reminiscence of the star-crossed fate of Romeo and Juliet is indicated again when Madeline finally enters the chamber where Porphyro has hidden himself: 'Out went the taper as she hurried in; / Its little smoke, in pallid moonshine, died' (199–200). As if the extinguished candle is not ominous enough, another association with death is made in contrast with her 'panting' (201) life and 'voluble' (204) heart: 'As though a tongueless nightingale should swell / Her throat in vain, and die, heart-stifled, in her dell' (206–7). The looming shadow of death is immediately expelled by a dazzling display of the window of Madeline's chamber:

A casement high and triple-arch'd there was,
All garlanded with carven imag'ries
Of fruits, and flowers, and bunches of knot-grass,
And diamonded with panes of quaint device,
Innumerable of stains and splendid dyes,
As are the tiger-moth's deep-demask'd wings; (208–13)

The visual extravagance presented in the rich diversity of 'imag'ries' in colour, shape, and light is accompanied by the vocal intricacy, with numerous interlaced alliterations conveying the exquisite splendour. This luxuriant setting prepares for Madeline's entrance which brings in more sensuousness, but at this point, Madeline is described as one who 'dreams awake' (232), in fear that 'all the charm is fled' (234), and soon falls asleep, to be 'blinded alike from sunshine and from rain' (242). Her carefulness to preserve the 'charm' calls one's attention to its very fragility.

When the romance is to culminate in the feast Porphyro prepares for Madeline, the door opens to another world: 'The boisterous, midnight, festive clarion, / The kettle-drum, and far-heard clarionet, / Affray his ears, though but in dying tone: – / The hall door shuts again, and all the noise is gone' (258–61). As the door has at the beginning led the tale into a bright warm setting, now it brings back, however momentarily, the threatening 'blood-thirsty' world to the lovers. When Madeline finally awakes from her dream and finds Porphyro, she sees in her lover a ghostly image, 'how pallid, chill, and drear!' (311), and pleads: 'if thou diest, my love, I know not where to go' (315). Then comes the consummation scene, but 'meantime the frost-wind blows / Like Love's alarum pattering the sharp sleet / Against the window-panes; St. Agnes' moon hath set' (322–4). The setting of the moon accompanying the fulfilment at the same time concludes the romantic night, and it also darkens all the brilliance once displayed on the window. The spell is about to be broken, when the storm sets in to give further threat. The sense of urgency delivered by 'Love's alarum' is immediately picked up when Porphyro tells Madeline, 'Arise – arise! the morning is at hand' (345), as Romeo pressed to flee at hearing the morning lark. The lovers then move on in haste:

> She hurried at his words, beset with fears,
> For there were sleeping dragons all around,
> At glaring watch, perhaps, with ready spears –
> Down the wide stairs a darkling way they found. –
> In all the house was heard no human sound. (352–6)

Once out of the dream chamber, the story revolves to darkness and silence, but perils are still constantly menacing, with the 'glaring watch' and 'ready spears' of the hostile human force, and the natural world that is no more welcoming, with the arras blown up and the carpets rising in the storm. Their way out also seems awfully long when their movement to reach the door is meticulously described in each step:

> They glide, like phantoms, into the wide hall;
> Like phantoms, to the iron porch, they glide;
> Where lay the Porter, in uneasy sprawl,
> With a huge empty flaggon by his side:
> The wakeful bloodhound rose, and shook his hide,
> But his sagacious eye an inmate owns:

By one, and one, the bolts full easy slide: –
The chains lie silent on the footworn stones; –
The key turns, and the door upon its hinges groans. (361–9)

The ease of their glide becomes ponderous in its repetition, which seems to
send them back to where they were, and the comparison of them to 'phantoms'
is repeated as if for fear that the readers would forget their illusory nature. The
sprawling porter anticipates the deformed face of the dead Angela, while the
'bloodhound' calls back the 'blood-thirsty race', as the 'footworn' stones con-
jure up all the 'sleeping dragons'. The 'easy slide' of the bolts is slowed down by
each pause in 'by one, and one', while the door's groan gives the final men-
acing note. Even if there is any sense of relief when one reaches the end of the
stanza as the lovers have finally taken leave of the claustrophobic interior, it is
immediately deflated by the concluding stanza. The romance, therefore, for all
its extravagant beauty, draws attention to its disagreeable background. Without
such a background, its beauty would lose the intense focus, and the problem
Romance might be but a cloying fairy tale.

When Keats relates his dissatisfaction with 'Isabella' in his comment, 'in my
dramatic capacity I enter fully into the feeling: but in Propria Persona I should
be apt to quiz it myself', he applies this criticism to 'The Eve of St. Agnes' as
well: 'There is no objection of this kind to Lamia – A good deal to St Agnes
Eve – only not so glaring' (*KL* II:174). He mentions the poem again in a later
letter: 'I wish to diffuse the colouring of St Agnes eve throughout a Poem in
which Character and Sentiment would be the figures to such drapery' (*KL* II:234).
What Keats seems to suggest is that 'The Eve of St Agnes' is dramatic only on
the superficial level of its 'colouring' and 'drapery', while its 'characters' and
'sentiments' are not depicted with equal finesse and intricacy, for his true
self has not fully entered into the characters and their sentiments. Indeed,
Madeline and Porphyro are phantom-like; they do not exemplify any complex
'sentiments', and in this sense, the romance is like 'Isabella', a bit 'smokeable'.

Keats's comment also reveals the essential difference between the two narra-
tives composed in 1819. If 'The Eve of St. Agnes' has an anti-romantic under-
tone, then 'Lamia', which in the first place can hardly be counted as a Romance,
is at times openly satirical. If the fate of Madeline and Porphyro is portentous,
then 'Lamia' does end in disillusionment and death, already foretold by the
'palely loitering' (2) knight haunted by la belle dame sans merci. Composed
from June to September, 'Lamia' exemplifies Keats's evolution within this great
year in its departure from 'The Eve of St. Agnes' written in January. Reporting
his progress on 'Lamia' to Reynolds on 11 July, Keats wrote, 'I have great hopes
of success, because I make use of my Judgment more deliberately than I yet
have done' (II:128). This 'healthy deliberation' (*KL* II:128) is most clearly
manifested in the refusal of 'Lamia' to commit to either affirmation or denial

of an enchanting but illusory experience, as well as the narrator's equivocation between these two opposite stances.

Lamia herself emerges as a strange combination of beauty and beast, yet being neither:

> She was a gordian shape of dazzling hue,
> Vermilion-spotted, golden, green, and blue;
> Striped like a zebra, freckled like a pard,
> Eyed like a peacock, and all crimson barr'd;
> And full of silver moons, that, as she breathed,
> Dissolv'd, or brighter shone, or interwreathed
> Their lustres with the gloomier tapestries – (I:47–53)

What is seen is a being of a chameleon nature encompassing multiple lives, which constantly shifts between 'brighter' and 'gloomier' shades of colouring. Dazzling and volatile, her identity is difficult to pin down. Being '[s]o rainbow-sided' (I:54), she embodies romantic fantasy in her very shape, colourful but transitory, spectacular yet insubstantial. With this indefinable identity, 'She seem'd, at once, some penanced lady elf, / Some demon's mistress, or the demon's self' (I:55–6). The incongruous combination of the fairy and the beastly shapes makes it uncertain whether her nature is benignant or malignant, but the serpentine association with the demon is too strong to be rid of, which is reinforced by the falling tone of the couplet that at the same time closes the issue with a sardonic finality, reminiscent of the satirical couplet at the tail of each *ottava rima* stanza of *Don Juan*. Consequently, when she is about to discard the demonic shape, the very metamorphosis she is undergoing reveals only more clearly her demonic nature:

> Her mouth foam'd, and the grass, therewith besprent,
> Wither'd at dew so sweet and virulent;
> Her eyes in torture fix'd, and anguish drear,
> Hot, glaz'd, and wide, with lid-lashes all sear,
> Flash'd phosphor and sharp sparks, without one cooling tear. (I:148–52)

These repulsive and horrendous images of her convulsion intentionally forbid sympathy for her pain, which seems alien to human suffering ('without one cooling tear'), and destructive to nature as well (the grass is 'withered' by her poisonous dew). As the metamorphosis continues, the transformation seems only to have taken away her former dazzling appearance,

> So that, in moments few, she was undrest
> Of all her sapphires, greens, and amethyst,

And rubious-argent: of all these bereft,
Nothing but pain and ugliness were left. (I:161–4)

The process is recorded in a series of reductive or negative verbs, until the final 'bereft' makes the desertion of the demonic, or elfish, disguise and the adoption of womanhood a lamentable change of deprivation and loss. Therefore, when Lamia takes on a human shape to entice Lycius, the narrator's celebration of her womanhood conveys only dramatic irony:

Let the mad poets say whate'er they please
Of the sweets of Fairies, Peris, Goddesses,
There is not such a treat among them all,
Haunters of cavern, lake, and waterfall,
As a real woman, lineal indeed
From Pyrrha's pebbles or old Adam's seed. (I:328–33)

The satirical tone is apparent and manifold. The obvious dramatic irony is pointed to Lycius, who does not know that Lamia is anything but 'a real woman'. The narrator, knowing better than Lycius, pokes fun at 'the mad poets' as well, thus distancing himself from the poet. The reminder that the narrator is another dramatic persona gives the narrative a thematic uncertainty, as here it is difficult to judge whether Lamia's temptation of Lycius in human shape is an act of love or an exemplification of her demonic deceptive nature.

At the other extreme from Lamia, who is on the border between a fairy enchanter and a devilish deceiver, stands the philosophic Apollonius, who from the first suspects her and soon sees through her as the latter. As soon as he reaches the conclusion, he 'laugh'd' (II:159) to his satisfaction, 'As though some knotty problem, that had daft / His patient thought, had now begun to thaw, / And solve and melt: – 'twas just as he foresaw' (II:160–2). For Apollonius, any mystery in life is a 'knotty' problem to be solved, to be put under the 'consequitive' analysis made by 'his patient thought', which impatiently reaches for a resolution that is inevitably abstract and reductive. The validity of Apollonius's philosophy, as Lamia's charm, is questioned by the intrusive narrator:

. . . Do not all charms fly
At the mere touch of cold philosophy?
There was an awful rainbow once in heaven:
We know her woof, her texture; she is given
In the dull catalogue of common things.
Philosophy will clip an Angel's wings,
Conquer all mysteries by rule and line,
Empty the haunted air, and gnomed mine –
Unweave a rainbow, as it erewhile made
The tender-person'd Lamia melt into a shade. (II:229–38)

The 'rainbow-sided' Lamia is posed against the cold philosopher Apollonius. The enchantment of the former cannot be perceived by the latter, nor the mysteries of the former be borne by the latter. While sympathy is obviously given to the 'tender-person'd' Lamia by the narrator, the very epithet suggests irony, for she is only an impersonator of humanity despite all her charms. The ambivalence is further intensified in the fact that Apollonius does turn out to conquer her mysteries which are indeed illusory, as if to confirm that 'the poetry of the rainbow' can after all be reduced to 'the prismatic colours'.

Caught in the middle of the antithesis between Lamia and Apollonius, Lycius establishes a triangular shape for the narrative that cannot be resolved by a clean dichotomy between the two sides of the antithesis. As Apollonius's student, Lycius has the same philosophical mindset, but he is also fascinated with the mysteries Lamia presents to him. His duality differentiates him from the single-minded Endymion who takes the pilgrimage and fulfils his love for his goddess, or Madeline who elopes with her dream lover, though to an unknown fate. Unlike these romances and the opening episode of Hermes and the nymph, the tale of Lycius and Lamia does not stop right at the fulfilment of love but goes on to the subsequent decline and even plunges into the final disaster. Already prophesied when Hermes 'flew' with his nymph 'into the green-recessed woods' (I:144) where they would not '[grow]' 'pale, as mortal lovers do' (I:145), the lovers in Book II find themselves in a mundane human world where love produces surfeit after the most passionate culmination. As the noise from the outside world invades the romantic chamber of Madeline, Lycius '[starts]' at 'a thrill / Of trumpets' (II:27–8) and is left with 'a thought' (II:29). The 'consequitive' mind cannot rest in innocent blissful immersion: 'His spirit pass'd beyond its golden bourn / Into the noisy world almost forsworn' (II:32–3). Unable to enjoy the idyllic existence unreflectively, Lycius proves himself a man of this world, and his proposal of the wedding is but an act of reclaiming the worldliness that he has 'almost forsworn'. By forcing Lamia to expose herself to the worldly Corinth, Lycius has unwittingly allied himself with Apollonius, and he, as much as Apollonius, has doomed the serpentine Lamia to vanish in the end.

The feast, preceding the fulfilment of imagination and consummation of love in other Keatsian romances, now leads to the catastrophe:

> Soft went the music the soft air along,
> While fluent Greek a vowel'd undersong
> Kept up among the guests, discoursing low
> At first, for scarcely was the wine at flow;
> But when the happy vintage touch'd their brains,
> Louder they talk, and louder come the strains
> Of powerful instruments . . .
> Now, when the wine has done its rosy deed,
> And every soul from human trammels freed,

No more so strange; for merry wine, sweet wine,
Will make Elysian shades not too fair, too divine. (II:199–205, 209–12)

As the music plays louder within the scene, the vocal force of the narrative increases gradually to achieve a hymnal effect for the overwhelming power of enchantment to break through 'human trammels' to enjoy Elysian bliss. On the other hand, the music increases in volume as the boisterous guests of this 'noisy world' become louder, while the wine pours forth Dionysian freedom together with worldly voluptuousness. The crescendo is juxtaposed with the gradual silencing in the final scene of disillusionment, when Lamia turns cold at Apollonius's penetrating sight: 'the loud revelry / Grew hush; the stately music no more breathes; / The myrtle sicken'd in a thousand wreaths. / By faint degrees, voice, lute, and pleasure ceased; / A deadly silence step by step increased' (II:262–6). At this moment, Lycius shrieks, 'Begone, foul dream!' (II:271). His double-edged shout transforms his former enchanting dream to something foul, as at his later echo of Apollonius's 'A Serpent!' (II:305) Lamia finally vanishes. Now Lycius finds in Lamia's face 'no azure vein / Wander'd on fair-spaced temples; no soft bloom / Misted the cheek; no passion to illume / The deep-recessed vision: – all was blight; / Lamia, no longer fair, there sat a deadly white' (II:272–6). Lamia's gradual transformation to a ghostly shade, contrary to her initial metamorphosis, is a process of losing human traces alike to a human death, thus betraying mournfulness and inviting sympathy. Lycius's immediately following death gives the narrative a further twist: is he killed by the grief of love, or by the shocking realization of the 'blight'? While he accuses Apollonius of 'his demon eyes' (II:289), has he not insistently gazed at Lamia himself which finally earns him the deadly vision, but then is not Lamia 'the demon's self'?

If Lamia's fanciful banquet can be exorcized, does it indicate that Porphyro's feast is but illusory as well, as is the beautiful romance itself? Does it also put into question Endymion's dream of his goddess, suspicious of his pilgrimage after an imaginative beauty? On the other hand, Apollonius's 'dissecting' intellect and 'consequitive' philosophy only end up killing Lycius whom he wishes to save. Does it not affirm 'the holiness of the Heart's affections and the truth of Imagination'? The poem provokes these debates but carefully avoids taking sides, leaving itself in ambiguity and refusing to close the issue. Such a maturing of negative capability characterizes Keats's major poems composed in this great year.

The Drama in the Odes

The spring of 1819 was the blossoming season for Keats the poet, but his long journal letter to George and Georgiana written from 14 February to 3 May reveals a soul going through a hard ordeal. 'Ode to Psyche' was found in the letter, copied a few days after the 'soul-making' part written on 21 April. Keats's reference to the poem indicates that he follows Lempriere's explanation of Psyche as signifying the soul (*KPA* 515), and after copying the poem together with a handful of sonnets, he finishes the long letter in a cheerful tone: 'this is the 3ᵈ of May & every thing is in delightful forwardness; the violets are not withered, before the peeping of the first rose' (*KL* II:109). Thus unfolded the spring of the great odes. This sudden outburst of creativity does seem to be provoked by the tragic vision of the soul-making world, but the bright-coloured ode to the soul does not translate that grim vision, nor do the other odes readily fit in with the soul-making prose except 'Ode on Melancholy', which reads like a natural conclusion of all the other odes which are interrelated thematically among themselves. The spring odes therefore may very well be read, as they often are, as a whole, and the whole needs to be viewed in a dramatic light because of this gap between the speaking 'I' and the poet himself. This drama is played out within the human consciousness itself, posing what Faulkner calls 'the problems of the human heart in conflict with itself' (119), and in the process, the speaker-poet moves towards the tragic vision the poet himself has gained. 'Ode to Psyche' as the prologue establishes the exposition of the conflict with its antithetical 'Ode on Indolence'. The conflict develops into intensity in 'Ode to a Nightingale' and 'Ode on a Grecian Urn', each of which unfolds a drama within itself, and it finally concludes in 'Ode on Melancholy'. This odic drama, naturally grown out of the problem Romance of 'The Eve of St. Agnes', discloses a contestation about the value of imagination – whether it has a valid creative power, or only preys on the mind as a demonic force – and intensifies into a contention of poetic imagination with human experience itself, asking whether by its power human beings may hope to be delivered from their miserable existence, or will only be brought to face the painful human reality in a sharper clarity. The questioning process is finally resolved in the embrace of the conflict itself for being the most intense human experience. The triumphantly tragic denouement in the spring, however, is only eventually fulfilled with negative capability in the final ode 'To Autumn', which concludes with no conclusion.

'Ode to Psyche' opens the drama in a dream-vision framework, with the speaker-poet narrating: 'Surely I dreamt to-day, or did I see / The winged Psyche with awaken'd eyes?' (5–6). With the receptive mind open to vision, the speaker enters into the realm of Flora and Pan: 'I wander'd in a forest thoughtlessly, / And, on the sudden, fainting with surprise, / Saw two fair creatures, couched side by side / In deepest grass' (7–10). Rather than an unconscious regression to his immature poetry, as argued by some critics, this return to the Arcadian idyll is, as the speaker makes clear in his opening invocation, 'remembrance dear' (2), a retrospection to the passage of human life from 'the infant or thoughtless Chamber' to 'the Chamber of Maiden-Thought', when 'I' was wandering 'thoughtlessly' before being revealed of the sight of wonder. It is in the awakening of imagination that one grows out of innocence, which, as Keats puts it in his explication of the metaphor, '[sharpens] one's vision into the heart and nature of Man'. Thus the innocent speaker sees Cupid and Psyche, who, looking back to Diana and Endymion, incarnate 'fellowship divine', while Psyche, paralleling Endymion, is a mortal deified for this 'fellowship with essence'. The speaker thus ordains himself to be the poet-priest for the new goddess, 'I see, and sing, by my own eyes inspired' (43), endeavouring to transform the vision into poetic imagination. The worship of the goddess becomes then at once the celebration of his own new role as a poet, both of which are realized by no other force but the mind: 'Yes, I will be thy priest, and build a fane / In some untrodden region of my mind, / Where branched thoughts, new grown with pleasant pain, / Instead of pines shall murmur in the wind' (50–3). 'The mind alone is formative', transfiguring itself into a virgin land for the 'fane' to be built on, and turning its interlaced thoughts into trees, rooted in the newly awakened experience of the heart in 'pleasant pain'. In the very process of asserting the imagination, the fane seems built up when it becomes 'a rosy sanctuary', which the speaker-poet will 'dress / With the wreath'd trellis of a working brain, / With buds, and bells, and stars without a name, / With all the gardener Fancy e'er could feign, / Who breeding flowers, will never breed the same' (59–63). The new poet's 'untrodden' mind has grown into 'a working brain', which, plotted by the gardener Imagination, is able to create a realm of richer charm than the actual world of nature subject to mutability. Imagination thus 'breeding flowers, will never breed the same'; like the immortals' 'aurorean love' (20), it is ever refreshed. The worship is fulfilled in the fulfilment of love, which, recapitulating the theme in *Endymion*, is 'the chief intensity' achieved by imagination.

Thus the first act of the odic drama concludes in the triumphant celebration of the active assertion of imaginative power, which then shifts in 'Ode on Indolence' to present a passive state of mind that refuses to be delivered out of its 'indolence':[6] 'Ripe was the drowsy hour; / The blissful cloud of summer-indolence / Benumb'd my eyes; my pulse grew less and less; / Pain had no sting, and pleasure's wreath no flower' (15–18). This suspension of the active power of the mind resembles a waning life with a weakening pulse, but it also suggests fertility with its 'ripeness'. It is a blissful state of numbness that senses no pain, but it is also deprived of the intensity to feel any joy. This delicate state of indolence, however, is under threat, haunted by the shadows of Love, Ambition, and Poesy, all of which are celebrated in 'Ode to Psyche'. They are 'like figures on a marble urn' (5), emerging and fading alternately. So does the speaker-poet's view of them keep shifting, as he first complains: 'why did ye not melt' (19), but soon 'burn'd / And ached for wings' 'to follow them' (23–4). The contradictory moods here are no different from the thematic contrast of the two odes. Love, what he has seen incarnate, is now questioned: 'What is Love? and where is it?' (32). Ambition, that which has inspired him to worship the neglected goddess and to make himself a poet-priest, now becomes 'a man's little heart's short fever-fit' (34). But the most violent turn occurs with Poesy. While the 'Ode to Psyche' celebrates the self-making of a poet, the present speaker curses '[his] demon Poesy' (30): 'For Poesy! – no, – she has not a joy, – / At least for me, – so sweet as drowsy noons, / And evenings steep'd in honied indolence' (35–7). Poesy is abandoned for the lotos-eaters' oblivious resignation, for the mind wishes to be 'shelter'd' from the knowledge of this world that 'annoys', be it 'how change the moons' or 'the voice of busy common-sense' (38–40). Ironically, the celebration of indolence becomes increasingly anticipatory of the worship of Psyche, with the 'sleep' 'embroider'd with dim dreams' (42) preparing for 'the wreath'd trellis of a working brain', and the soul, as 'a lawn besprinkled o'er / With flowers, and stirring shades, and baffled beams' (43–4), calling forth the silent plotting of the gardener Fancy. 'Ripe was the drowsy hour'; the very act of enjoying the richness of indolence draws it ever closer to the state of creativity. So indolence becomes the 'sleep' preceding 'poetry', the passive receptiveness storing up the outpouring creative energy. When the speaker-poet claims that he 'yet [has] visions' (57) for the night and the day, commanding, 'Vanish, ye phantoms, from my idle spright' (59), his visions become indistinguishably blurred with the phantoms he tries to dispel, forming the very force which is about to disrupt his 'idleness'. The 'blissful' state of suspension soon collapses, and the 'drowsy numbness' is found to be painful in the next act.

'My heart aches, and a drowsy numbness pains / My sense, as though of hemlock I had drunk, / Or emptied some dull opiate to the drains / One minute past, and Lethe-wards had sunk' (1–4). So the speaker in the next ode starts. In contrast to the state of indolence which is 'a rare instance of advantage in the body overpowering the Mind' (*KL* II:79), now it is the mind that over-powers the body: the aching heart transforms its pain to the physical sense, making the very numbness painful. The state of indolence has lost its fragile equilibrium insulated from pain and pleasure, and the weakening pulse is no longer easeful but perilously close to death. Opening with a forthright confes-sion of his aching heart and declining physicality, the speaker enters onstage as a mortal being preyed upon by a painful awareness of his own mortality. He then addresses his antagonist, an utterly alien being which brings him the pain: ''Tis not through envy of thy happy lot, / But being too happy in thine happi-ness' (5–6). The fairy bird, singing 'in full-throated ease' (10) of the summer as its world is 'melodious' (8) and 'green' (9), exists in its ever-present here and now in a complete absence of self-awareness and knowledge of mutability and time. Its distinct state of being engages the human speaker so much as to take him up in its happiness, but unlike the bird's single-minded joy, the human speaker's happiness, ever prone to 'its neighbour pain' ('Lamia' I:192), makes his heart 'ache'. The speaker, therefore, with his 'all too human' consciousness, longs to enter into the bird's existence. This longing to leave the painful self to take part in the bird's happy otherness is a purely imaginative effort. The resignation of the mind in 'Ode on Indolence' is abandoned for an active assertion in 'Ode to Psyche' and so the odic drama continues. The drama within the drama also begins, with the speaker making one trial of imaginative participation with the bird's being after another, for every effort turns out to be self-defeating and thus has to be remade.

The very first attempt the mind makes is self-contradictory. It calls forth 'a draught of vintage' (11) to immerse itself in forgetful intoxication, thus asserting itself only to regain its state of resignation. The speaker, quite unaware, conjures up a sensuous scene of Dionysian mirth, hoping to 'drink, and leave the world unseen, / And with thee fade away into the forest dim' (19–20). The wish seems granted when the following stanza opens with the confirmation of 'fade away': 'Fade far away, dissolve, and quite forget / What thou among the leaves hast never known' (21–2). But the very act of forgetting turns into a process of remembering that drags him back to the world he seems to have left:

> The weariness, the fever, and the fret
> Here, where men sit and hear each other groan;
> Where palsy shakes a few, sad, last gray hairs,
> Where youth grows pale, and spectre-thin, and dies;
> Where but to think is to be full of sorrow
> And leaden-eyed despairs,
> Where Beauty cannot keep her lustrous eyes,
> Or new Love pine at them beyond to-morrow. (23–30)

In justifying his wish to reject the world by enumerating human sufferings, he only relives each painful experience vividly, from the cruel mortality in either the miserably long process of ageing or the sudden termination of young lives, to the fleeting existence of beauty, and easily satiated human nature itself that makes any permanent happiness impossible. Insisting on telling the bird what it '[has] never known', the speaker, instead of bringing them closer, only removes himself further away. The failure of his engagement with the bird is made manifest when he is found to be still staying in this world and beckoning himself to depart: 'Away! away! for I will fly to thee, / Not charioted by Bacchus and his pards, / But on the viewless wings of Poesy' (31–3). Having to resort to a more powerful form of imagination than passive intoxication, the speaker turns to the demonic Poesy, though he still has to struggle with the 'dull brain' that either 'perplexes' pleasure with pain or 'retards' (34) pain into numbness. Immediately after invoking poetic imagination, the speaker finds his wish fulfilled: 'Already with thee!' (35).

The magical power of poetic imagination gives him wings, lifting his 'Lethe-wards'-sinking body from the painful human world to the same height with the nightingale. Finally taking part in its existence, the speaker feels the 'breezes' (39) with the bird, and sees with it the 'verdurous glooms' and 'winding mossy ways' (40). 'But here there is no light' (38); he has to see the nightingale's world in his mind's eye:

> I cannot see what flowers are at my feet,
> Nor what soft incense hangs upon the boughs,
> But, in embalmed darkness, guess each sweet
> Wherewith the seasonable month endows
> The grass, the thicket, and the fruit-tree wild;
> White hawthorn, and the pastoral eglantine;
> Fast fading violets cover'd up in leaves;
> And mid-May's eldest child,
> The coming musk-rose, full of dewy wine,
> The murmurous haunt of flies on summer eves. (41–50)

The deprivation of sight paradoxically endows him with a powerful synaesthesia, bringing forth a luxuriant bloom in colour, shape, scent and taste, all of which turn the imaginative participation with the nightingale's being into a truthful experience. At the very moment of fulfilment, however, a dramatic reversal has also imperceptibly taken place. Taking the imagined perspective of the bird, he ends up seeing the world 'at [his] feet', the luxuriance of which only betrays an earthly being's deep relish in this world. While the scene is blossoming in an increasing richness, the speaker's mind is also growing more vigorous and exhilarated, and he is literally carried away by his imagination when he visualizes the violets as 'fast-fading' and the musk-rose as 'coming'. The same viewless wings of Poesy have taken him out of the immediate realm of the nightingale's, and the irony is just as the epistle to Reynolds describes: '– It is a flaw / In happiness to see beyond our bourn – / It forces us in summer skies to mourn: / It spoils the singing of the nightingale' (82–5).

This consciousness of process and time peculiar to the human mind again marks him off as a separate being from the bird, who sings for the present season with no sense of urgency. The apartness of the speaker from the bird, however, is not recognized by the speaker yet, and the dramatic irony becomes more evident when the speaker is then found to start musing on death, a completely alien idea to the bird: 'Now more than ever seems it rich to die, / To cease upon the midnight with no pain' (55–6). The longing for death at this 'rich' moment derives from no other source than his full awareness of its transience, and to perpetuate a rich moment by death only betrays a desperate human effort to approximate to eternity. In the midst of his thoughts on death, he finds the bird to be 'pouring forth thy soul abroad / In such an ecstasy!' (57–8). The contrast between his vain effort to arrest an imaginary rich moment and the nightingale's natural ecstatic enjoyment of its eternal present becomes too glaring to ignore, and the speaker finally recognizes his dissociation from the bird that has already happened: 'Still wouldst thou sing, and I have ears in vain – / To thy high requiem become a sod' (59–60).

Again cut away from the bird, the speaker is sent back to where he was at the opening of the poem, thus again finding the bird an alien other: 'Thou wast not born for death, immortal Bird! / No hungry generations tread thee down; / The voice I hear this passing night was heard / In ancient days by emperor and clown' (61–4). At the same time, the attempt to join the bird is resumed. Imagining the bird's immortal life, the speaker transcends his own mortality and lives with the generations of the future and past that will still listen and have listened to the bird. While he seems finally reunited with the bird, however, the imaginary participation proceeds in an ominous direction: 'Perhaps the self-same song that found a path / Through the sad heart of Ruth, when, sick for home, / She stood in tears amid the alien corn' (65–7). Participating in the nightingale's eternal presence by transfiguring himself into the solitary reaper, the speaker's sympathetic identification with her brings him back to the human world of longing and loss she has lived in. Passing then to 'magic casements' (69), he faces 'perilous seas', finding himself in a 'faery land' that has become 'forlorn' (70), no longer capable of producing charm. The disenchanting vision betrays his own distrust in the power of imagination, thus disengaging him again from the immortal bird: 'Forlorn! the very word is like a bell / To toll me back from thee to my sole self!' (71–2). Just as the return to the 'sole self' announces his final failure to join the nightingale's otherness, so does it signal the defeat of the gardener Fancy, immediately cursed as the 'deceiving elf' (74). The speaker, in contrast to his earlier self-beckoning 'Away! away!', now bids the bird, 'Adieu! adieu! thy plaintive anthem fades / Past the near meadows, over the still stream, / Up the hill-side; and now 'tis buried deep / In the next valley-glades' (75–8). Recognizing the futility of all his efforts, the speaker is finally resigned to letting the bird go. Yet in seeing the bird 'fade away', he is at the same time following its disappearing track, or taking an imaginary flight with it by his viewless wings of Poesy again. The see-saw movement thus repeats itself, as yet again in the final lines of equivocation: 'Was it a vision, or a waking dream? / Fled is that music: – Do I wake or sleep?' (79–80). The drama is thus left open-ended, with the speaker neither completely rejecting his imaginary experience as a 'dream', nor affirming it as a 'vision'. The 'fierce dispute', unsettled, is yet to go on.

As the odes to Psyche and Indolence provide oppositional perspectives from two poles of a spectrum, so do 'Ode to a Nightingale' and 'Ode on a Grecian Urn' compose a complimentary pair. Like 'Nightingale', 'Grecian Urn' is also built on the irreconcilable conflict between immortality and transience, and presents the conflict by a dramatic confrontation between a human speaker and a symbol of permanence. In both odes, the speaker attempts to engage his self with the existence of this ideal Other, and in both, the very fulfilment of the engagement sets the dissociation in motion, dramatizing the irony of the paradox of an imaginative effort. In neither of these two odes, however, is the conflict finally resolved, and both end in an ambiguity about the value of an imaginary experience as against human experience itself.

Rather than alternating between engagement and separation as in 'Nightingale', 'Grecian Urn' develops the conflict in a classical dramatic structure: the speaker's engrossment with the urn describes a continuous rising curve until it reaches the climax, when it reverses to a process of dissociation that becomes gradually manifest, until it descends to the point of recognition of the separation, and finally ends in a conclusion that is again equivocal. Unlike 'Nightingale', defined by the speaker's opening voice of 'my heart aches' as a drama of consciousness with the first-person-I's inner world playing the major role, 'Grecian Urn' resembles a more archetypal drama in the effacement of the first-person speaker and the more autonomous development of the other.

It opens with the urn placed right at the centre, displaying itself as an artistic entity, while the speaker is an invisible voice: 'Thou still unravish'd bride of quietness, / Thou foster-child of silence and slow time, / Sylvan historian, who canst thus express / A flowery tale more sweetly than our rhyme' (1–4). The speaker's apostrophes to the urn, however, also make his presence strongly felt, for the ways in which he finds the urn's otherness in turn define himself. Unlike the nightingale, which is completely insulated from humanity, the urn is characterized by its duality of being both human and alien. As the 'still unravish'd bride of quietness', the urn remains intact and unscathed by the assault of time, but it is also ever threatened by the danger of falling into historical oblivion. Being the 'foster-child of silence and slow time', it survives time yet is not a lineal heir of immortality. Being 'sylvan', it contains a sweeter 'flowery tale', but it is also a 'historian', whose narrative, however 'flowery', can only be sequenced in time. But its ambiguous identity makes its existence all the more mysterious, so the speaker casts himself directly into the world it presents, enquiring how to access it:

What leaf-fring'd legend haunts about thy shape
Of deities or mortals, or of both,
In Tempe or the dales of Arcady?
What men or gods are these? What maidens loth?
What mad pursuit? What struggle to escape?
What pipes and timbrels? What wild ecstasy? (5–10)

The urn unfolds a world that gradually regains life in the speaker's increasingly contracted questions that quicken the pace, and the world is set back in the flow of time by the speaker's focus on motion and life.

The speaker, quite unconscious of this, continues to explore its world:

Heard melodies are sweet, but those unheard
Are sweeter; therefore, ye soft pipes, play on;
Not to the sensual ear, but, more endear'd,

Pipe to the spirit ditties of no tone:
Fair youth, beneath the trees, thou canst not leave
Thy song, nor ever can those trees be bare;
Bold lover, never, never canst thou kiss,
Though winning near the goal – yet, do not grieve;
She cannot fade, though thou hast not thy bliss,
For ever wilt thou love, and she be fair! (11–20)

In the speaker's addresses to each subject on the urn, subtle turns of his mind
are submerged. The pipes are told to 'play on', because with his 'sensual ear',
the speaker has first found the 'unheard' music strange, but concludes that it is
'more endear'd' only after the thought that the sensual ear is but a part of 'this
mortal body of a thousand days'. Similarly, he reassures the 'fair youth' that
he is to stay in the prime season, only because it is an inconceivable idea in the
actual world in which the prime hour is always followed by decline. And the
bold lover is told not to 'grieve', exactly because the speaker sees his need to be
consoled for being forever deprived of his 'bliss', and can only console him with
his knowledge of this world: 'Where Beauty cannot keep her lustrous eyes / Or
new Love pine at them beyond to-morrow'. Therefore, in this one-sided dia-
logue with the urn, what is heard is rather a voice persuading itself. The speech,
instead of presenting the actual scene on the urn, reveals a process of adjusting
his perspective in looking at the urn, in which he drives away the doubt about
its reduction of experience by conceding to its simultaneous reduction of the
painful aspects of experience, and thus comes to regard the very reduction as
an artistic triumph. All of this indicates that the speaker, resembling an unreli-
able narrator, is biased by his human perspective, and is only taking a restricted
view of the urn.

   Thus, what is seen next is a re-view of the urn from his adjusted, filtered point
of view:

Ah, happy, happy boughs! that cannot shed
Your leaves, nor ever bid the spring adieu;
And, happy melodist, unwearied,
For ever piping songs for ever new;
More happy love! more happy, happy love!
For ever warm and still to be enjoy'd,
For ever panting, and for ever young (21–7)

'[T]oo happy in thine happiness', the speaker yields himself to the 'wild ecstasy'
of the urn, and the urn in turn becomes the happiest state imaginable in
remaining ever promising and anticipant. As he becomes increasingly exalted
with his imagination of the urn's eternal present, so does his imagination
become ever closer to actual experience, with the lovers coming to life with

their imagined 'panting' 'warmth'. As in 'Ode to a Nightingale', at the very moment when his imagination triumphs in achieving truthfulness, the dramatic irony sets in, with the forever 'warm' and 'panting' life permanently frozen on the lifeless urn, and that which always expects fulfilment never to be fulfilled. The irony reaches its climax when the speaker from his self-willed point of view firmly asserts the urn's supremacy over human reality: 'All breathing human passion far above, / That leaves a heart high-sorrowful and cloy'd, / A burning forehead, and a parching tongue' (28–30). As in 'Nightingale', when trying to forget the world, he only remembers, here too his unfavourable comparison of human reality with the urn only evokes it with a vivid life. For all its 'weariness', 'fever' and 'fret', human experience is characterized by the heat the urn does not possess. The contradiction is not admitted by the speaker, but the shift of the scene implicitly suggests the dead end of his imagination, which demands a re-adjustment of perspective: 'Who are these coming to the sacrifice? / To what green altar, O mysterious priest, / Lead'st thou that heifer lowing at the skies, / And all her silken flanks with garlands drest?' (31–4). The formal, solemn scene silences the former 'wild ecstasy', and stills the 'mad pursuit', falling gradually to a mood that is irrevocably 'forlorn':

What little town by river or sea shore,
Or mountain-built with peaceful citadel,
Is emptied of this folk, this pious morn?
And, little town, thy streets for evermore
Will silent be; and not a soul to tell
Why thou art desolate, can e'er return. (35–40)

Capable of arresting a transitory moment of ecstasy, the same urn can also negate the flow of life, permanently evacuating the townsfolk and leaving the town in eternal desolation deprived of history. As the figures in 'Ode on Indolence' appear and disappear while the urn turns, the two scenes on this urn also provide two oppositional perspectives to look at eternity, which is a double-edged sword. Gradually coming to the recognition of the bitterness of this 'artifice of eternity', the speaker is at the same time 'tolled back' to his 'sole self' by the permanently 'forlorn' little town. Cut away from the imaginary world of the urn, the speaker has reached the end of his imaginary journey.

His revised addresses to the urn bespeak the transformation his mind has gone through in this imaginary experience. The urn personified at the beginning now loses its life, becoming 'Attic shape', 'Fair attitude' (41) and 'silent form' (44). The identity of 'men and maidens' enquired at the beginning is confirmed to be 'marble' (42), while the leaf-fring'd legend becomes 'the trodden weed' (43), shadows of the lives that are no more. The flowery tale turns to the anticlimax of 'Cold Pastoral' (45), which, signalling the speaker's final recognition of its lifelessness, brings the drama to its zenith. But then,

instead of pursuing this negative inclination to a complete denial, the speaker
turns back to reconcile himself with the urn:

> When old age shall this generation waste,
> Thou shalt remain, in midst of other woe
> Than ours, a friend to man, to whom thou say'st,
> 'Beauty is truth, truth beauty', – that is all
> Ye know on earth, and all ye need to know. (46–50)

So, 'immortal urn! / No hungry generations tread thee down'. For all the bitter-
ness he has experienced falling from unreserved happiness to disconsolate
desolation, the speaker finally maintains that the urn, as the ideal of poetry, is
'a friend / To sooth the cares, and lift the thoughts of man'. Offering a glimpse
of 'a fine isolated verisimilitude caught from the Penetralium of mystery', the
urn provides a moment of solace for feverish human existence, and 'the sense
of beauty' it provokes 'overcomes every other consideration'. Therefore,
'Beauty is truth, truth beauty', even if it is only half knowledge. After all, human
knowledge, confined by its mortality, can only be half knowledge. Reaching out
for the omniscience of eternity then is a futile attempt to reach after something
impossible. Therefore, no matter who says what in the last two lines, the end
seems to deliver a message of negative capability from the poet. The beauty on
the urn, captured from the instantaneous experience of earthly happiness,
when finely repeated in art, turns into an imaginative truth that transcends
its earthly existence, as Keats writes himself: 'we shall enjoy ourselves here after
by having what we called happiness on Earth repeated in a finer tone and so
repeated' (*KL* I:185).

So the two internal dramas are both concluded in a negatively capable light,
neither completely affirming the triumph of imagination over human reality
nor repudiating it, though human experience constantly intrudes to question
the transcendence of imagination. The unsettled conflict is finally resolved
in the last spring ode, 'Ode on Melancholy', which fully accepts the inherently
paradoxical and painful nature of human experience itself. It is a celebration of
tragic intensity by fully recognizing the necessity of disagreeables for 'Beauty &
Truth', and a poetic expression of a thorough embrace of human sufferings for
their soul-making power.

'No, no, go not to Lethe' (1): the ode starts by addressing the seeker of
Melancholy in a tone of admonishment. The speaker thus is a man of experi-
ence, who has gained an insight into 'Melancholy', like the poet himself.
Melancholy is not found in death, darkness or gloom, he expostulates, 'For
shade to shade will come too drowsily, / And drown the wakeful anguish of the
soul' (9–10). One does not experience Melancholy when the human world
is seen as 'a vale of tears', which only creates 'a drowsy numbness'. Instead,
Melancholy exists only for the soul that is 'wakeful' of its 'anguish', keen to be

constantly sharpened by the 'World of Pains and troubles', what Keats calls 'touchstones of his heart' (*KL* II:103). Melancholy therefore can only be found in this world of the vale of soul-making, which is full of 'disagreeables' interdependent with and indispensable for the sense of beauty. As Keats writes in his long letter before he comes to the tragic vision of the making of the soul: 'Circumstances are like Clouds continually gathering and bursting – While we are laughing the seed of some trouble is put into <he> the wide arable land of events' (*KL* II:79). The speaker here also reminds us, 'the melancholy fit shall fall / Sudden from heaven like a weeping cloud' (11–2). Yet it is this world of fickle 'circumstances' that whets the heart, keeps the anguish wakeful for the soul. The speaker now comes to see, it is exactly the distinctness of the human world from the nightingale's and the urn's eternal bliss that makes it the only habitat for Melancholy:

> She dwells with Beauty – Beauty that must die;
> And Joy, whose hand is ever at his lips
> Bidding adieu; and aching Pleasure nigh,
> Turning to poison while the bee-mouth sips:
> Ay, in the very temple of Delight
> Veil'd Melancholy has her sovran shrine. (21–6)

As Keats illustrates his vision of the soul-making world:

> Let the fish philosophise the ice away from the Rivers in winter time and they shall be at continual play in the tepid delight of summer. Look at the Poles and at the sands of Africa, Whirlpools and volcanoes – Let men exterminate them and I will say that they may arrive at earthly Happiness – (*KL* II:101)

Paradoxically, the sober view of the impossibility of 'earthly Happiness' also reconciles one with human experience, and this grand drama of the spring wrestling with human experience can now come to its end. The last act of the odic drama is closed by a tragic-hero-like figure, 'whose strenuous tongue / Can burst Joy's grape against his palate fine; / His soul shall taste the sadness of her might, / And be among her cloudy trophies hung' (27–30). Though finally defeated by Melancholy, he triumphs in gaining the most intense experience by plunging himself into the fierce dispute between the keenest joy and sharpest pain. The speaker himself has wandered from innocence to experience, vacillated between an intense experience of the mind and a passive indolence, wrestled with the impulse to 'leave the world unseen' and the relish in its beautiful luxuriance, and struggled with the fascination with an eternal bliss and the love for a life of process. Now he reaches his conclusion: embrace human experience with its inherent contradictions and paradoxes and accept the conflict of the heart with itself, for they give the soul the tragic identity.

Dramatic Interlude

The odic drama was followed by actual dramatic attempts. Keats's awareness of distancing the self from poetry can be clearly seen in the spring odes, but his interest in drama started earlier and remained constant. Back in January 1818 when revising *Endymion*, we remember, Keats had mentioned the plan for 'the chief Attempt in the Drama', and he dabbled with the dramatic form ever since in various pieces. In the summer of 1819, he finally produced a real play, *Otho the Great*, and he revealed when he finished it, 'One of my Ambitions is to make as great a revolution in modern dramatic writing as Kean has done in acting' (*KL* II:139). But *Otho the Great* itself was not written out of dramatic ambition, being a practical attempt to pull himself out of financial difficulty, and he was but the 'Midwife to [Brown's] plot' (*KL* II:157). The play has many promising aspects, but perhaps too many to achieve intensity for any. The plot itself is well-constructed enough, love and betrayal interwoven with political schemes and ambition, but also brought in are many interests that are left undeveloped. The filial relationship composes the initial conflict but is easily resolved. The main character, in the course of the play, shifts from Otho to Ludolph, whose madness, rather than being dramatically inevitable, seems more like Keats's own interest. The Richard III- or Edgar-like villainy of Conrad, the Lady Macbeth and femme fatale combination in Auranthe, and the conscience-stricken Albert all suggest ambitious attempts at characterization, but they are not filled in with enough 'bye-writing' to reveal their psychological complexity. Obviously, Keats was constantly hearing Shakespeare's characters while composing, but his speeches with Shakespearean echoes, more often than not, seem to be put into the characters' mouths rather than spoken by themselves.

But the second play, *King Stephen*, is on a remarkably different level, though with only four scenes finished. It is breath-taking as soon as it starts, and unlike Ludolph in *Otho the Great*, King Stephen speaks with a gusto that fits in with the dramatic context, and in turn gives the play momentum. His opening speech immediately sets the stage with a sense of urgency, which at the same time brings out his own character:

> If shame can on a soldier's vein-swoll'n front
> Spread deeper crimson than the battle's toil,
> Blush in your casing helmets! – for see, see!
> Yonder my chivalry, my pride of war,
> Wrench'd with an iron hand from firm array,
> Are routed loose about the plashy meads,
> Of honour forfeit. O, that my known voice
> Could reach your dastard ears and fright you more! (I.i.1–8)

While in *Otho the Great* speeches are mostly directly descriptive of events or emotions, the speeches in *King Stephen* become more projective of happenings and characters. Further, there is also a dexterous shift of point of view in characterizing Stephen, and this greatly expands the dimension of both the character and the play itself. The second scene takes place in the enemy camp, but Stephen remains firmly in the limelight. First, there rushes in a Captain, who describes King Stephen in fearful wonder:

> He sole and lone maintains
> A hopeless bustle 'mid our swarming arms;
> And with a nimble savageness attacks,
> Escapes, makes fiercer onset, then anew
> Eludes death, giving death to most that dare
> Trespass within the circuit of his sword. (I.ii.10–15)

Then follows a Knight, who exclaims, 'From Stephen, my good Prince – Stephen – Stephen – ' (I.ii.29). Annoyed, Glocester asks, 'Why do you make such echoing of his name?' (I.ii.30), and he answers, 'Because I think, my lord, he is no man, / But a fierce demon 'nointed safe from wounds / And misbaptised with a Christian name' (I.ii.31–3). After this, he gives a full report of Stephen's fight, and Stephen's valour reverberates on the stage without the role's physical presence. By filing in messengers to report on the battle from various perspectives, Keats also manages to conjure up the sweeping span of the battlefield by this heteroglossia, which might be something he picked up from Shakespeare's historical plays.

Around the time when *King Stephen* was composed, Keats wrote in his letter:

> The little dramatic skill I may as yet have however badly it might show in a Drama would I think be sufficient for a Poem – I wish to diffuse the colouring of St Agnes eve throughout a Poem in which Character and Sentiment would be the figures to such drapery – Two or three such Poems, if God should spare me, written in the course of the next six years, would be a famous gradus ad Parnassum altissimum – I mean they would nerve me up to the writing of a few fine Plays – my greatest ambition – (*KL* II:234)

King Stephen, though unfinished, strongly promises his ambition to be fulfilled, but it remains forever only a promise.

The Entrance and Exit of the Self

The Great Year drew to its end with two accomplishments of very different kinds. After all the dramatic trials in actual plays and poems, Keats put the self back at the centre again in his last grand project. *The Fall of Hyperion* is Keats's *Prelude*, his *Purgatorio*, in which the self replaces the god of poetry in the first *Hyperion*. It is retrospective, with the narrating self looking back on the narrated self going through all the struggles on his poetic journey, from 'Sleep and Poetry' to *Endymion*, on to the first *Hyperion* and the great odes. But it is also prospective,[7] as a vision 'straining at particles of light in the midst of a great darkness' (*KL* II:80), looking for ways to make the self a true tragic poet, 'a miserable and mighty Poet of the human Heart' like his presider. As the most 'autobiographical' of Keats's poems, it also most lucidly decrees that the self become a non-egotistical poet, a 'physician to all men'. Partly owing to this contradiction, the recast epic was again left unfinished. But at the time when he decided to abandon it, he composed 'To Autumn', a poem in which the self of the poet is completely effaced, and thus in a sense accomplished what he has decreed for himself in the unfinished epic.

The revised epic opens with an induction which already speaks of it as a posthumous work: 'Whether the dream now purposed to rehearse / Be poet's or fanatic's will be known / When this warm scribe my hand is in the grave' (I:16–18). The induction thus defines the perspective of the narrator to be retrospective, so the flashback in the narrative also symbolizes the poet's reflection on his past poetic career. The narrated 'I' first finds himself in 'an arbour' (I:25), emblematic of his early poetry encapsulated in the setting of a Spenserian 'Bower', and then sees 'a feast' (I:29), suggesting the recollection of his romances where a feast first precedes the consummation of love and later only forebodes disillusionment. It now becomes the 'refuse of a meal' (I:30), no longer bountiful and extravagant as his former feasts, just as the realm of Flora and Pan has become the 'faery lands forlorn' in his own poetry. But the poet still drinks from the remnants, and the juice makes him 'swoon' (I:55), as all his personae have fallen into sleep before being endowed with a vision of beauty or of horror. The poet then sees the altar and the steps, where he receives the oracle that demands his ascension of the steps with the threat of death. Recapitulating Apollo, who has to 'die into life' as the god of poetry, the poet undergoes the purgatorial ordeal for his aspiration to the higher realm of poetry dealing with 'the agonies' and 'the strife of human hearts'. Unlike Apollo who then becomes 'celestial', the human poet only 'dated on / [his] doom' (I:144–5) after going through the pains of mortality. With seeing his conductress, 'the veiled shadow' (I:141) of Moneta, the poet has reached the threshold of knowledge that Apollo arrives at before going through his 'immortal death'. While Apollo sought for the knowledge of this world, the poet first seeks from Moneta self-knowledge: 'What am I that should so be sav'd from death?' (I:138). Moneta's following reply and the narrated poet's self-defence therefore act out the narrating poet's self-enquiry about his role as a poet, which also recasts the fierce debate about the value of poetic imagination going on throughout the spring odes.

Moneta's first reply affirms sympathetic imagination for human sufferings as the foremost decree for a poet: 'None can usurp this height . . . / But those to whom the miseries of the world / Are misery, and will not let them rest' (I:147–9).

The poet claims his identity first of all by his capability to take 'the miseries of the world' as his own, but sympathetic imagination alone is not sufficient to confirm his identity as a poet. The doubt is posed by the poet himself when he compares his identity as a 'sufferer' for humanity with the 'humanists' who also 'feel the giant agony of the world' (I:157) but 'labour for mortal good' (I:159). This is reminiscent of Keats's own humanistic concern, repeatedly expressed around the time just before he started the first *Hyperion*, that 'there is no worthy pursuit but the idea of doing some good for the world' (*KL* I:271).[8] While Moneta's reply confirms the narrated poet's doubt, it also indicates the narrating poet's own questioning about the 'good' of his poetry, and in a broader sense, his scepticism about the 'worth' of imaginative experience in general. This is made clearer by the more disturbing challenge Moneta puts forward: 'Thou art a dreaming thing; / A fever of thyself' (I:168–9). While common men have 'the pain alone; the joy alone; distinct: / Only the dreamer venoms all his days' (I:174–5). The dreamer, cursed by his bounteous vision that perplexes pain and joy, recollects the speaker-poet who experiences both ecstasy and disillusionment in his imagination of the nightingale and the Grecian urn. As the paradox of imagination is not resolved in those odes, here too, the scepticism about the value of imagination is turned over when the poet refuses to accept Moneta's verdict, objecting that an imaginative experience can be dismissed for bringing no visible 'benefit' to the world: 'sure a poet is a sage; / A humanist, physician to all men' (I:189–90). But Moneta refuses to confer on him the title of poet in the first place: 'The poet and the dreamer are distinct, / Diverse, sheer opposite, antipodes. / The one pours out a balm upon the world, / The other vexes it' (I:199–202). For all his vehement protest, the poet does not deny that he has not become a poet of the nobler kind, who can not only feel the 'miseries of the world' but alleviate them, thus 'benefiting' the world as a humanist, though poetic 'balm' is intangible. The 'great end of Poesy' is to 'sooth the cares' of men, – that is the ideal he has held for himself from the outset of his poetic career. With more exposure to 'the weariness, the fever, and the fret' of humanity, the poet came to hold the healing effect of poetry only more dearly. What Moneta is to reveal to him therefore will bring him closer to this ideal and transform him from a dreamer to a poet in the higher sense. At this point, the narrated 'I' turns his attention from himself to the altar and Moneta, and symbolically shifts from the search for self-knowledge to the search for 'knowledge enormous', and Moneta, touched by his 'good will' (I:242), offers him the revelation.

The poet is then allowed to see the agonies of the fallen Titans, which epitomize 'the miseries of the world'. The gods' 'giant agony' is encapsulated in Moneta's face:

... a wan face,
Not pin'd by human sorrows, but bright blanch'd

By an immortal sickness which kills not;
It works a constant change, which happy death
Can put no end to; deathwards progressing
To no death was that visage. (I:256–61)

As Apollo is deified by the 'knowledge' gained from Mnemosyne's face, the
narrated 'I' has to acquire the knowledge needed to be a tragic poet from
Moneta's countenance, which she literally unveils for him. Shaped by the agon-
izing experience of the fallen Titans, Moneta's face reveals a vision of supreme
suffering. It conveys the eternity of pain, which will never be relieved by death.
Therefore it also conveys the pain of eternity, which makes the suffering end-
less. The cruelty of immortality[9] overturns the eternal bliss embodied in the
nightingale and the lovers on the Grecian urn, developing the permanent
desolation of the little town to a painful climax. The fearful 'immortal sickness'
Moneta is for ever suffering from provokes the equally powerful sympathy of
the poet which overcomes his fear, and he is brought closer to being a 'phys-
ician' poet by his urge to know the cause of her suffering: 'I ached to see what
things the hollow brain / Behind enwombed: what high tragedy / In the dark
secret chambers of her skull / Was acting' (I:276–9). Like Apollo tortured by
'aching ignorance', the poet '[aches]' to know her painful experience, and
in feeling the pain with her, he is already on his way to becoming a tragic poet
and turning her experience into 'high tragedy' in his imagination. The intense
sympathy then immediately brings him 'side by side' (I:292) with the goddess,
endowing him with the vision of the figure of Saturn. The poet relates: 'there
grew / A power within me of enormous ken, / To see as a God sees, and take the
depth / Of things as nimbly as the outward eye / Can size and shape pervade'
(I:302–6). As 'knowledge enormous' has made Apollo the God of poetry, now
'enormous ken' makes the dreamer a tragic poet. The knowledge of the most
painful miseries of the world, gained from the vision allowed him for his
sympathy, in turn gives him the tragic vision to see beyond the perceptible and
penetrate into 'the burden of the mystery', thus conceiving of 'the lofty theme'
(I:306) for the tragic poetry he is to create, which will make him 'see, / And
seeing ne'er forget' (I:309–10).

   But to accomplish the transformation, he has yet to go through a giant agony
himself, indicating that the knowledge of suffering has to be intensely experi-
enced before it can be finally turned into tragic power. Watching the motion-
less fallen gods for 'a long awful time' (I:384), the poet feels overwhelmed by
the terrible oppression of their stillness: 'Without stay or prop / But my own
weak mortality, I bore / The load of this eternal quietude' (I:388–90). What
the poet then experiences is exactly the feeling of 'immortal sickness' that
Moneta's visage has expressed, and in bearing the formidable weight of the
'eternal quietude' which conveys the fallen gods' agony, the poet shares the suf-
fering of the Titans who are overwhelmed by their pain. Only after knowledge

has turned into experience, when seeing the suffering intensely enough trans-
forms the seeing into feeling, does he finally become a tragic poet who can now
feel that Saturn is like a feeble 'old man of the earth' (I:440), and sympathize
with his 'earthly loss' (I:441).

All this stress on the power of sympathy, the truthfulness of imagination and
the embrace of suffering is consistent with the central concerns pervading
Keats's poetry, but they are wrought together to an extreme in *The Fall of
Hyperion*, where sympathetic imagination entails fellow suffering of the most
agonizing kind, and has to be exerted to the degree of becoming truthful
experience, and the experience is not Adam's dream but the nightmarish
vision of Moneta's eternal pain. The second canto continues with the poet
being shown the vision of Hyperion, whose light enables the poet to see with his
'quick eyes' (II:53) Hyperion raging in fear. '[O]n he flared' (II:61), but the
poet then stopped.

On 21 September 1819, Keats wrote to Reynolds that he had given up the
reconstructed *Hyperion*: 'there were too many Miltonic inversions in it – Miltonic
verse cannot be written but in an artful or rather artist's humour. I wish to give
myself up to other sensations'. Interestingly enough, Keats describes the aban-
donment of the poem as an act of submission of the self. Does that indicate that
he eventually felt the self in it too prominent? He then asks Reynolds to pick
out lines and mark which are 'the false beauty proceeding from art', and which
are 'the true voice of feeling' (*KL* II:167). What chiefly bothered him seems to
be the epic form, the too consciously 'artistic' stance the poem takes, which
goes against the poem's central concern about the humanistic nature of poetry.
On the same day, he wrote to George and Georgiana about the decision, giving
the same reason, 'Life to [Milton] would be death to me' (*KL* II:212), and he
also describes his general creative temper at the time:

> Some think I have lost that poetic ardour and fire 't is said I once had – the
> fact is perhaps I have: but instead of that I hope I shall substitute a more
> thoughtful and quiet power. I am more frequently, now, contented to read
> and think – but now & then, haunted with ambitious thoughts. Qui[e]ter in
> my pulse, improved in my digestion; exerting myself against vexing specula-
> tions – scarcely content to write the best verses for the fever they leave behind.
> I want to compose without this fever. I hope I one day shall. (*KL* II:209)

One wonders whether Keats felt the second *Hyperion*, though among his
'best verses', had not really left behind the fever, thus defeating the aim of
poetry which he claims, within the poem, to be that it should heal the world.
As a poem examining his own role as poet and defining his future direction,
the fever may have been inevitable, for it aspired to a grand goal he had laid
before himself. As with the first *Hyperion*, Keats left the second most probably
because his negatively capable mind felt sceptical about the tendency of a grand

endeavour to strive too hard towards an end too definite, however grand that end might be.

In the same letter to Reynolds, Keats told him that he had just composed 'To Autumn':

> How beautiful the season is now – How fine the air. A temperate sharpness about it. Really, without joking, chaste weather – Dian skies – I never lik'd stubble fields so much as now – Aye better than the chilly green of the spring. Somehow a stubble plain looks warm – in the same way that some pictures look warm – this struck me so much in my sunday's walk that I composed upon it. (*KL* II:167)

The word 'temperate' captures the tone of the poem, as he writes in his sonnet 'On Fame', 'How fever'd is the man who cannot look / Upon his mortal days with temperate blood' (1–2); and 'To Autumn' is, as Keats wishes, 'without fever'. It portrays a season characterized by the paradox of consummation and consumption, but it neither celebrates the consummation nor mourns for the consumption. Unlike the speaker in the spring odes who tells about his own imagination of an object, the speaker here gives the actual experience of the season with images that are tangible, perceptible and audible in their fullest strength. While the scenes on the Grecian urn are frozen moments snatched out of the passage of time, the autumnal scenes here are flowing on, as autumn does in experience. While the ode on Melancholy vehemently urges for acceptance of human experience, 'To Autumn' calmly accepts it. It is an epitome of Keats's poetry of experience, concluding not only the spring odes but his whole poetic career with the expression of a negative capability that had finally ripened.

> Season of mists and mellow fruitfulness,
> Close bosom-friend of the maturing sun;
> Conspiring with him how to load and bless
> With fruit the vines that round the thatch-eves run;
> To bend with apples the moss'd cottage-trees,
> And fill all fruit with ripeness to the core;
> To swell the gourd, and plump the hazel shells
> With a sweet kernel; to set budding more,
> And still more, later flowers for the bees,
> Until they think warm days will never cease,
> For summer has o'er-brimm'd their clammy cells. (1–11)

It is a season of natural benignancy with its bounteous offering, loading all beings with its generosity, though its kindness is also a 'conspiracy', as it will later take away what it now gives. With the weight of the load ever increasing, all lives grow and ripen while the poem proceeds, as they do in the season that constantly moves towards fulfilment. As the season will eventually progress from bountiful plenitude to bleak desolation, the flowers' ever increasing budding will bring the process to the point of 'overbrimming' that goes beyond the apex of fulfilment. The bees, like the nightingale that sings of summer 'in full-throated ease', are not aware of the ongoing process, but the human speaker here is reticent, not expressing envy of their happy lot, nor revealing any other feelings of his own.

Autumn then is seen as a harvester 'sitting careless on a granary floor' (14), a role growing out of its benign role of a loader, but the harvester also entails a more merciless role of reaper. Yet, as the harvester is 'careless', so is the reaper nonchalant, leaving half of the furrow and '[sparing] the next swath' (18). The season itself is neither deliberately kind nor malicious, like all natural processes that provide and take away. The reaper then develops into the figure of a gleaner, who '[keeps] / Steady [the] laden head across a brook' (19–20). As a gleaner, the season will take back its offerings, but the 'laden head' also calls back its role of the generous loader. The 'steady' stance across the brook keeps the figure balanced between the endowing loader and the relentless reaper, like the poem itself maintains equilibrium between the dual natures of the season. The equilibrium culminates in the image of 'by a cider-press, with patient look, / Thou watchest the last oozings hours by hours' (21–2). Recapitulating the role of the loader that has filled 'all fruit with ripeness to the core', the figure here achieves a perfect composure, receiving the harvest with all content, accepting the gradual loss of life with all calmness. The 'patient look' follows the process to pass the last moment of fulfilment to go on to the subsequent decline, not wincing at the accumulation of hours which will finally make the beauty fade, trees bare, lovers no longer young. It is an image of a human being who looks at his experience with all the cherishing of its endowment and all the equanimity towards its deprivation. The 'patient look' in autumn heals the aching heart of the spring odes, offering quiet fortitude to accept mortality in return for the vivid flow of life that it also enjoys.

As the season moves on from the loader to the harvester, reaper and gleaner, so does the poem proceed to the end of the season that forebodes decay and death. With the season slowly declining, the day is also 'soft-dying' (25) to the autumnal hour. While the nightfall is approaching, the gnats' 'wailful choir' (27) mourning for their ephemeral lives gives the first elegiac note of the autumnal music. But it is joined by voices of more diverse lives, the 'full-grown' lambs which recall the generosity of the ripe season, the hedge-crickets whose song will warm the drowsy listener in wintry silence, the whistling red-breast, and 'gathering swallows' which 'twitter in the skies' (30–3). Together, they perform an ensemble that is as rich and grand as the season. The swallows about to take leave gives the poem a sense of finality, but their departure seen in the 'skies' also leaves the poem ever expanding in inconclusiveness. The autumnal ode thus closes 'the living year' of Keats with its bounteous harvest of negative capability, realizing his invocation of the old bards made back in 1818 in his first spring ode to May, which turned out to be a sad prophecy: 'my song should die away, / Content as theirs, / Rich in the simple worship of a day' ('Mother of Hermes! and still youthful Maia' 12–14).

Chapter 4

Modernist Heritage of Negative Capability

More than two decades after Keats's death, his letters were published by Lord Houghton and his poetry began to be reprinted. As outlined in the introduction, the reputation of both Keats and his idea of negative capability rose steadily after this, but it was not until the 1920s that critics began to show serious interest in the idea itself. In a certain sense, the currency of negative capability grew together with modernism, and with its evident affinity with the modernist precepts of impersonality and dramatic presentation, its appeal to the modernists should not be surprising. Among the theories of the modernist poets, Yeats's of poetic mask and Eliot's of impersonality are apparently connected with Keats's notion. To explore the legacy of negative capability in their poetry will therefore give us a more holistic picture of the idea, for the history of an idea lies as much in its contemporariness as in its pastness.

Yeats's 'Radical Innocence'

In 1915, W. B. Yeats wrote in 'Ego Dominus Tuus':

Hic.　　　　　And yet
No one denies to Keats love of the world;
Remember his deliberate happiness.
Ille. His art is happy, but who knows his mind?
I see a schoolboy when I think of him,
With face and nose pressed to a sweet-shop window,
For certainly he sank into his grave
His senses and his heart unsatisfied,
And made – being poor, ailing and ignorant,
Shut out from all the luxury of the world,
The coarse-bred son of a livery-stable keeper –
Luxuriant song. (51–62)[1]

Many critics are rather put off by Yeats's condescending stance in viewing Keats as driven to sensuous pleasure by his 'coarse-bred' background, but Yeats's 'condescension' should be read in the context of the whole poem. By stressing Keats's 'coarse breeding', Yeats, through his persona 'Ille', aims to suggest that it is just the actual 'poverty' in Keats's life that makes his poetry 'luxuriant', which is an instance of the paradox between the artist's self and his 'anti-self' poetic mask as rehearsed in the whole poem. It is appropriate enough, in this sense, for Yeats to choose Keats as an example, and even if this picture of Keats betrays a sense of superiority in Yeats, it still indicates Yeats's recognition that Keats's poetry is distinct from mere self-expressiveness. This awareness of the non-egotistical quality of Keats's poetry also exemplifies the inheritance of negative capability in Yeats himself, who thinks that poetry is made out of 'the quarrel with ourselves' while 'the quarrel with others' only makes 'rhetoric' (*Mythologies* 331); and who holds that 'we sing amid our uncertainty' (*Mythologies* 331) in a time and place pervaded by bigotry and bitterness; who sees the world as an embodiment of a 'great mind' (*EI* 28) of which the self is only a part; and who seeks for 'tragic joy' in an age of hysteria, which is exactly why he chooses to see Keats's 'happiness' as 'deliberate'.[2]

No evidence suggests that Yeats had read Keats's letters or knew Keats's notion of negative capability, but it is hardly surprising that the quality should be passed down to Yeats, who thinks that 'many minds can flow into one another' and 'our memories are a part of one great memory' (*EI* 28); negative capability could be part of the great poetic memory he inevitably inherited. For Yeats, this memory is the source of his own poetry, and he, as much as Eliot if not more so, stresses the indebtedness of the individual talent to the poetic tradition, as he puts it:

> I have never said clearly that I condemn all that is not tradition, that there is a subject-matter which has descended like that 'deposit' certain philosophers speak of . . . . This subject-matter is something I have received from the generations, part of that compact with my fellow men made in my name before I was born. I cannot break from it without breaking from some part of my own nature. (*EI* viii)

In 'A General Introduction for My Work', Yeats expresses the view more vehemently: 'Talk to me of originality and I will turn on you with rage. I am a crowd, I am a lonely man, I am nothing' (*EI* 522). As he recollects, at the beginning of his poetic career, 'I read nothing but romantic literature' (*EI* 510), which is one of the most important parts of the tradition from which Yeats's poetry grew, and he pledges his allegiance to this tradition even in a much later poem: 'We were the last romantics – chose for theme / Traditional sanctity and loveliness' ('Coole and Ballylee, 1931' 41–2).

It is well-known that if there is *the* Romantic ancestor for Yeats, it is not Keats but Shelley. As Yeats reveals in '*Prometheus Unbound*' written in 1932, '[Shelley] and not Blake, whom I had studied more and with more approval, had shaped my life' (*EI* 424). But in his letter dated 14 March 1916, not long after 'Ego Dominus Tuus' was composed, Yeats wrote to his father:

> I think Keats perhaps greater than Shelley and beyond words greater than Swinburne because he makes pictures one cannot forget and sees them as full of rhythm as a Chinese painting. Swinburne's poetry, all but some early poems, is as abstract as a cubist picture. Carlyle is abstract – ideas, never things or only their common worn out images taken up from some preacher. (*YL* 608)

Slightly before this, Yeats was discussing Wyndham Lewis's 'Cubist pictures', in which he finds 'an element corresponding to rhetoric arising from his confusion of the abstract with the rhythmical'. 'Rhythm', Yeats explains, 'implies a living body, a breast to rise and fall, or limbs that dance, while the abstract is incompatible with life'. After making the above comment on Keats and the other poets, he continues:

> I separate the rhythmical and the abstract. They are brothers but one is Abel and one is Cain. In poetry they are not confused for we know that poetry is rhythm, but in music-hall verses we find an abstract cadence . . . . This cadence is a mechanism, it never suggests a voice shaken with joy or sorrow as poetical rhythm does. It is but the noise of a machine and not the coming and going of the breath. (*YL* 609)

In this brief reference to Keats, many important ideas of Yeats are touched upon. For Yeats, the abstract murders the rhythmical, because it aims at 'ideas' instead of 'things'. This insistence on reducing things to ideas is synonymous with what Yeats calls 'rhetoric', a mind busy 'quarreling' with others. As Ille tells Hic in the poem: 'The rhetorician would deceive his neighbours, / The sentimentalist himself; while art / Is but a vision of reality' (46–8). Poetry is opposed to rhetoric, offering instead 'a vision of reality', or the rhythm that embodies the life of 'things'. Thus the mind must follow actual experience as it constantly shifts between opposites, being capable of holding 'quarrels' occasioned by these conflicts within itself. As Yeats writes in 'Anima Hominis': 'The other self, the anti-self or the antithetical self, as one may choose to name it, comes but to those who are no longer deceived, whose passion is reality' (*Mythologies* 331). Therefore in 'Ego Dominus Tuus', while Hic 'would find [himself] and not an image' (10), Ille would 'seek an image' (66) being both 'most like me' (72) and 'most unlike, being my anti-self' (74). By regarding Keats as an exemplar in making poetry out of images of anti-self, Yeats expresses a similar view to his comment in this letter, that Keats has 'passion' for 'reality', which enables his imagination to go beyond the self and entertain the anti-self or other of experience itself. His poetry therefore articulates the rhythm of life which alternates between opposites, and gives 'a vision of reality' by its truthful intensity. Yeats's view of Keats thus captures the essential qualities of Keats's negative capability and conversely, it also exemplifies qualities of his own that are affinitive.

Though Yeats never claimed direct influence from Keats as he did with Shelley or Blake, Keats was a generally constant presence for him. His essay on Shelley written in 1900 opens with a very Keatsian statement: 'I . . . am now certain that the imagination has some way of lighting on the truth that the reason has not' (*EI* 65), and in it he characterizes Keats with 'his love of embodied things, of precision of form and colouring, of emotions made sleepy by the flesh' (*EI* 91), which is exactly what Eliot finds lacking in Shelley. Yeats shares this 'love of embodied things', as he writes:

> Art bids us touch and taste and hear and see the world, and shrinks from what Blake calls mathematic form, from every abstract thing, from all that is of the brain only, from all that is not a fountain jetting from the entire hopes, memories, and sensations of the body. (*EI* 292–3)

It is almost a Yeatsian recapitulation of 'O for a Life of Sensations rather than of Thoughts'. This conviction that 'art is sensuous' (*EI* 293) gives him the notion equivalent to Eliot's 'objective correlative', that 'an emotion does not exist, or does not become perceptible and active among us, till it has found its expression, in colour or in sound or in form, or in all of these' (*EI* 157). It is perhaps his 'terror of the abstract' (*Memoirs* 37) and emphasis on the embodiment of imagination that made Yeats feel an affinity with Keats in the first place, and these qualities also provide the premises for Yeats to re-articulate negative capability, though in a distinctively Yeatsian fashion.

In a journal entry of 9 March 1909, commenting on A. H. Hallam's view that 'poetry was the impression on the senses of certain very sensitive men', Yeats writes, 'It was such with the pure artists, Keats and Shelley, but not so with the impure artists who, like Wordsworth, mixed up popular morality with their work' (*Memoirs* 179). He expresses a similar view in his essay 'Art and Ideas' written in 1913, in which he recalls, 'When I began to write I avowed for my principles those of Arthur Hallam in his essay upon Tennyson', that is, the early Tennyson who 'was an example of the school of Keats and Shelley' (*EI* 347), 'the aesthetic school' (*EI* 348). According to Yeats, 'Keats and Shelley, unlike Wordsworth, intermixed into their poetry no elements from the general thought, but wrote out of the impression made by the world upon their delicate senses' (*EI* 347), while Wordsworth 'condescended to moral maxims, or some received philosophy, a multitude of things that even the common sense could understand' (*EI* 348). So here again, as in his above-quoted letter which juxtaposes Keats with the 'abstract' Swinburne and Carlyle, Yeats stresses the absence of the 'palpable' moral or philosophical 'design' in Keats, though here he does not yet make any distinction between Keats and Shelley, as he does in that letter written a few years later.

This label of 'pure artist' was used again by Yeats in 1920 when he was invited to contribute to the *Memorial Volume* for Keats:

> Of the group of romantic poets at the start of last century he was the one pure artist, without any intermixture of doctrine or fanaticism, 'so crammed with life he can but grow in life with being', as Ben Jonson said of some unknown poet, possibly Shakespeare. (*MV* 216)

Again stressing the 'life', or the rhythm of 'things' in Keats's poetry which does not give in to doctrinaire 'ideas', Yeats is actually commenting on Keats's negative capability, only not using the term. His association of Keats with Shakespeare makes one wonder whether the idea was his own or influenced by the view of Keats's Shakespearean quality pioneered by Matthew Arnold. Interestingly enough, here Keats becomes the only 'pure artist' among the Romantics. The exclusion of Shelley does not seem merely a polite gesture made for the occasion, for it is consistent with the view expressed in the above-mentioned letter and a few other references to Keats and Shelley made around the 1910s. Put together, they do seem to suggest a subtle change in Yeats's view of Keats, or rather of the role of the poet in general, for Keats is often measured against Shelley, who is a constant reference point in Yeats's eyes.

In the essay memorializing John Synge written in 1910, Yeats puts Keats and Shelley as different types of artists:

> There are artists like Byron, like Goethe, like Shelley, who have impressive personalities, active wills and all their faculties at the service of the will; but [Synge] belonged to those who, like Wordsworth, like Coleridge, like Goldsmith, like Keats, have little personality, so far as the casual eye can see, little personal will, but fiery and brooding imagination. (*EI* 328–9)

Whether faithful to the actual personalities of these artists or not, Yeats here distinguishes Keats from the egotistical poetic characters, which is in line with his portrayal of Keats in 'Ego Dominus Tuus'. The distinction he makes, strikingly close to Keats's categories of 'Men of Power' and 'Men of Genius', also corresponds to his own increasing concerns with the dramatic quality of poetry. On 17 October 1918, Yeats wrote to his father about the difference between Keats and Shelley again:

> I look on them as two distinct types of men, who could not exchange methods . . . . If you accept metempsychosis, Keats was moving to greater subjectivity of being, and to unity of that being, and Shelley to greater objectivity and to consequent break-up of unity of being. (*YL* 653)

What Yeats contemplates here gives a rather accurate picture of Keats at his later stage when his poetry reveals the paradoxical relationship between the identity of the poet and the non-egotistical nature of poetry more clearly. Yeats's changing perceptions of Keats and Shelley, therefore, seem to be focused on the issue of the poet's identity and how it is manifested in his poetry, which coincide with his own growing preoccupations with the antithetical mask a poet necessarily assumes in his poetry.

Judging from these sporadic remarks, Yeats's view of Keats as the only 'pure' Romantic 'artist' seems to be a genuine tribute, and after all, it is also his own conviction that art should not be 'intermixed' with 'doctrine or fanaticism', as he writes in objection to the Young Ireland Society:

> Even if what one defends be true, an attitude of defence, a continual apology, whatever the cause, makes the mind barren because it kills intellectual innocence; that delight in what is unforeseen, and in the mere spectacle of the world, the mere drifting hither and thither that must come before all true thought and emotion. (*EI* 314)

This 'intellectual innocence', putting the open receptiveness of the mind as the prerequisite to artistic creation, is strikingly congenial to Keats's notion of negative capability.[3]

For all these expressions of closer affinity with and higher esteem of Keats, however, Yeats declined the request to contribute to the *Keats Memorial Volume*. He writes to Dr. Williamson, the editor, 'I cannot write on Keats. I have not read Keats during the last five years, and I should have to fill my mind with him' (*MV* 216). So it seems that Yeats did not want to immerse himself in the poetry he had been perhaps too familiar with, and this might have something to do with the changes he was making to his own poetry around the time. His letter to his father written on 5 August 1913 indicates such a concern:

> Of recent years instead of 'vision', meaning by vision the intense realization of a state of ecstatic emotion symbolized in a definite imagined region, I have tried for more self portraiture. I have tried to make my work convincing with a speech so natural and dramatic that the hearer would feel the presence of a man thinking and feeling.

He then adds that Keats's poetry belongs to 'the type of vision' (*YL* 583). In this light, it was quite natural for him not to want to 'fill his mind' with Keats's poetry, for he needed to resist the influence of the kind of poetry he was trying to stop writing. Claiming himself a descendant of the Romantic tradition as much as he did, Yeats, like Eliot, also had to break from the tradition while inheriting it. Because of this urge to write 'new' poetry, Yeats and Eliot, even more so, manifest a rather mixed attitude towards their Romantic predecessors. George Bornstein argues, 'Yeats wrote Greater Romantic Lyrics only in his maturity, when he had cast off derivative romanticism of the nineties and was creating a modern variety' (53). And I propose that it is just in these mature, modern Romantic lyrics that Yeats demonstrates particularly evident Keatsian qualities of negative capability, which does not seem irrelevant to all the above-mentioned reflections he had made about Keats around this time.

The parallels between the golden bird in 'Sailing to Byzantium' and Keats's nightingale and the Grecian urn have been much noticed, and these two odes were frequently on Yeats's mind.[4] Yeats's recapitulation of Keats's immortal bird and artifice of eternity is actually already evident in 'The Wild Swans at Coole', and further develops in many other key poems in his later career. It also needs to be stressed that both these two key lyrics, and their extensions in other poems of the mature Yeats, are mostly indebted to Keats not only in their verbal echoes and parallel symbols, but in their adoption of a negatively capable stance to reveal conflicting impulses. Throughout these poems, there runs a vacillation between the aspiration for a symbol of timelessness and the clinging to actual human experience in all its earthly complexity. Like Keats's poetry of experience, these poems of Yeats are also more oriented to unfolding conflict than probing for resolution. They exemplify Yeats's 'self-quarrelling' poetry, or in another figure of his, poetry of 'warfare', as he puts it: 'all noble things are the result of warfare; great nations and classes, of warfare in the visible world, great poetry and philosophy, of invisible warfare, the division of a mind within itself' (*EI* 321).

The opening scene of 'The Wild Swans at Coole' sets the immortal birds in a world of flux: 'The trees are in their autumn beauty, / The woodland paths are dry, / Under the October twilight the water / Mirrors a still sky; / Upon the brimming water among the stones / Are nine-and-fifty swans' (1–6). The season, like Keats's autumn, is paradoxical, displaying 'beauty' but also impregnating decline, with the 'dry' woodland paths forecasting a scene of desolation like that Keats's knight finds himself in, where 'the sedge has wither'd from the lake / And no birds sing' ('La Belle Dame sans Merci' 3–4). The time of the day is the characteristic Yeatsian twilight, corresponding with the autumnal season, recalling the 'soft-dying day' in Keats's autumn. The spatial setting is liminal too, caught between water and land. The water reflects 'a still sky', but the symmetry is offset by the odd number of the swans. They are found among the stones, steady against the brimming water as if impervious of the flow of time, but also ironically reminiscent of the stone in 'Easter, 1916' that '[troubles] the living stream' (44).

The speaker then continues in a 'Tintern Abbey' elegiac tone: 'The nineteenth autumn has come upon me / Since I first made my count; / I saw, before I had well finished, / All suddenly mount / And scatter wheeling in great broken rings / Upon their clamorous wings' (7–12). The immortal birds only bring the human spectator a keener awareness of time, as Keats's speaker is preyed upon by his own mortality at hearing the nightingale's singing 'in full-throated ease'. He had not 'finished' his count in the past, nor has he finished his recounting in the present, when the tense shifts abruptly back to the now before he 'had well finished' his recollection. The swans' indifference to the human spectator's emotional state resembles the nightingale which '[has] never known' the pains in the human world. Their sudden motion and 'clamour', disrupting both the external tranquility and the internal reverie, make their symbolic constancy suspicious, indicating that the human viewer might be too wishful in his perspective on them. The irony is also suggested in the 'broken rings' they form, a sign of incompleteness, as their number, being odd, flatly contradicts the human spectator's unreliable account of them as 'lover by lover'. Like Keats's speaker, Yeats's viewer seems also unaware of the irony. Looking at 'those brilliant creatures' (13) which seem to be alien to his own autumnal mood, his 'heart is sore' (14), as Keats's speaker's 'heart aches' at the nightingale's 'happiness': 'All's changed since I, hearing at twilight, / The first time on this shore, / The bell-beat of their wings above my head, / Trod with a lighter tread' (15–8).

Resembling Keats's speaker, Yeats's viewer also projects onto the swans what he is not: 'Unwearied still, lover by lover, / They paddle in the cold / Companionable streams or climb the air; / Their hearts have not grown old; / Passion or conquest, wander where they will, / Attend upon them still' (19–24). As the 'still unravish'd bride' forever has the potential to be ravished and the 'happy melodist' is 'unwearied' only on the urn, so are the swans 'unwearied still', but only in the human viewer's eye, whereas their actual beings are constantly subject to mutability. The speaker, in seeing the swans as the ideal other, can only adopt human terms to imagine their alien existence, as Keats's speaker can only visualize the nightingale's world with his human perspective. Thus 'their hearts have not grown old', 'still' driven by 'Passion or conquest', which, ironically, are exactly the impulses to make them 'wearied', as Keats's speaker's imaginative participation with the bird removes him from it by its very powerfulness. 'Still wouldst thou sing, and I have ears in vain': Keats's 'still' signals the dissociation of the speaker from the bird, while Yeats's 'still' as the last word of the stanza highlights the disparity between the changed human viewer and the unchanged swans, thus preparing for their departure in the final stanza: 'But now they drift on the still water, / Mysterious, beautiful; / Among what rushes will they build, / By what lake's edge or pool / Delight men's eyes when I awake some day / To find they have flown away?' (25–30). As the nightingale 'fades' away, the swans 'drift' ahead. Like Keats's speaker following the bird with the viewless wings, Yeats's viewer sees them move into other scenes in his mind's eye. While Keats's speaker asks himself, 'Was it a vision, or a waking dream?', Yeats's speaker also indicates that he sees the swans when he is not 'awake'. Countering the actuality of his overall poetic experience, the speaker concludes the whole poem in uncertainty and ambivalence.

The tension in 'The Wild Swans at Coole', evident enough, is still restrained and understated, whereas 'Sailing to Byzantium', like 'Ode on a Grecian Urn', develops the submerged tension into a more conspicuous dramatic irony.

With the distant reference of 'That', the poem opens with the speaker look-
ing back on the world he has already left:

That is no country for old men. The young
In one another's arms, birds in the trees,
– Those dying generations – at their song,
The salmon-falls, the mackerel-crowded seas,
Fish, flesh, or fowl, commend all summer long
Whatever is begotten, born, and dies.
Caught in that sensual music all neglect
Monuments of unageing intellect. (1–8)

As Keats's speaker relives 'the weariness, the fever, and the fret' of the mortal
world that he avows to forget, the old speaker here recasts himself into the
sensual country that he has apparently forsaken. The 'dying generations', echo-
ing Keats's 'hungry generations', appear vigorous and thriving in the long
catalogue, overwhelming the 'unageing intellect' that does seem negligible,
as Keats's speaker's assertion of 'all breathing human passion far above' calls
attention to the unbreathing lovers on the urn. The natural beings sing 'all
summer long', unaware of process and time like Keats's nightingale singing in
its eternal summer, whereas it is only the human speaker who constantly hears
the sound of mortality. His rejection of their 'sensual music' therefore is as sus-
picious as Keats's speaker's claim that the melodies 'unheard' by 'the sensual
ear' are 'more endear'd'. He then continues: 'An aged man is but a paltry
thing, / A tattered coat upon a stick, unless / Soul clap its hands and sing, and
louder sing / For every tatter in its mortal dress' (9–12). 'Paltry' has a faint echo
of Keats's 'palsy' aged men, while the soul's louder singing is reminiscent of the
nightingale's 'pouring forth thy soul abroad / In such an ecstasy!'. But the
stronger though less obvious Keatsian echo lies in the irony of the physicality
the soul takes to 'clap its hands', as Keats's urn triumphs over human passion by
freezing a most passionate moment in human experience.

Paralleling Keats's speaker's 'Already with thee!', the aged speaker of Yeats
announces, 'I have sailed the seas and come / To the holy city of Byzantium'
(15–16). Keats's speaker joins the nightingale by the power of poesy, while
Yeats's old man reaches Byzantium by discarding the 'mortal dress' of the soul
and 'studying / Monuments of its own magnificence' (13–4). Keats's speaker,
after uniting with the nightingale, only sees a luxuriant human world, while
Yeats's old speaker, attending to the soul's spirituality, gives it a vigorous physical
form. Keats's speaker believes that the urn, as 'Sylvan historian', can 'express / A
flowery tale more sweetly than our rhyme', and Yeats's old man invokes the
'sages': 'be the singing-masters of my soul. / Consume my heart away; sick with
desire / And fastened to a dying animal / It knows not what it is; and gather
me / Into the artifice of eternity' (20–4). His 'heart', 'sick with desire', reminds
one not only of Keats's 'heart high-sorrowful and cloy'd', but the spectator of

the swans whose heart is 'sore' with the sense of loss and mutability, all being
'fastened to a dying animal' as the 'dying generations' 'caught in that sensual
music'. His invocation thus unwittingly turns into a confession, acknowledging
his identity as 'a dying animal' when he seeks to sing for the 'unageing' soul.
The double-edged 'artifice of eternity', as Keats's urn is a 'foster-child' of time-
lessness, only simulates immortality by its make-believe fictionality. The speak-
er's elaboration of this 'artifice of eternity' therefore develops the irony to a
climax in the concluding stanza:

> Once out of nature I shall never take
> My bodily form from any natural thing,
> But such a form as Grecian goldsmiths make
> Of hammered gold and gold enamelling
> To keep a drowsy Emperor awake;
> Or set upon a golden bough to sing
> To lords and ladies of Byzantium
> Of what is past, or passing, or to come. (25–32)

As the Grecian urn bears indelible human traces, Yeats's artifice can only be
made by human 'goldsmiths'. The golden bird will 'keep a drowsy Emperor
awake', as the nightingale 'was heard / In ancient days by emperor and clown'.
Discarding the dying body, the aged speaker aspires to be the perpetually 'happy
melodist' as the piper on the Grecian urn, 'for ever piping songs for ever new'.
But what it can sing is only of 'what is past, or passing, or to come', which,
though reversing the order of 'begotten, born, and dies', is but the same pro-
cess sequenced in time, as the Grecian urn can only 'express / a flowery tale' by
arresting a scene of 'wild ecstasy' from the human world.

As Keats's Grecian urn '[teases] us out of thought', Yeats's 'artifice of eternity'
concludes with such ambivalence that it only provokes doubts about the soul's
'own magnificence' independent of its 'mortal dress' and 'sick heart'. The
tension becomes more fierce when the artifice of eternity, including the immor-
tal bird, recurs in Yeats's poetry composed in an increasingly more violent
historical setting.

The swan comes back in 'Nineteen Hundred and Nineteen', against a back-
ground where 'days are dragon-ridden, the nightmare / Rides upon sleep' (25–6):

> Some moralist or mythological poet
> Compares the solitary soul to a swan;
> I am satisfied with that,
> Satisfied if a troubled mirror show it,
> Before that brief gleam of its life be gone,
> An image of its state;
> The wings half spread for flight,

The breast thrust out in pride
Whether to play, or to ride
Those winds that clamour of approaching night. (59–68)

The poet accepts the association of the swan with 'the solitary soul' only on the condition of reflecting the swan by 'a troubled mirror', emblematic of his own mental state troubled by the chaotic world, thus calling attention to his conscious making of the image of the swan into a poetic symbol. If the wild swans at Coole are made into a poetic artifice of eternity, then the swan here becomes 'fastened to a dying animal', whose 'solitary soul' is manifested only at the last moment of its transient life. The autumn twilight has turned into the ominous 'approaching night' of 'winter', and the clamorous wings now beat against the clamorous winds of peril and catastrophe. The 'mysterious, beautiful' swans aloof from human grief now take on 'pride', having to confront the experience of unknowable vicissitudes. Even when the swan does turn into 'the solitary soul' taking flight from this world, it 'has leaped into the desolate heaven' (79), as Keats's 'magic casements' only open to 'faery lands forlorn'. While Keats's speaker realizes then that imagination is a 'deceiving elf', the poet here finds that the image he makes through the 'troubled mirror' turns out to unsettle his whole world of poetic imagination: 'That image can bring wildness, bring a rage / To end all things, to end / What my laborious life imagined, even / The half-imagined, the half-written page' (80–3). The image of the swan has evolved from mystery and beauty into 'wildness' and 'rage', bringing forth an apocalyptic vision of human history, in face of which the poet's imaginative world appears only too 'laborious' and lame. This image of apocalypse metamorphosizes into the almighty god in 'Leda and the Swan', who, by performing a deed of violence, 'engenders' (9) chains of violence and destruction in human history. The 'brute blood of the air' (12) becomes blurred with the 'rough beast' (21) that 'slouches towards Bethlehem to be born' (22) in 'The Second Coming', and the image of the swan in cyclical historical processes revolves to the very origin of the 'mere anarchy' (4) of the human world.

This ominous association of the swan is revised again in 'The Tower', when the poet, writing his will, bequeaths to his imagined descendants his 'pride' (127), which is compared to 'that of the hour / When the swan must fix his eye / Upon a fading gleam, / Float out upon a long / Last reach of glittering stream / And there sing his last song' (139–44). The swan now recovers its tranquility, but it is no longer 'unwearied still'. Unaccompanied by its 'lover', it is a 'solitary soul' reaching the end of its life. Its heart has 'grown old', clearly envisioning that both its own life and the flux of history have only 'a fading gleam'. Yet instead of evoking 'wildness' and 'rage', the swan becomes an image of tragic majesty, proudly facing waning life and glory by singing the last song at the moment of catastrophe. In Keatsian terms, it is an image of Melancholy, wakeful at both its own anguish and the miseries of the soul-making world.

The swan, therefore, with its shifting associations that are dissonant and opposing, reveals the negatively capable mind of the poet which constantly exposes itself to violently changing experience and encompasses the conflicting visions consequently provoked. Not only the immortal bird, but other artifices of eternity undergo similar trials of experience in Yeats's poetry as well. In 'Meditations in Time of Civil War', the artifice takes the form of 'a changeless sword' (III:2), and 'A bit of an embroidered dress/Covers its wooden sheath' (III:6–7). But this time, the poet is unequivocal about the ambivalence of the symbol: 'In Sato's house,/Curved like new moon, moon-luminous,/It lay five hundred years./Yet if no change appears/No moon; only an aching heart/Conceives a changeless work of art' (III:9–14). The poet here acknowledges that a 'changeless' artefact can only be 'conceived' by an artist with a mortal body and a heart 'sick with desire', thus reconciling himself with the human existence caught in continuous cycles of being 'begotten, born, and dies'. Even the changeless artefact has to take a shape out of changing experience, symbolized by the new moon, as the golden bird can only sing of life in process. By recognizing the paradox of the artifice of eternity, the poet turns the sword into a symbol of synthesis, which, as his 'rose upon the rood of time', signifies the crux of history and eternity, change and fixation. Encompassing the warring aspects in itself, the sword becomes one of the 'emblems of adversity' (II:30) the poet searches for to confront the overall stormy and dark surroundings.

But the synthesis falls apart when the sword recurs in 'A Dialogue of Self and Soul', an exemplar of Yeats's self-quarrelling poetry, with the self and the soul playing antagonistic roles as the poet's dramatic personae engaged in the warfare within the poet's mind itself. The soul starts by summoning the self to its symbols of 'the winding ancient stair' (1), 'the broken, crumbling battlement' (3), 'the breathless starlit air' (4) and 'the star that marks the hidden pole' (5), asking it to abandon the human world for 'the steep ascent' (2). The self counters:

> The consecrated blade upon my knees
> Is Sato's ancient blade, still as it was,
> Still razor-keen, still like a looking-glass
> Unspotted by the centuries;
> That flowering, silken, old embroidery, torn
> From some court-lady's dress and round
> The wooden scabbard bound and wound,
> Can, tattered, still protect, faded adorn. (9–16)

The sword now becomes a symbol the self sets as an antithesis of the symbols of the soul. It is as 'ancient' as the winding stair, but unlike the ruinous 'battlement', it remains 'razor-keen'. While the emblems of the soul reach upward to the ethereal, the self's blade looks at the image of this world and keeps itself 'unspotted'. It wears a 'mortal dress', tattered and faded as the 'aching heart' that conceived it had long been dead, but 'round', 'bound' and 'wound', it vocally makes the disappeared life still hauntingly present. The self's symbol is despised by the soul:

> Why should the imagination of a man
> Long past his prime remember things that are
> Emblematical of love and war?
> Think of ancestral night that can,
> If but imagination scorn the earth
> And intellect its wandering
> To this and that and t'other thing,
> Deliver from the crime of death and birth. (17–24)

The soul, echoing the old speaker of 'Sailing to Byzantium' who urges for the soul to 'sing / For every tatter in its mortal dress', accuses the self of being occupied by the fleeting human experience when it is already 'a paltry thing'. Yet 'only an aching heart / Conceives a changeless work of art', and the sword and embroidery become artifice of eternity exactly by being 'emblematical of love and war', as 'passion or conquest' 'still' 'attend upon' the immortal birds. The soul refuses to recognize this paradox, and its subsequent admonishment, preceded by 'if but', indicates its own doubt about whether imagination can really 'scorn the earth', and intellect be kept from 'wandering'. Reining the mind by force from drifting with the fluid experience, the soul will only 'kill' the 'intellectual innocence' of the mind, in fact making itself the very antithesis of negative capability.

The self confronts the soul by reaffirming his earthly symbols:

> Montashigi, third of his family, fashioned it
> Five hundred years ago, about it lie
> Flowers from I know not what embroidery –
> Heart's purple – and all these I set
> For emblems of the day against the tower
> Emblematical of the night,
> And claim as by a soldier's right
> A charter to commit the crime once more. (25–32)

Naming the specific individual who designed the sword, the self reasserts its allegiance to human experience by embracing its concreteness and particularity. Going back to its origin, the self returns the changeless artefact to the once-existing life with the 'aching heart' that 'conceives' it, and by comparing the embroidery to 'Heart's purple', regains the human passion that is woven into this 'mortal dress'. Recovering their lives, the self claims them to be emblems of 'the day', symbolic of the light engendering life, to oppose the soul's symbol of the night, which is the tower overwhelming in its dark lifelessness, monumental of the soul's 'own magnificence'. Confronting the soul's advice to be delivered from the 'crime of death and birth', the self takes up its sword to guard its right to 'commit the crime once more'.

Challenged by the vigorous, belligerent self, the soul falls into a meditative mood. Comparing its ascension to Heaven with a state of the intellect that 'no longer knows / Is from the *Ought*, or *Knower* from the *Known*' (36–7), it acknowledges its rejection of the state of being and its dissociation from experience, thus betraying a doubt about its sole pursuit of the 'steep ascent', as that expressed by the poet in 'Easter, 1916': 'Too long a sacrifice / Can make a stone of the heart' (57–8). And not only is the heart turned into a stone, the soul continues: 'Only the dead can be forgiven; / But when I think of that my tongue's a stone' (39–40). With the soul vocally defeated, the self takes over the dialogue completely. Its subsequent long turn, however, is taken up by all kinds of foulness, striving, blindness and suffering in human life, almost echoing the soul's account of it as 'the crime of death and birth'. But it concludes with a triumphant celebration of human experience for all its follies:

> I am content to follow to its source
> Every event in action or in thought;
> Measure the lot; forgive myself the lot!
> When such as I cast out remorse
> So great a sweetness flows into the breast
> We must laugh and we must sing,
> We are blest by everything,
> Everything we look upon is blest. (65–72)

By its unreserved and all-inclusive embrace of human experience, the self achieves a unity of being with the great other, thus replacing the 'ache' of the heart with 'sweetness'. In Keatsian terms, the self has found out the use of the soul-making world. The warfare is concluded by the triumph of the self's thorough affirmation of earthly existence, but the conclusion is not final, for the poet returns to Byzantium and makes the self and the soul intricately mingled rather then distinctly dichotomized.

In 'Byzantium', the sequel of 'Sailing to Byzantium', the ambivalence of the artifice of eternity, instead of being indicated, is openly acknowledged by the poet, addressing it ambiguously as 'miracle, bird, or golden handiwork' (17), which, 'by the moon embittered, scorn aloud / In glory of changeless metal / Common bird or petal / And all complexities of mire or blood' (21-4). 'Scorning' the earth, it takes the soul's stance, but its association with the moon also makes it intimately related with the self's artefact which is also 'changeless'.

What it 'scorns' is also 'disdained' by the 'dome' of the 'great cathedral' (4) at the opening: 'A starlit or a moonlit dome disdains / All that man is, / All mere complexities, / The fury and the mire of human veins' (5–8). Reaching upward, the dome, like the tower signifying 'steep ascent', belongs to symbols of the soul. Overwhelmed by the forces of the soul, the self seems vanquished when the human reality it dearly embraces is rejected as 'mere complexities'. But when the makers of the artifice emerge in the last scene, one cannot be certain whether they create symbols for the soul or the self: 'The golden smithies of the Emperor! / Marbles of the dancing floor / Break bitter furies of complexity, / Those images that yet / Fresh images beget, / That dolphin-torn, that gong-tormented sea' (35–40). The human smiths make 'marbles of the dancing floor', which 'break' 'All that man is' together with human passions of 'bitter furies'. But they at the same time conjure up images that take on the power of the dying generations to beget images that still regenerate, which flow into a vast sea of experience. The sea itself is a mixture of contrarieties, haunted by both dolphins, creatures of 'mire or blood' belonging to the self's sensual world, and the clamorous gong of the 'great cathedral', the symbol of the soul's steep ascent.

As opposition and paradox become an essential theme in Keats's poetry, Yeats's vacillation between his antithetical selves constitutes a major pattern in his poetry. The poem entitled 'Vacillation' sets the soul quarrelling with the self again, urging it to 'Seek out reality, leave things that seem' (72), but the heart retorts, 'What theme had Homer but original sin?' (77), pledging to commit the 'crime' of existence yet again. Keats forsakes the bright star in 'lone splendour' ('Bright star' 2) for the 'sweet unrest' (12) of human love, so does Yeats's poetry make the final 'vacillation' back to the heart, as the poet writes in his *Last Poems*: 'I must lie down where all the ladders start / In the foul rag and bone shop of the heart' ('The Circus Animals' Desertion' 39–40).

In Keats's poetry, the contrarieties have never been really reconciled, nor has Keats attempted to unify them into syntheses. Yeats, on the other hand, has been seeking for some kind of resolution among his antitheses and vacillations. One may adopt Richard Ellmann's term 'affirmative capability' here to describe their difference. After all, they lived in radically different times, and when the age was dominated by 'mere anarchy' and hysteria, it was only natural for Yeats to search for a kind of affirmative order to impose on and with which to confront the all too chaotic reality.

Ellmann bases the term on a journal entry of Yeats in January 1929, in which Yeats comments on Pound's 'scepticism' as arising 'out of search for complete undisturbed self-possession'; he considers Eliot's scepticism in the same way: 'there is a tendency to exchange search for submission'. Yeats then writes, 'if I affirm that such and such is so, the more complete the affirmation, the more complete the proof, and even when incomplete, it remains valid within some limit. I must kill scepticism in myself' (qtd. in Ellmann 1964: 239). Further on,

Yeats reflects on the necessity of tradition for a poet and writes: '[t]he "modern man" is a term invented by modern poetry to dignify our scepticism' (qtd. in Ellmann 1964: 240).

Ellmann holds that Yeats 'hovered for a time near' Keats's stance of negative capability, but eventually 'moved beyond' it. He calls it 'affirmative capability', 'for it begins with the poet's difficulties but emphasizes his resolutions of them . . . . Neither the intellect nor the emotions can be satisfied to remain in "uncertainties, mysteries, and doubts"; they demand the more solid fare of affirmations' (1964: 238). He then explains, 'In a world where no sort of truth is common, and where complete truth is impossible, incomplete truths must be put forward as the best we have' (1964: 241). Interestingly enough, in the anthology *The Modern Tradition* Ellmann compiled with Charles Feidelson, he collects both Keats's negative capability passage and the above journal entry of Yeats, including the former in the section called 'the State of Doubt', the latter, 'the State of Affirmation'.

It is essential, I would stress, to distinguish Keats's 'state of doubt' from what Yeats comments on as modernist 'scepticism'. Keats makes it very clear that the state of 'doubts' is experienced in 'uncertainties' and 'mysteries', and a negatively capable mind is opposed as much to dogmatic scepticism as to doctrinaire belief. In this sense, what Ellmann calls the affirmative capability of Yeats is actually negative capability in an affirmative form, for when scepticism becomes the fact and reason the mind irritably reaches after, then the ability to doubt scepticism and to search for affirmation is being capable of staying open to the uncertain and mysterious nature of experience. If we agree with Yeats that scepticism is a modern disease, then maybe negative capability, when passed down to modernity, can only take an affirmative shape.

This affirmative capability of Yeats is clearly manifested in 'A Prayer for My Daughter', where the father, against the 'howling' 'storm' (1) outside and 'the great gloom' (8) in his mind, prays for the daughter:

> May she become a flourishing hidden tree
> That all her thoughts may like the linnet be,
> And have no business but dispensing round
> Their magnanimities of sound
> . . .
> O may she live like some green laurel
> Rooted in one dear perpetual place. (41–4, 47–8)

The laurel tree of course anticipates the chestnut tree: 'great rooted blossomer, / Are you the leaf, the blossom or the bole?' ('Among School Children' 61–2). Here, the laurel tree, too, is a symbol of all-encompassing plenitude. It is made up of the steadfast root, the flourishing leaf, blossom and the bole, as well as the linnet which can take free flights and thus utter its 'magnanimities of sound'. The prayer expresses the anxiety for order and tradition, but more importantly, it puts on top an accommodating mind open to the experience of 'all complexities'. In this sense, it echoes Oceanus's speech to the fallen Titans, which, in very similar images, urges for a disinterested perspective to envision the rich diversity of the universe:

> . . . doth the dull soil
> Quarrel with the proud forests it hath fed,
> . . .
> Can it deny the chiefdom of green groves?
> Or shall the tree be envious of the dove
> Because it cooeth, and hath snowy wings
> To wander wherewithal and find its joys? (*Hyperion* II:217–8, 220–3)

Yeats's thoughts thus pass from the image of disinterested magnitude to its antithesis, pondering the mind confined by hatred, which is in essence fanatic egotism: 'If there's no hatred in a mind / Assault and battery of the wind / Can never tear the linnet from the leaf. / An intellectual hatred is the worst, / So let her think opinions are accursed' (54–8). Only by a mind of affirmative openness within can one resist the wind of destructive violence without, which is actually a consequence of hatred and bigotry broken loose on a massive scale. The lines here also shed light on Yeats's comment on scepticism, that it results from a 'search for complete undisturbed self-possession', one which reveals an opinionated mind that the self is 'possessed' with so as not to be 'disturbed' by the complexities of experience. Similarly, 'intellectual hatred' may be seen as a variant of what Yeats calls 'rhetoric', both resulting from the 'quarrel with others', when the mind is armed with the 'opinions' of the self to fight against all the discordant and the opposite. It is the antithesis of Keats's 'neutral intellect', or Yeats's poetic mind of 'intellectual innocence' that is capable of engaging in 'quarrel with ourselves', both bespeaking a mind like 'the Horn of Plenty' (32), an image of magnitude both poets are fond of. Thus the father continues, 'all hatred driven hence, / the soul recovers radical innocence' (65–6), which, like his notion of 'intellectual innocence', is an affirmative innocence to counter 'the murderous innocence of the sea' (16), the chaotic, destructive world outside pervaded by intellectual hatred. In this light, Yeats's comment on Keats as 'the one pure artist, without any intermixture of doctrine or fanaticism' is a translation of Keats's negative capability into Yeatsian terms: a negatively capable mind is a 'soul' of 'radical innocence'.

The poem is concluded in prayers for 'custom' and 'ceremony': 'For arrogance and hatred are the wares / Peddled in the thoroughfares' (75–6). One almost feels that Yeats is echoing Keats's 'let the mind be a thoroughfare for all thoughts'. Then he continues: 'How but in custom and in ceremony / Are innocence and beauty born? / Ceremony's a name for the rich horn, / And custom for the spreading laurel tree' (77–80). If innocence is synonymous with negative capability, then custom and ceremony equate to affirmative capability, the search for tradition and order as ramparts against the assaulting storm outside.

It is this affirmative capability that gives Yeats the resources to make 'tragic joy' ('The Gyres' 8) out of disastrous experience, which parallels Keats's tragic vision of the soul-making world gained from a mind of negative capability. An exemplar of this is a later poem on the artifice of eternity, 'Lapis Lazuli', in which the artefact is juxtaposed with a background of even more horrifying 'murderous innocence', as the sounds of 'hysterical women' (1) are mingled with the noise of 'Aeroplane and Zeppelin' (6): 'Two Chinamen, behind them a third, / Are carved in Lapis Lazuli, / Over them flies a long-legged bird / A symbol of longevity; / The third, doubtless a serving-man, / Carries a musical instrument' (37–42). The bird of longevity recapitulates the immortal bird, while the musician parallels both Keats's melodist on the urn and Yeats's singing bird in Byzantium. But the setting is distinct from the pastoral Arcady or the holy city:

> Every discolouration of the stone,
> Every accidental crack or dent
> Seems a water-course or an avalanche,
> Or lofty slope where it still snows
> Though doubtless plum or cherry-branch
> Sweetens the little half-way house
> Those Chinamen climb towards. (43–9)

As with his former deliberate making of an image, the poet now is also consciously re-making the artefact which is itself a product of imagination. He projects 'water-course', 'avalanche', or snowy 'lofty slope' on the actual 'discolouration', 'crack or dent', planting 'plum or cherry-branch' on the mountain by his mind. The artefact that is ruinous and worn out by time is thus turned into a landscape of sublimity by the poet, and he further transforms it by setting the figures inside to motion, as Keats has done with the scenes on the Grecian urn. But unlike Keats, who ends up in an ambivalent attitude about the artifice of eternity, Yeats emphasizes the fulfilment of his imagination of the artefact:

>   and I
> Delight to imagine them seated there;
> There, on the mountain and the sky,
> On all the tragic scene they stare.
> One asks for mournful melodies;
> Accomplished fingers begin to play.

Their eyes mid many wrinkles, their eyes,
Their ancient, glittering eyes, are gay. (49–56)

By stressing his 'delight' in imagining their scene to be a 'tragic' one in which
they nevertheless remain 'gay', the poet is calling attention to the tragic joy
he is deliberately creating in his imagination. The poem becomes a refracted
mirror of his mind, which projects onto the artefact, invents for it a tragic
setting, and consequently transforms the internal figures into tragic heroes.
The musician in turn becomes a tragic artist, reflecting the image of the poet
himself. His remade 'Lapis Lazuli' thus becomes a poetic artefact he presents to
his readers, asserting his 'delight' in confronting his immediate tragic scene.
As Keats embraces the pains and troubles of the world for their soul-making
power, Yeats affirms 'Tragedy wrought to its uttermost' (20) for its paradoxical
force to create 'gaiety transfiguring all that dread' (17). He writes elsewhere:
'He only can create the greatest imaginable beauty who has endured all imagin-
able pangs, for only when we have seen and foreseen what we dread shall we be
rewarded by that dazzling, unforeseen, wing-footed wanderer' (*Mythologies* 332).
This is strongly reminiscent of Keats's notion of tragic intensity achieved by
transforming the most 'disagreeable' pains into their opposite, the greatest
'Beauty & Truth'. And Lear and Cordelia are among Yeats's exemplars of tragic
joy as well, who 'do not break up their lines to weep', but 'are gay; / Gaiety trans-
figuring all that dread' (15–7).

Eliot's 'Wisdom of Humility'

The legacy of negative capability is most often traced in the modernist notion
of impersonality, chiefly propagated by T. S. Eliot in his ground-breaking
'Tradition and the Individual Talent', published exactly one hundred years
after Keats's Great Year.[5] The most well-known expression of impersonality is
probably the following statement: 'Poetry is not a turning loose of emotion,
but an escape from emotion; it is not the expression of personality, but an
escape from personality' – so often quoted on its own that the following qualifi-
cation tends to be ignored: 'But, of course, only those who have personality
and emotions know what it means to want to escape from these things' (*SE* 21).
Just as negative capability does not preclude self-identity, so is personality indis-
pensable for Eliot's notion of impersonality, as emotion precedes the 'escape'
from it. Eliot's thought resembles not only Keats's idea of the non-egotistical
poet, but the paradox in the relation between the artist's self and the imper-
sonal artistic product contained in the conception of negative capability. This
paradox is more clearly expressed by Eliot later in his career. In his essay on
Yeats published in 1940, commenting on 'the superiority of Yeats's later work'
for 'the greater expression of personality in it', Eliot realizes that he may be

causing confusion among his readers: 'I have, in early essays, extolled what I called impersonality in art, and it may seem that . . . I am contradicting myself' (*PP* 255). He then explains:

> There are two forms of impersonality: that which is natural to the mere skilful craftsman, and that which is more and more achieved by the maturing artist. The first is that of what I have called the 'anthology piece' . . . . The second impersonality is that of the poet who, out of intense and personal experience, is able to express a general truth; retaining all the particularity of his experience, to make of it a general symbol. And the strange thing is that Yeats, having been a great craftsman in the first kind, became a great poet in the second. (*PP* 255)

It is hardly surprising that when enjoying an established status, Eliot could afford to express his modernist precepts in a less provocative manner,[6] but even in 'Tradition and the Individual Talent', he has not equated impersonality with objectivity, as indicated in the sentence tailing the famous statement quoted above.

The famous catalyst-artist metaphor also encompasses both sides of the issue. Adopting the analogy that platinum is catalytic in forming oxygen and sulphur dioxide into sulphuric acid, Eliot writes:

> This combination takes place only if the platinum is present; nevertheless the newly formed acid contains no trace of platinum, and the platinum itself is apparently unaffected: has remained inert, neutral, and unchanged. The mind of the poet is the shred of platinum. (*SE* 18)

Not only does the target of the analogy coincide with Keats's idea of the camelion poet, but the source of the analogy itself is strikingly close to the chemical metaphor used by Keats when he distinguishes 'Men of Power' from 'Men of Genius', who 'are great as certain ethereal chemicals operating on the Mass of neutral intellect' but who 'have not any individuality, any determined character'. No wonder when Eliot exalts Keats's letters as 'the result of genius' (*UP* 101), he singles out this passage to quote, which must have struck him as articulating his own thoughts. Summing up his catalyst metaphor, Eliot writes: 'The poet's mind is in fact a receptacle for seizing and storing up numberless feelings, phrases, images, which remain there until all the particles which can unite to form a new compound are present together' (*SE* 19). The mind being a 'receptacle' fits in with the receptive openness of a negatively capable mind as well. To form this 'compound', Eliot illustrates, 'the fusion takes place' through 'the intensity of the artistic process', and Keats's nightingale that '[brings] together' 'a number of feelings' (*SE* 19) is among his examples. Though his 'intensity' does not mean exactly the same as Keats's 'intensity', the fusing together of disparate elements is congenial to Keats's emphasis on the inclusion of both sides of the opposition in order to achieve intensity. On a similar ground, Eliot also argues for 'a degree of heterogeneity of material compelled into unity by the operation of the poet's mind' (*SE* 283) when he defends the Metaphysical poets against Johnson's accusation that 'the most heterogeneous ideas are yoked by violence together' (*Lives* 14) in their poetry. Of course, Eliot makes the apology not only for metaphysical poetry but for his own and modernist poetry in general, which is often a montage yoking together highly heterogeneous elements.

Eliot concludes the essay by restating impersonality: 'The emotion of art is impersonal. And the poet cannot reach this impersonality without surrendering himself wholly to the work to be done' (*SE* 22). One is reminded of Keats's similar comment: 'Poetry should be great & unobtrusive, a thing which enters into one's soul, and does not startle it or amaze it with itself but with its subject'. The note of self-surrender chimes with Keats as well, as expressed in the introductory remark of his thoughts on 'Men of Power' and 'Men of Genius', 'I must say of one thing that has pressed upon me lately and encreased my Humility and capability of submission', which Eliot also includes in his quote.

All these parallels, however, only suggest Eliot's affinity with instead of indebtedness to Keats, for he had not read Keats's letters when he wrote the essay. In his letter dated 3 February 1921, Eliot tells Mary Hutchinson, 'You have made me want to read Keats's letters' (*EL* 436). We do not know whether he read them then, but obviously he had by 1933, when he delivered the lecture on 'Shelley and Keats'.

The first half of the lecture deals with Shelley, but it is pertinent to Keats as well, for, according to Eliot, Shelley 'makes an astonishing contrast with the attractive Keats' (*UP* 89). Eliot disapproves of the priority of 'ideas' in Shelley's poetry, calling it 'abuse of poetry' (*UP* 89), because his ideas are not 'founded on the facts of experience' (*UP* 96). Instead, 'Shelley seems to have had to a high degree the unusual faculty of passionate apprehension of abstract ideas' (*UP* 89), and his ideas are also 'fixed' (*UP* 90). In contrast to Shelley and his contemporaries who make use of poetry to express 'ideas', Keats is 'a singular figure in a varied and remarkable period' (*UP* 100). What Eliot sees as 'singular' in Keats, therefore, is his antithetical stance to the irritable reaching after 'abstract ideas' that Eliot attributes to Shelley and other Romantics, which is the very essence of negative capability. Eliot then makes the comment that would become a milestone in Keats criticism:

> Keats seems to me also a great poet . . . . But I am not so much concerned with the degree of his greatness as with its kind; and its kind is manifested more clearly in his Letters than in his poems; and in contrast with the kinds we have

been reviewing, it seems to me to be much more the kind of Shakespeare. The Letters are certainly the most notable and the most important ever written by any English poet. (*UP* 100)

To support this, Eliot quotes two passages from Keats's letters: one is mentioned above, and the other is Keats's comment on Wordsworth's 'Gipsies' as 'a kind of sketchy intellectual Landscape – not a search for Truth',[7] which is exactly what Eliot has just accused Wordsworth of together with Shelley. He thus cheers it as being 'of the finest quality of criticism' (*UP* 100). Eliot concludes the lecture by restating Keats's distinctness from his contemporaries and his Shakespearean lineage:

> Wordsworth and Shelley both theorise. Keats has no theory, and to have formed one was irrelevant to his interests, and alien to his mind. If we take either Wordsworth or Shelley as representative of his age . . . we cannot so take Keats. But we cannot accuse Keats of any withdrawal, or refusal; he was merely about his business. He had no theories, yet in the sense appropriate to the poet, in the same sense, though to a lesser degree than Shakespeare, he had a 'philosophic' mind. He was occupied only with the highest use of poetry. (*UP* 102)

The tribute, however, is chiefly paid to Keats the correspondent, whom Eliot exalts above Keats the poet. While recognizing Keats is 'a great poet', Eliot claims that he is 'not happy about *Hyperion*', though admitting that, 'The Odes – especially perhaps the *Ode to Psyche* – are enough for his reputation' (*UP* 100). Such a grudging affirmation characterizes Eliot's attitude towards Keats's poetry. In 'Imperfect Critics', commenting on the discontinuity of the Elizabethans' 'quality of sensuous thought, or of thinking through the senses, or of the senses thinking', or what would come to be known as the 'dissociation of sensibility', Eliot continues: 'There is a trace of it only in Keats' (*SW* 23), making the exception very sparingly. In 'The Metaphysical Poets', he expresses the point again, that in Shelley's *Triumph of Life* and Keats's second *Hyperion*, 'there are traces of a struggle toward unification of sensibility. But Keats and Shelley died, and Tennyson and Browning ruminated' (*SE* 288). Interestingly enough, Eliot describes the conception of 'unification of sensibility' in a very Keatsian manner: to 'feel [the] thought as immediately as the odour of a rose' (*SE* 287). Christopher Baker speculates that Eliot 'could have recalled' (58) Keats's line, 'Sudden a thought came like a full-blown rose' (136), in 'The Eve of St. Agnes'. Whether this is the case or not, Eliot's emphasis on the unification of sensibility is congenial with Keats's affirmation for 'Sensations' against 'consequitive' 'Thoughts'. A slightly more generous remark is found in 'Philip Massinger', where Eliot comments on the camelion quality of a poet: 'Of Shakespeare notably, of Jonson less, of Marlowe (and of Keats to the term of life allowed him), one can say that they *se transvasaient goutte à goutte*' (*SE* 218).

As Eliot would later express his idea of 'impersonality' less radically, his attitude towards Keats's poetry, and indeed towards Romantic poetry in general, cannot be taken at face value. A remark in his letter to Richard Aldington written on 6 July 1921 is quite revealing:

[A]ny innuendos I make at the expense of Milton, Keats, Shelley and the nineteenth century in general are part of a plan to help us rectify, so far as *I* can, the immense skew in public opinion toward our pantheon of literature. (*EL* 460)

The complex motives behind Eliot's anti-Romantic stance have been increasingly noted by critics, Bornstein among them, who sees both Eliot and Yeats as posing in their attitudes towards romanticism:

Yeats and Eliot made opposite public uses of romanticism to define their own poetic stances. While Yeats projected himself as the last romantic, Eliot posed as an anti-romantic modern; and whereas Yeats strove to rescue romanticism from its own defects, Eliot worked to purge literature as a whole of the contamination of romanticism. Both these postures exaggerate, for Yeats' rescue meant transformation and Eliot's overt wreckage masked covert salvage. (94–5)

He calls attention to Eliot's belated confession of his adolescent passion for the Romantics made in 1932 in the introduction to *The Use of Poetry and the Use of Criticism*, where Eliot recollects 'the almost overwhelming introduction to a new world of feeling' Edward Fitzgerald's *Omar* gave him, and reveals, 'It was like a sudden conversion; the world appeared anew, painted with bright, delicious and painful colours. Thereupon I took the usual adolescent course with Byron, Shelley, Keats, Rossetti, Swinburne' (33). Bornstein also goes into Eliot's adolescent poems, which are chiefly imitations of Romantic poetry, including Keats's odes and 'Lamia'. He maintains that 'Eliot often works through to romantic positions in the name of anti-romanticism', and sums up the argument of what he calls 'revisionist critics': 'Eliot's high valuation of evoking immediate experience, exaltation of Image and of image making over purely rational powers of mind, emotive origin of poetry, and struggle to recombine aesthetic and moral stances' all '[place] him firmly in romantic tradition' (106).[8]

Though Eliot's inheritance of the Romantic tradition is not our immediate concern, the disguise of Eliot's ostentatious stance applies to his inheritance of Keats as well. Patrick D. Murphy argues for 'Eliot's [p]olemic with Keats' in his essay on the satirical allusions to Keats in *The Waste Land*, but as Eliot's stance towards Romanticism is more complicated than 'polemical', his specific subversions of Keats should not blind one from the much deeper affinity between them. After all, which allusion in *The Waste Land* is not subversive? Under the poem's overall satirical surface, I would argue, negative capability lies at its very core, and it is not only exemplified in its thematic essence, but embodied in its poetic form. Further, as the central concerns in *The Waste Land* are consistently developed in Eliot's later poetry, negative capability also runs on to his post-conversion poems, which, stripped of the early satirical tone, reveal negative capability more conspicuously. It evidently draws towards the spiritual dimension, but it should not be taken only as a religious doctrine. Indeed, Eliot's negative capability is not obtained from Keats, but proceeded from religious thinking, as his criticism shows kinship with Keats without receiving direct influence from him. With his mind as a capacious 'receptacle', Eliot makes a 'new compound' of negative capability by 'seizing and storing up numberless' particles, not only from Christianity or religions east and west, but from all kinds of traditions he believes an individual talent is indebted to, religious, artistic or philosophical. The evolution of negative capability from Keats to Eliot allows us to see that a truly comprehensive genealogy of negative capability would extend further back in history than I have been able to trace in this book, and its roots are spread out across cultural boundaries.

The Waste Land, for example, exemplifies negative capability not in Eliot's verbal and symbolic echoes of Keats, the first of which is found in 'A Game of Chess':

> Above the antique mantel was displayed
> As though a window gave upon the sylvan scene
> The change of Philomel, by the barbarous king
> So rudely forced; yet there the nightingale
> Filled all the desert with inviolable voice
> And still she cried, and still the world pursues,
> 'Jug Jug' to dirty ears. (II:97–103)

Of course 'Jug Jug' is a twisted echo of Keats's nightingale, as Eliot's 'sylvan scene' turns the 'mad pursuit' on Keats's 'sylvan historian' into a violent rape, the brutality of which is already anticipated by the nightingales in the Sweeney poem. Keats's Romantic sorrow, 'Still wouldst thou sing, and I have ears in vain', is also distorted into the eternal shrill of Eliot's nightingale which 'still' 'cried' to the modern world that 'still' 'pursues' in cruel menace. The satire is conspicuous in the other allusion as well. In 'The Fire Sermon', Tiresias looks at the typist's room: 'Out of the window perilously spread / Her drying combinations touched by the sun's last rays' (III:224–5). Keats's 'magic casements' opening to 'perilous seas' become the mundane window revealing only a sordid private life caught in ennui and lust. Both are among the 'heap of broken images' (I:22) on the 'ruins' (V:430) of the waste land, which can only be 'set' 'in order' (V:425) by the healing rain and the revelatory thunder in the end. And not until 'What the Thunder said' does one hear the voice of negative capability. After the first 'DA', we read: '*Datta*: what have we given? / My friend, blood shaking my heart / The awful daring of a moment's surrender / Which an age of prudence can never retract / By this, and this only, we have existed' (V:401–5). To 'give' is to give up all the 'prudence' that the ego encloses itself in, so the thunder is actually calling forth 'surrender' of the ego, or self-annihilation in Keatsian terms, which can only be achieved by a 'daring' break-through from the egocentric insulation and a fearless exposure of the self to a greater other. It thus leads to the second 'DA', sympathy, which will release the self from its confinement: '*Dayadhvam*: I have heard the key / Turn in the door once and turn once only / We think of the key, each in his prison / Think-ing of the key, each confirms a prison' (V:411–4). The predicament of modern consciousness lies in the egotism each self is imprisoned in, which cannot be opened by the 'key' from outside but only by 'sympathy' engendered from inside the mind itself. Only by making the 'daring' surrender can the ego set itself free and reach out in sympathy.

The dramatic personae in *The Waste Land* are all self-imprisoned modern egos, including the 'bored' (III:236) typist and her equally apathetic lover inside the 'perilous' window, and the monologic voice making futile communi-cations heard after the nightingale's 'Jug Jug': 'My nerves are bad to-night. Yes, bad. Stay with me. / 'Speak to me. Why do you never speak. Speak. / 'What are you thinking of? What thinking? What? / I never know what you are thinking. Think' (II:111–4). In this sense, Eliot's 'polemics' with Keats disclose a much deeper affinity, for they are employed to portray characters who are victims of inertia and need to be 'shaken' by 'blood' in their hearts, and whose symptom is egotistic 'prudence' that can only be healed by self-surrender. Such charac-ters are not only found in *The Waste Land*, but pervade Eliot's early poetry: Prufrock who is confined in his claustrophobic mind where 'decisions and revisions' constantly 'reverse' to 'indecisions', haunted by the self-questioning 'Do I dare?' that is finally resolved in the desolate 'I was afraid'; the youth pos-sessed by 'self-possession' in 'Portrait of a Lady'; Gerontion, whose 'thoughts of a dry brain in a dry season' are analogous to 'tenants of the house'; or on the other end, 'apeneck Sweeney', driven by carnal desire with no spiritual concern. Together, they form a lifeless crowd '[flowing]' (I:62) in the 'Unreal City' (I:60), each '[fixing] his eyes before his feet' (I:65), preyed upon by egotism yet dispossessed of a true self. They all need to be released from their egocentric prison cell, making the awful daring surrender. The 'Thunder' spoke to Eliot's waste land as it had done to Keats's 'faery land forlorn' or 'world of miseries', for the renunciation of the self is the source of spirituality deeply embedded in human thinking from ancient times.

The symptom of modernity does not only lie in the egotism of individual human beings, but in national and cultural egocentrism as well. As Eliot writes: 'Religious thought and practice, philosophy and art, all tend to become isolated areas cultivated by groups in no communication with each other' (*SP* 293–4), which is exactly why *The Waste Land* chooses to close by moving to the culture and religion of a distant time and place. On the other hand, 'give', 'sympathize' and 'control' should not be taken only as a sermon of Hinduism, just as 'Unreal City' refers to other metropolises as well as London. In 'What the Thunder Said', Eliot conveys a hope for union and fusion when European culture was falling apart, and just as he is against the dissociation of sensibility, Eliot also sees 'perils' in 'cultural disintegration' (*SP* 293). As he says, 'I refused to draw any absolute line between East and West, between Europe and Asia' (*SP* 303–4). This thought is embodied in the very form of *The Waste Land*, which adopts various languages and alludes to a human past of diverse cultural sources, thus amalgamating a compound comprehensive and synthetic. In this sense, Eliot's negative capability, like Yeats's, also takes an affirmative form against the 'mere anarchy' of modernity, and this 'affirmative capability' was seen more clearly in his conversion, for he believes that religion 'gives an apparent meaning to life, provides the frame-work for a culture, and protects the mass of humanity from boredom and despair' (*SP* 299–300). On the other hand, his conversion did not confine his spirituality to orthodox Christianity. As indicated in *The Waste Land*, 'the whole history of religion is behind Eliot's Christianity' (Smidt 191).

In *Ash-Wednesday*, written soon after his conversion in 1927, a more evident echo of Keats is found when Eliot describes the veiled lady in Part II: 'Lady of silences / Calm and distressed / Torn and most whole'. These lines recall the 'wan face' Moneta unveils for the poet in *The Fall of Hyperion*: 'Not pin'd by human sorrows, but bright blanch'd / By an immortal sickness which kills not; / . . . deathwards progressing / To no death was that visage'. Eliot makes the catalogue of paradoxes even more elaborate: 'End of the endless / Journey to no end / Conclusion of all that / Is inconclusible / Speech without word and / Word of no speech / Grace to the Mother / For the Garden / Where all love ends'. Of course their common source is Dante's Beatrice, but Eliot's lady of paradox is more likely to derive from Keats's conductress, and the parallel is not fortuitous. It is from sympathizing with Moneta and experiencing her pain that Keats transforms himself into a tragic poet, 'physician to all men', while self-sacrificial suffering is epitomized in Jesus Christ's death for mankind in Christianity. Thus for Eliot, the lady, encompassing and reconciling paradoxes, incarnates divine 'goodness' and 'loveliness' and 'honours the Virgin in meditation'. The 'single Rose' transforms into 'the Garden', while 'I', forgetful of the self, 'Thus devoted, concentrated in purpose', achieves a moment of union with the divine. This rose garden at the intersection of time and timelessness anticipates the one in *Four Quartets*, where Keatsian echoes are also found in moments of divine revelation.

The very theme of *Four Quartets* centred on the paradox of time and eternity has a Keatsian touch, though it is rendered in a religious framework, and its meditative lyrical form also lends itself to reminiscences of Romantic poetry. As Bornstein says, '*Four Quartets* is romantic against the grain' (154). Yet as with

The Waste Land, Eliot's negative capability in *Four Quartets* goes beyond the sporadic Keatsian echoes or Romantic touches but pervades its overall pattern. It is exemplified not only in its emphasis on self-surrender to achieve the moment of Incarnation, but in that on the experience of this moment as 'a fine isolated verisimilitude caught from the Penetralium of mystery', with the mind freed from self-assertiveness. The receptive openness to the mysterious, ineffable vision of the divine links negative capability with *via negativa*, which is 'the matrix of [Eliot's] late poems and plays' (Hay 1).[9] The whole poem also puts greater weight on the acceptance of suffering for the purification of the spirit, which is akin to Keats's notion of soul-making.

At the beginning of 'Burnt Norton' a bird appears, but instead of uttering the dull 'Jug Jug', 'the bird called, in response to / The unheard music hidden in the shrubbery' (I). The 'sweeter' 'unheard music' belongs to the Edenic rose garden, leading to the first moment of epiphany. When 'Burnt Norton' moves to the end, it presents a transfigured Grecian urn also embodying a paradox of movement and stillness: 'Only by the form, the pattern, / Can words or music reach / The stillness, as a Chinese jar still / Moves perpetually in its stillness' (V). Not only does the jar recall Keats's artifice of eternity,[10] but the play with the word 'still' reminds one of Keats. The jar is emblematic of 'the still point of the turning world', as 'the dance is', which is also 'neither arrest nor movement' (II), recapitulated by the phantasmal dance in 'East Coker'.

The imaginary dance conjured up by Eliot, with the faint pipe and drum vocalizing the 'unheard' music, recalls the wild ecstasy on the Grecian urn enlivened by Keats's imagination:

> On a summer midnight, you can hear the music
> Of the weak pipe and the little drum
> And see them dancing around the bonfire
> The association of man and woman
> In daunsinge, signifying matrimonie –
> A dignified and commodious sacrament. (I)

As the dance in 'Burnt Norton' is a symbol of a timeless moment, the poet, by envisioning the ancient dance, transcends the linear temporal scale and reaches 'the still point' in his mind. With the language shifting back to the old time, the poet, as Keats's speaker, enters into the imagined world of the invisible dancers, whose union in holy matrimony celebrated by communal rituals juxtaposes with the modern egos caught in isolation on the waste land. As Keats's urn regains life while the human viewer's imagination grows more vigorous, Eliot's dancers become more vivid with life in his quickened mind:

> Two and two, necessarye coniunction,
> Holding eche other by the hand or the arm

Whiche botokeneth concorde. Round and round the fire
Leaping through the flames, or joined in circles,
Rustically solemn or in rustic laughter
Lifting heavy feet in clumsy shoes,
Earth feet, loam feet, lifted in country mirth
Mirth of those long since under earth
Nourishing the corn. (I)

The rise and fall of the imagination parallel the dramatic movement in Keats's
ode: the imperceptible encroachment of time creeps in together with the
regained motion and life, as Keats's urn finally reveals a cold pastoral. The
'mirth' abruptly buried 'under earth' turns the reversed passage of time back
to the present moment, depriving the poet of the regained past together with
the still point, which is drowned in the flux of time revolving in nature's cycle.
But the poet continues:

Keeping time,
Keeping the rhythm in their dancing
As in their living in the living seasons
The time of the seasons and the constellations
The time of milking and the time of harvest
The time of the coupling of man and woman
And that of beasts. Feet rising and falling.
Eating and drinking. Dung and death. (I)

His time keeping maintains the presence of the past in his mind, perpetuating
their dancing pace by his verbal music, as the Chinese jar encapsulates the
'pattern' by arresting movement, but at the same time it also throws him back
into their living time which is linear, thus ending up revolving to 'dung and
death'. In the association of the 'coupling' of human beings with that of 'beasts',
the simple ritualistic country life becomes ambivalently blurred with the urban
waste land that 'moves / In appetency' ('Burnt Norton' III). Eliot at this
point recalls both Yeats's aged speaker who still sings the sensual music of
'what is past, or passing, or to come' in Byzantium, and Keats's listener of the
nightingale who finds his imagination frustrated by the linear human time:
'Still wouldst thou sing, and I have ears in vain −/ To thy high requiem
become a sod'.

The whole experience of vision and disillusion, however, is only a prepar-
ation for the revelation of negative capability in the next movement, which,
however, is opened with a confusion of seasonal cycle, 'the late November'
mixed with 'the disturbance of the spring', 'the summer heat' and winter 'snow-
drops', heading towards an apocalyptic 'destructive fire' (II). 'The only hope,
or else despair', the poet contemplates in 'Little Gidding', is 'to be redeemed

from fire by fire' (IV). The fire here, provoked by the human world consumed by the fire of senses, points towards the purgatorial fire of redemption. Its destructive intensity juxtaposes with 'the autumnal serenity / And the wisdom of age', which only provides the knowledge that is self-deceptive and deceitful: 'The knowledge imposes a pattern, and falsifies, / For the pattern is new in every moment / And every moment is a new and shocking / Valuation of all we have been' (II). The 'false' knowledge fails to 'keep time' with the fluidity of experience, for it is 'only a deliberate hebetude', as 'the wisdom of old men' is only 'prudence' to '[turn] their eyes' from the darkness of 'Their fear of fear and frenzy, their fear of possession, / Of belonging to another, or to others, or to God' (II). The world of Now and Past become merged with the waste land where 'winter kept us warm, covering / Earth in forgetful snow' (*The Waste Land* I:5–6), where human beings live in a serenity of ennui that keeps the self undisturbed in the prison of egotism.

> What a happy thing it would be if we could settle our thoughts, make our minds up on any matter in five Minutes and remain content – that is to build a sort of mental Cottage of feelings quiet and pleasant – to have a sort of Philosophical Back Garden, and cheerful holiday-keeping front one.

Whether Eliot remembers these words in Keats's letter, he arrives at a similar point as Keats, as he has at the end of *The Waste Land* in 'What the Thunder Said': 'The only wisdom we can hope to acquire / Is the wisdom of humility: humility is endless' (II). Now 'a moment's surrender' becomes 'endless' 'humility', and its true 'wisdom' repudiates the false wisdom enclosing the self in a comfortable 'mental cottage' surrounded by a 'garden' of prudence. Gregory S. Jay comments: 'This endless humility of the philosophical imagination repeats Keats, marking Eliot's own long-awaited arrival at negative capability' (219). And it brings him closer to Keats's soul-making vision as well, for it is followed by 'dark dark dark' that all human lives fall into in the following movement, when the poet tells his soul, 'be still':

> Wait without thought, for you are not ready for thought:
> So the darkness shall be the light, and the stillness the dancing.
> . . .
> The laughter in the garden, echoed ecstasy
> Not lost, but requiring, pointing to the agony
> Of death and birth. (III)

The wisdom of humility brings the mind to the state 'without thought', abnegating the conscious assertion of the ego, so that the vacated open mind of negative capability is ready to receive the divine illumination, which will transform the abysmal darkness into light and reinvigorate stillness into dancing.

But the rose garden 'at the still point of the turning world' can only be regained from the agony of experience, for 'Only through time time is conquered' ('Burnt Norton' II). Keats has come to a similar conclusion, realizing that beauty resides only in this world of transience and suffering, thus embracing this world as 'necessary' to keep the soul wakeful of its anguish, which is paralleled by Eliot's 'sin is Behovely' ('Little Gidding' III). Keats plunges into experience with his negatively capable mind for its tragic intensity, whereas Eliot throws himself into the agony of experience to strive for a moment of union with the divine. For Keats, the tragic poet is the 'physician' healing the fever of men, and for Eliot, Christ is the 'wounded surgeon' (IV). 'Our only health is the disease' (IV), so the soul tortured by its painful awareness of the sin offers the only hope for salvation: 'We must be still and still moving / Into another intensity / For a further union, a deeper communion / Through the dark cold and the empty desolation' (V).

As the mind has to suspend the self-consciousness to prepare for the union with the divine Other, the union itself can only be experienced by a mind of negative capability. At the end of 'The Dry Salvages', the poet reflects, 'to apprehend / The point of intersection of the timeless / With time, is an occupation for the saint – '(V), but

> For most of us, there is only the unattended
> Moment, the moment in and out of time,
> The distraction fit, lost in a shaft of sunlight,
> The wild thyme unseen, or the winter lightning
> Or the waterfall, or music heard so deeply
> That it is not heard at all, but you are the music
> While the music lasts. (V)

Only when the mind is purged of the self-interest attached to the temporal scale does it arrive at the timeless point, achieving, in Keatsian terms, 'fellowship divine', or Yeats's 'unity of being'. The subject becomes one with the object, and the music, internalized by the listener, turns the sensual music into the 'sweeter' music unheard. The epiphanic moment experienced by the mind of humility reaches the still point: 'The hint half guessed, the gift half understood, is Incarnation' (V). The union with the divine is thus perceived as mystic and ineffable, as Keats's glimpse of beauty 'caught from the Penetralium of mystery' is only 'half knowledge'. Eliot's negative capability becomes united with the Negative Way, which, by its almost universal roots in Christianity, ancient Greek philosophy, Hinduism, Buddhism and Taoism, shows negative capability as part of our oldest heritage.

In 'Tradition and the Individual Talent', Eliot defines the 'historical sense' as 'a sense of the timeless as well as of the temporal and of the timeless and of the temporal together', which, he claims, 'is what makes a writer traditional' (*SE* 14). And in *Four Quartets* when he experiences the 'sense of the timeless and the temporal together' in a mind of negative capability, he makes himself a traditional poet by not only taking after Keats's heritage, but recovering its deeper roots in history. As he writes at the end of the last quartet: 'A people without history / Is not redeemed from time, for history is a pattern / Of timeless moments' (V). He thus passes down negative capability as a living tradition which, by its recurrent pattern in human history, is 'redeemed from time'.

Conclusion

The Tradition of Negative Capability

Chapter 4 focuses on Eliot's negative capability centred on the abnegation of the ego running from *The Waste Land* to *Four Quartets*, and embodied in the dramatic nature of his poetry. The dominance of dramatic speeches in Eliot's poetry is obvious, but his poetry generally gives a dramatic feel because of his replacement of the 'personality' with a 'medium' (*SE* 20), or what he calls 'objective correlative'. As Keats claims that 'descriptions are bad at all times' (*KL* I:301), Eliot believes that '[p]ermanent literature is always a presentation' (*SW* 64), and his imagery is characterized by its evocative and non-discursive nature. One thinks of, among numerous examples, the feline yellow fog in 'Prufrock', the tangible 'strange synthetic perfumes' (II:87) in 'A Game of Chess', 'the last fingers of leaf' that 'clutch and sink into the wet bank' (III:173–4) in 'The Fire Sermon', the 'rhythm' of the river embodied in 'the rank ailanthus of the April dooryard' and 'the smell of grapes on the autumn table' (I) in 'The Dry Salvages'; even 'the still point' takes shape in the Chinese jar, the dancing, the rose garden, or the 'shaft of light'. Their concrete fullness is not unlike a Keatsian image of synaesthesia, both relying on a firm experiential basis to objectify the emotional tone and to efface the presence of the poet. The objectification and depersonalization are carried further in Eliot's poetry, which gives it a more radical dramatic form, but negative capability remains at the core. Similarly, its unconventional mosaic shape, especially conspicuous in his early poetry, also conveys negative capability in its own right, which, composed of discordant fragments, resists an overarching 'palpable design' to reach after fact and reason. In this light, negative capability has many formalistic descendants in modernist poetry, from Eliot's notion of 'objective correlative' to the more extreme stance of 'no ideas but in things', all of which emphasize the inconclusiveness of poetic experience, only putting on an increasingly grotesque form.

'I see Pope as Blake and Keats saw him' (*OBMV* xxi), is Yeats's view of Eliot. Insisting on 'traditional sanctity', Yeats cannot accept Eliot's radical form, and '[thinks] of him as satirist rather than poet' (*OBMV* xxii). Despite its drastically different form, Yeats's poetry too has a markedly dramatic quality built on the same solid experiential ground. We have seen his abhorrence of different forms of abstraction ranging from rhetoric to intellectual hatred, sentimentalism to scepticism, and the richness of his symbols exemplifies his 'passion' for the 'reality' of 'all complexities'. His constant assumption of an anti-self mask also gives his poetry a dialogic energy that creates a dramatic tension. As in Eliot's case, Yeats's negatively capable aspects are not limited to those poems discussed in the previous chapter, which does not include many dramatic pieces of his that take up a considerable proportion of his poetry.

The metamorphoses of negative capability in their poetry provide a historical perspective to look back on Keats's own poetry. As Eliot says, 'the past should be altered by the present as much as the present is directed by the past' (*SE* 15). What Yeats and Eliot inherit from Keats is not that isolated beauty of his sensuous and precise imagery for which the Victorians and Pre-Raphaelites had championed Keats. Instead, the life of Keats's poetry flows on in its firm grasp of experience, in which his compressed and synaesthetic poetic language is embedded; in its insistence on a truthful vision of experience by actively shifting between opposite perspectives to observe it; and by encompassing its inherent paradoxes and contradictions to avoid any reductive resolution: all of which are encapsulated in his notion of negative capability. We have seen, too, that Keats did not arrive at this negatively capable stage all at once. He had striven long in his short career, and he had never ceased striving for a vaster scope of poetry right up till the very end. From the outset, it was the largesse of his mind that cherished every detail of this copious world that endowed it at the same time with a finesse to identify with its diverse beings, and it was the same commitment to the rich complexity of human experience that gave him the strength to resist reaching after the kind of poetry that would fail to convey the fullness of human experience as it truthfully was.

Looking back from 'Lamia' to *Endymion*, one can see the long distance Keats had covered in less than three years' time, and his 'healthy deliberation' demonstrates itself not in repudiating the truthfulness of imagination but adding to it a further, and an antithetical, dimension. Similarly, the second *Hyperion* does not so much revise the first as supplement it by extending the gods' world to the human realm, and by putting the self into the experience of Apollo to test the truth of the speculative 'axioms' on his own pulses. The last ode, 'To autumn', too, in no way denies the tragic vision achieved from the endless debates going on in the grand drama of the spring odes, but actually adopts it to experience human life at the very moment when Beauty is indeed dying, and Joy's hand bidding adieu.

All the way through, Keats was driven by 'large limb'd visions' (*The Fall of Hyperion* I:445) beyond his immediate setting. It was the same magnitude of his mind that brought him to constantly look back to the ancient bards of vast territories, and his bardolatry was a most eloquent example of his camelion nature that led him to become a camelion poet himself. In becoming a negatively capable poet by first finding the quality possessed by his presider so enormously,

Keats most forcefully demonstrated Eliot's argument of the indebtedness of the individual talent to his tradition.

By reading the most important Shakespearean play with Keats, we have seen what a perfect exemplar of negative capability should be. The devastating catastrophe reveals the tenacious fortitude it takes to resist reaching after some comforting fact and reason, and the terrible agony a poet must go through in rendering human experience a truthful vision. The tragic intensity achieved by the fierce dispute between opposite forces gives us a glimpse of a capacious neutral intellect, and the vivid life of each of its diverse characters constantly shaped by the violent dramatic experience demonstrates the remarkable metamorphoses a camelion poet can accomplish. Keats's re-readings of the play became fruitful in his Great Year, when his inheritance of its negative capability matured in his own poetry, which created dramatic poetry out of a lyrical form.

As the central quality forming these '[Men] of Achievement, especially in Literature' at different times, negative capability makes itself an important part of the tradition in English poetry. It emphasizes a full expression of experience rather than a 'consequitive' resolution, and the transfiguration of the self into a vaster otherness instead of self-expressiveness, which can be said to be a dramatic poetic tradition, even when taking a lyrical form. Whether this tradition was continuous or disrupted depends on how to evaluate the time between Shakespeare and Keats, and that between Keats and modernism, as well as where Keats's contemporaries fit in, all leaving us much to explore.

Negative capability was at first a quality Keats ascribed to Shakespeare, or a poet's critical view on his predecessor, which became a poetic criterion for himself. The interconnection between a poet's critical concepts and creative principles can be seen in Yeats and Eliot as well, and all of their critical writings inform their own poetic creations. In Eliot's case, his criticism of Keats, as Keats's of Shakespeare, not only became an important part of the critical heritage of the poetic predecessor, but came to influence his contemporary poetic values as well. The controversy over *Lear* presents a similar case. The Romantic restoration of its tragic ending bespeaks the Romantics' critical attitude as much as their own creative value. The reputation of Keats in modernist times is also involved with both the modernist poets' critical taste and their poetic standard. It cannot be said how much Eliot's endorsement of Keats saved him from the anti-Romantic turn led by Eliot himself, but Keats was indeed much less discredited than his contemporaries in the twentieth century, and a number of key figures in both poetry and fiction have been ardent admirers of his, such as Stevens, Williams, Fitzgerald and Faulkner, just to name a few. From Yeats's and Eliot's inheritance of Keats, one can see that it was not accidental that the trajectory of the critical reception of negative capability began to rise at roughly the same time as modernism was emerging. With negative capability gradually gaining a central position in contemporary critical discourse, those qualities the modernists found congenial in it were further advocated.

The impact of criticism on creation, after all, was what happened in Keats's own case. It was Hazlitt who helped him formulate some of the central ideas constituting negative capability, leading him to turn away from his contemporaries to a more distant poetic tradition. Many of Hazlitt's critical views actually coincide with Eliot's, though Eliot refuses to acknowledge this,[1] which demonstrates the affinity of negative capability with modernism from another perspective. Hazlitt is against egotism as much as Eliot, and his emphasis on replacing abstraction with 'hieroglyphics' corresponds to Eliot's notion of objective correlative. Both of their critical writings are marked by the prominence of textual quotes, showing their common attention to detail and caution against generalization. Eliot's exaltation of dramatic above lyrical poetry is shared by Hazlitt too, and his disapproval of the Romantics and enthusiasm about the Elizabethans had been expressed by Hazlitt a hundred years before. When Eliot writes in 'Tradition and the Individual Talent' that the poet 'must be ... aware ... that art never improves' (16), is he not echoing Hazlitt's famous essay, 'Why the Arts are not Progressive' (IV:160–4)? And if we look at Eliot's commentary on Shakespeare:

[T]he work of a great poetic dramatist, like Shakespeare, constitutes a world. Each character speaks for himself, but no other poet could have found those words for him to speak. If you seek for Shakespeare, you will find him only in the characters he created .... The world of a great poetic dramatist is a world in which the creator is everywhere present, and everywhere hidden. (*PP* 102)

its closeness to Hazlitt's passage is apparent:

The striking peculiarity of Shakspeare's mind was its generic quality, its power of communication with all other minds .... He was just like any other man, but that he was like all other men .... He was nothing in himself; but he was all that others were, or that they could become.

And of course, both Eliot's and Hazlitt's passages remind one of Keats's letter on the camelion poet, who 'has no self – it is every thing and nothing – It has no character – it enjoys light and shade .... It has as much delight in conceiving an Iago as an Imogen'. The camelion poet is in the critical tradition as much as in the creative one.

But negative capability is not confined to aesthetics. We can see this in Keats's repeated readings of *Lear*, which became for him much more than an artistic exemplar – a resource for his own life. It is clearer in Eliot's case, where negative capability excavates its deeper layers in cultural and intellectual tradition. It is part of the Great Memory of mankind, for it is a way of being, conveying, ultimately, an attitude towards human experience. It can be traced back not only to ancient religious and philosophical thinking, but to the origin of imaginative literature. The pair of heroes in Homeric epics may very well be seen as juxtaposed by negative capability, who respectively represent the archetypal 'Man of Power' and 'Man of Genius', with Achilles having a firm proper self clinging to his rage that defines the tone for the *Iliad* from the very opening, and Odysseus ingenious in his metamorphic capability as the master artificer of identity. Similarly, among Shakespeare's tragic heroes, Lear and Hamlet also pose against each other in their contrasting measures of negative capability. Resembling Achilles, Lear is characterized by a strong identity distinguished in its ferocious power of fury that makes him unable to submit to his circumstances, while Hamlet may be said to possess so much negative capability that he almost becomes its victim, who, preyed upon by endless uncertainties, doubts, mysteries, loses the name of action. All these characters demonstrate negative capability as a human quality, as already seen in many other associations made with negative capability mentioned in the introduction.

Just as for Yeats intellectual innocence was part of his moral attitude, and Eliot's self-surrender went beyond the aesthetic realm to become the source of his spirituality, negative capability was not only a quality of Keats the poet, but evident in Keats the man. It explains the attraction of his letters, which reveal a man whose experience constantly reshaped his identity, whose open-mindedness reached the point of being able to welcome hardships for their trial of 'resources'[2] for the spirit, who loved life dearly despite its pains, yet who was only left to say bitterly at the end, 'how short is the longest Life' (*KL* II:293). Arnold comments that 'Keats had flint and iron in him' (288), and Murry associates him with Christ, while Trilling regards him as a tragic hero. But he was never a Byronic hero standing apart from humanity. His circle of friends invariably recalled him literally with 'love' (*KC* I:xiv), and Shaw speaks of his unique 'geniality'[3] (*MV* 176). His non-egotistical nature is evident in his frequent sayings in his letters: 'I wish I could enter into all your feelings' (*KL* I:242), and other people's identities 'pressed upon'[4] him, even a stranger, a consumptive girl travelling to Italy in the same cabin with him. As he recorded in his letter, 'all her bad symptoms have preyed upon me' (*KL* II:349), and Severn recalled how Keats, while suffering from his own symptoms, tried gallantly to cheer her up with his 'golden jokes' (*KL* II:341). It was his deep attachment to humanity that made him state firmly, 'Scenery is fine – but human nature is finer' (*KL* I:242), even being soberly aware that 'there lives not the Man who may not be cut up, aye hashed to pieces on his weakest side'. As he wrote in his letter, 'A Man's life of any worth is a continual allegory', and what he says of Shakespeare applies to himself as well: '[he] led a life of Allegory; his works are the comments on it'. And it was an allegory of negative capability.

Notes

Introduction

[1] All quotations from Keats's letters are from Rollins's edition, which keeps Keats's misspellings, inconsistent capitalizations and repetitions.

[2] *For* but. (Rollins's note)

[3] Bridges's 'new symbols' of spelling are substituted by standard ones.

[4] Bridges comments on Keats's two verse dramas: 'there is a succinctness and force about the whole, which forbid one to conclude that Keats would not have succeeded in drama' (148).

[5] Here as in Bate's case Murry seems alluded to.

[6] The annotation in the current 8th edition (2006) becomes:

> Keats coins [the phrase] so as to distinguish between, on the one hand, a poetry that is evidently shaped by the writer's personal interests and beliefs and, on the other hand, a poetry of impersonality that records the writer's receptivity to the 'uncertainties' of experience. This second kind of poetry, in which a sense of beauty overcomes considerations of truth versus falsehood, is that produced by the poet of 'negative capability'. (II:942)

The revision itself suggests the inaccuracy of the former annotation used for four decades.

[7] Similar problems appear in the translation of the term. Tu An, the most important contemporary Chinese translator of Keats, puts it as, literally, 'objective perception' (客体感受力). Another translator, Wang Xinruo, renders it 'passive perception' (消极感受力).

[8] This point will be addressed in Chapter 4.

Chapter 1

[1] R. T. Davies's 1957 essay is offered as 'a supplement' to Muir's with some 'further instances' (1), but not many.

[2] He states that his aim 'is not to trace any specific indebtedness owed by Keats to Hazlitt, but to use Hazlitt's well-formed precepts in order to build up some guidelines about Keats's central areas of interest in reading Shakespeare' (31).

[3] 'Intersubjectivity' is the term Kinnaird offers to replace Bate's 'sympathy' and 'disinterestedness' for their respective confusions with 'empathy' and 'objectivity' (7), but it seems to me that Bate is justified in using Hazlitt's original terms.

⁴ Many critics have not specified the time since it is uncertain. Gittings conjectures that the first meeting took place in November 1816; Bromwich places it in January 1818, but it should be earlier, since when Keats wrote to Reynolds on 9 March 1817, 'It's the finest thing by God – as Hazlitt wo^d say' (*KL* I:123), he seemed to have already met Hazlitt in person.

⁵ Hazlitt describes Keats in such a tone whenever he attacks the reviewers: 'Poor Keats', 'young, sensitive, delicate' in *Table-Talk* (VIII:99, 211); 'pale shade of Keats' in *Notes of A Journey through France and Italy* (X:247); 'Poor Keats' again in 'Is Genius Conscious of Its Powers' (XII:123); Keats '[vilified]' in 'Qualifications Necessary to Success' (XII:208); 'poor Keats' yet again 'crushed' in 'The Periodical Press' (XVI:237), and the 'blighted' Keats who 'died young' by the 'shaft' of the reviewers in 'Shelley's Posthumous Poems' (XVI:269).

⁶ All quotations of Keats's poems are from Stillinger's edition.

⁷ Rollins has provided extremely useful annotations to Keats's possible borrowings from or allusions to Hazlitt in Keats's letters.

⁸ Bate has no doubt that Keats read the book: 'Keats read, undoubtedly at Bailey's suggestion, Hazlitt's *Essay on the Principles of Human Action*, and bought a copy that was still in his library at his death' (1964: 255–6). Muir, however, states with reservation that 'Keats is known to have possessed and admired' the book, 'but curiously enough, there is no evidence that Keats had studied [it] with great attention' (156). But it seems to me that even if Keats had not closely studied this book, he would have been familiar with Hazlitt's general argument of 'disinterestedness', which Hazlitt also outlined in *Letter to Gifford* and consistently upheld in his other writings.

⁹ He probably intended *righter*. (Rollins's note)

¹⁰ Abbey's attitude would have been particularly hard to swallow if Keats was reminded of Abbey's former dismissal of his own first volume of poems: 'John I have read your Book, & it reminds me of the Quaker's Horse which was hard to catch, & good for nothing when he was caught – So your Book is hard to understand & good for nothing when it is understood'. Abbey was well aware of the effect of his words, recollecting, 'I don't think he ever forgave me for uttering this Opinion' (*KC* I:308).

¹¹ One of Keats's favourite phrases. For instance, he uses it in the camelion poet letter, 'When I am in a room with People if I ever am free from speculating on creations of my own brain, then not myself goes home to myself: but the identity of every one in the room begins to to press upon me that, I am in a very little time anhilated – ' (*KL* I:387). When Tom was seriously ill, Keats wrote to Dilke, 'His identity presses upon me so all day' (*KL* I:369).

¹² Shelley writes this in his letter inviting Keats to stay with him in Pisa after learning about Keats's sickness. Though eventually they did not meet in Italy, the fact that Shelley died with Keats's *1820 Poems* in his pocket gives their relationship a poignant touch (*KL* II:323n).

¹³ *For* but. (Rollin's note)

¹⁴ This is *The Dramatic Works of William Shakespeare* in seven volumes, edited by Johnson and Steevens, printed by C. Whittingham, Chiswick in 1814, which he also took to Italy in 1820. It is now at the Houghton Library, Harvard University. Keats had another edition of Shakespeare's plays, the 1808 facsimile reprint of

the First Folio, which was kept at the library of the Keats House, Hampstead and is now moved to the London Metropolitan Archives. The former is inscribed with 'John Keats – April 1817' on the title page, while the latter, 'John Keats 1817' (see Figure 1.1). (Rosenbaum 405)

15 Keats's copy of *The Poetical Works of William Shakspeare* is inscribed with 'John Hamilton Reynolds to John Keats 1819' by Reynolds and 'Given me by Keats Jan. 1820' by Joseph Severn, which is now kept at the London Metropolitan Archives. At the time of this letter, then, the book was lent to Keats.

16 Keats indeed copied the poem on the page preceding *Lear* in his Folio (see Figure 1.3), so presumably, he started to re-read the play only after making this 'preparation'.

17 Rollins annotates that Keats owned a copy of *La nouvelle Héloïse*, and that Jacques Voisine in his *J.-J. Rousseau en Angleterre* (1956) 'is impressed by the fact that, alone among the great romantics, Keats pokes fun at Rousseau and gives no praise to his eloquence' (*KL* II:266n).

Chapter 2

1 S. R. Swaminathan in a very short essay published in 1969 proposes that 'it is probable that Keats is referring not to Shakespeare's play but to Benjamin West's painting of the storm scene in *King Lear*' (15). He makes the proposition in a very tentative manner, and his conjecture is based on no other evidence but that the topic at hand is West. Though the possibility cannot be ruled out, it is unlikely, with Keats's strong attachment to Shakespeare and the play and his not altogether reverent tone when referring to West ('It is a wonderful picture, when West's age is considered'), that he would regard one of West's paintings as an exemplar of 'the excellence of every Art'.

2 The copy is now at the Houghton Library, Harvard University, and transcriptions can be found in Amy Lowell's *John Keats* (II:545–605), which are corrected by later critics.

3 All the subsequent references to Keats's underlinings and annotations of *Lear* are also found in Keats's Folio copy, since *Lear* in his seven-volume Shakespeare is not marked (White 169). Keats's markings and marginalia in *Lear* have not been reproduced in full in any publication. Caroline Spurgeon gives an account with selected transcriptions which do not include those in *Lear*. The Oxford edition of *John Keats* edited by Elizabeth Cook provides the transcribed marginalia in the Folio, but does not include the markings. R. S. White describes the markings more closely, but presents only some of them. The subsequent descriptions of Keats's Folio are based on my own research at the London Metropolitan Archives, though I am indebted to all the above-mentioned authors.

4 Most of the subsequent quotations from the play are from the conflated text in the *Norton Shakespeare*, but when Keats's marginalia are introduced, I quote from Keats's Folio. Though Keats's reading was only recorded in his Folio copy, it is fair to assume that he was familiar with the Quarto text in his seven-volume edition as well.

⁵ White makes a similar point in his book, though his account is a bit exaggerated: 'Although she says little, virtually everything is noticed' (176).

⁶ S. L. Goldberg in his book on *Lear* also suggests reading the play 'in a "negative capability" of the spirit' (9), arguing, 'The play does not offer us anything like a single, straightforward, clear-cut attitude to life, or a guaranteed moral vantage point . . .; part of its integrity . . . is precisely that it does not' (2–3).

⁷ It might be interesting to compare Keats's markings with Hazlitt's comments on these scenes. Act III Scene ii, most of which Keats has marked, is specifically mentioned by Hazlitt as 'not so fine' (IV:268), though he highly regards the other two storm scenes, Act III Scenes iv and vi. Probably, the former scene may seem to Hazlitt relatively uniform in its 'grand and terrible' (Hazlitt IV:268) tone, whereas the latter two scenes are more dramatic by bringing in more complex and oppositional forces, such as Tom and the 'trial', to intensify Lear's pathos. Keats, as a poet instead of a critic, would not read these scenes in exactly the same light, naturally.

⁸ The illusory trial (III.vi.15–51) is not in the Folio, but Keats would know these lines from the Quarto text in his other edition, a point mentioned by White as well (172).

⁹ In the Folio, the scene ends when Cordelia and Lear exit, not including the last twelve lines, the talk between Kent and the Gentleman about the war.

¹⁰ Hazlitt picks up the topic again in his later lecture 'On Wit and Humour' given in 1819, the manuscripts of which were read by Keats: 'Lear and the Fool are the sublimest instance I know of passion and wit united, or of imagination unfolding the most tremendous sufferings, and of burlesque on passion playing with it, aiding and relieving its intensity by the most pointed, but familiar and indifferent illustrations of the same thing in different objects, and on a meaner scale' (VI:24). The view, it should be noted, still contains 'a little contradiction', regarding the Fool as both 'aiding' and 'relieving' the intensity.

¹¹ White makes the same point when summarizing Keats's markings: 'the greatest concentration is upon Lear himself' (177).

Chapter 3

¹ Douglas Bush's phrase to refer to the period from September 1818 to September 1819 (1967), or 'the living year' in Robert Gittings's term (1954). W. J. Bate claims that the time 'may be soberly described as the most productive in the life of any poet of the past three centuries' (1964: 388).

² I borrow the term from Robert Langbaum, who defines it as 'a poetry constructed upon the deliberate disequilibrium between experience and idea, a poetry which makes its statement not as an idea but as an experience from which one or more ideas can be abstracted as problematical rationalizations' (35–6).

³ All quotations from Keats's poems are from *KPS*, with line numbers cited in brackets.

⁴ It is reminiscent of T. S. Eliot's 'place of disaffection' ('Burnt Norton' III) in *Four Quartets*, though Eliot's 'neither-nor' state is a Modernist ironic version of this cave of Romantic agony.

5 Shaw claims, 'if Karl Marx can be imagined as writing a poem instead of a treatise on Capital, he would have written *Isabella*', which 'contains all the Factory Commission Reports that Marx read, and that Keats did not read because they were not yet written in his time' (*MV* 175).

6 The date of composition of 'Ode on Indolence', as the other spring odes, is conjectural. Though it recapitulates the prose description of a similar scenario in the section of the journal letter to George and Georgiana dated 19 March, it was probably composed in May after 'Ode to Psyche', which was written in April. My sequencing of the spring odes is mainly thematic, having no intention to suggest that it is the actual order of composition.

7 Paul de Man argues that '[t]he pattern of Keats's work is prospective rather than retrospective . . . . None of the larger works . . . can in any sense be called finished. The circle never seems to close' (181). *The Fall of Hyperion*, however, does not fit in with this pattern exactly, being both prospective and retrospective.

8 This is found in the letter dated 24 April 1818, and in the letter written on 9 April, there is a similar assertion, 'I would jump down Ætna for any great Public good' (*KL* I:267). On 10 June 1818, Keats wrote again, 'I am never alone . . . without placing my ultimate in the glory of dying for a great human purpose' (*KL* I:293).

9 One wonders whether Tennyson's 'Tithonus' was inspired by Moneta's face, 'Me only cruel immortality / consumes'.

Chapter 4

1 All quotations from Yeats's poems are from Finneran's edition, *The Collected Poems of W. B. Yeats*, with line numbers cited in brackets.

2 James Land Jones's *Adam's Dream* is the only book-length study of Yeats's connections with Keats, which focuses on their common mythic consciousness. A few Yeatsian critics adopt the term 'negative capability' to describe Yeats, but they use it to refer to Yeats the prose writer. Hazard Adams calls *Reveries over Childhood and Youth* 'an excellent example of Keats's "negative capability" exhibited in autobiographical circumstances' (Finneran 54). T. R. Henn proposes that Phase Twenty-Seven in *A Vision* 'suggests something of Keats' "negative capability"' (185), which is described by Yeats as follows: 'If he possesses intellect he will use it but to serve perception and renunciation. His joy is to be nothing, to do nothing, to think nothing; but to permit the total life, expressed in its humanity, to flow in upon him and to express itself through his acts and thoughts' (180). Richard Ellmann does refer to Yeats the poet by Keats's notion of negative capability, but he applies its antonym, 'affirmative capability', to Yeats, which will be discussed more closely below.

3 Douglas Bush also mentions this point in his essay 'Keats and His Ideas' (244).

4 See, for example, 'The Celtic Element in Literature' in *Essays and Introductions*, p. 176, 177, and the journal of 9 March 1909 in *Memoirs*, p. 180.

5 As mentioned in the Introduction, this has become a commonly accepted view, included in the entry of negative capability in *The New Princeton Encyclopedia of*

Poetry and Poetics. Many critics have made this point, though handling it rather briefly. Douglas Bush mentions in his essay 'Keats and His Ideas' (1957) that Eliot's 'emphasis on the impersonality of the artist, or Yeats's "intellectual innocence"' may be seen 'as parallels to' Keats's negative capability (244). Brian Lee writes in his book *Theory and Personality: The Significance of T. S. Eliot's Criticism* (1979) that Keats's term '[corresponds] to Impersonality' (89). Edward Lobb discusses it in his book *T. S. Eliot and the Romantic Critical Tradition* (1981): 'The most important influence on Eliot's historiography is the one which seems, at first glance, least likely – that of Keats' (63). M. A. R. Habib in *The Early T. S. Eliot and Western Philosophy* (1999) makes the point that 'Of the Romantics, Eliot found Keats the most congenial' (185). Christopher Baker's essay 'Porphyro's Rose: Keats and T. S. Eliot's "The Metaphysical Poets"' (2003) claims, 'No predecessor could have modeled the virtues of negative capability for Eliot better than Keats' (58).

6 In the 1951 preface to *Selected Essays* in which 'Tradition and the Individual Talent' appears first, Eliot writes: 'On reviewing the contents of this book, I find myself at times inclined to quarrel with my own judgments, and more often to criticise the way in which they were expressed' (8). In the 1964 preface to *The Use of Poetry and the Use of Criticism*, Eliot calls 'Tradition and the Individual Talent' 'perhaps the most juvenile' (9) of his writings, 'though', he says, 'I do not repudiate' it (10).

7 For a closer discussion of the passage, see Chapter 1, pp. 81–2.

8 Northrop Frye concludes his book on Eliot by mentioning that 'Since the nineteen-twenties, critics have become increasingly aware of the continuity of the English Romantic Tradition and Eliot's place in it' (98), and adds, 'the greatness of his achievement will finally be understood, not in the context of the tradition he chose, but in the context of the tradition that chose him' (99). Helen Gardner in *T. S. Eliot and the English Poetic Tradition* calls Eliot 'a poet of feeling', 'like the great Romantic and Victorian poets' (12). Robert Langbaum in *The Poetry of Experience* also stresses the connection between Romanticism and Modernism: 'Whatever the difference between the literary movements of the nineteenth and twentieth centuries, they are connected by their view of the world as meaningless, by their response to the same wilderness. That wilderness is the legacy of the Enlightenment' (11).

9 The two notions are connected, but *via negativa* obviously also differs from negative capability in its denial of the ordinary facts of experience in order to achieve a vision of God.

10 Many critics have noted this, for example, Grover Smith, in *T. S. Eliot's Poetry and Plays: A Study in Sources and Meaning*, p.266, and Bornstein in his book, p.156.

Conclusion

1 Eliot calls Hazlitt 'perhaps the most uninteresting mind of all our distinguished critics' (*SE* 309) in his essay on Dryden, accusing Hazlitt of '[committing] at least four crimes against taste' 'in one sentence' (*SE* 310). Eliot's attack is unjust,

totally ignoring the context of Hazlitt's statement. There is another reference to Hazlitt in 'Imperfect Critics', again unfavourably (*SW* 17, 18).

2 Keats expressed the thought many times in his letters, for example, pp. I:186, II:115, II:181.

3 Shaw continues by satirizing other literary men for their lack of geniality: 'Dante is not notably genial. Milton can do a stunt of geniality . . . but one does not see him exuberantly fighting the butcher, as Keats is said to have done. Wordsworth, cheerful at times as a pious duty, is not genial . . . . Even the thought of Shelley kills geniality . . . . Byron's joy is derision . . . . Keats alone remains for us not only a poet, but a merry soul, a jolly fellow' (*MV* 176). Trilling comments on this and develops the idea at great lengths in his essay.

4 See Chapter 1, Note 11.

Bibliography

Abrams, M. H. *The Mirror and the Lamp*. Oxford: Oxford University Press, 1953.
—ed. *The Norton Anthology of English Literature (The Major Authors)*. 1st edn. New York: Norton, 1962.
—ed. *The Norton Anthology of English Literature*. Vol. 2. 7th edn. New York: Norton, 2000.
Aristotle. *Poetics*. Trans. Gerald F. Else. Ann Arbor: The University of Michigan Press, 1970.
Arnold, Matthew. *Essays in Criticism. First and Second Series*. London: Everyman's Library, 1906.
Baker, Carlos. 'The Poet as Janus: Originality and Imitation in Modern Poetry'. *Proceedings of the American Philosophical Society* 128:2 (1984): 167–72.
Baker, Christopher. 'Porphyro's Rose: Keats and T. S. Eliot's "The Metaphysical Poets"'. *Journal of Modern Literature* 27:1–2 (Fall 2003): 57–62.
Bate, Jonathan. *Shakespeare and the English Romantic Imagination*. Oxford: Clarendon Press, 1986.
— and Russell Jackson, eds. *Shakespeare: An Illustrated Stage History*. Oxford: Oxford University Press, 1996.
Bate, Walter Jackson. *The Burden of the Past and the English Poet*. New York: Norton, 1972.
— ed. *Criticism: The Major Texts*. New York: Harcourt, 1970.
— *From Classic to Romantic: Premises of Taste in Eighteenth-Century England*. New York: Harper, 1961.
—*John Keats*. Cambridge: The Belknap Press of Harvard University Press, 1964.
—'Keats's Style: Evolution toward Qualities of Permanent Value'. *The Major English Romantic Poets*. Ed. Clarence D. Thorpe, Carlos Baker and Bennett Weaver. Carbondale: Southern Illinois University Press, 1957.
—*Negative Capability: The Intuitive Approach in Keats*. Cambridge, MA: Harvard University Press, 1939.
—*The Stylistic Development of Keats*. 1945. New York: Humanities Press, 1962.
Bloom, Harold. *The Anxiety of Influence*. New York: Oxford University Press, 1973.
—'Keats and the Embarrassments of Poetic Tradition'. *From Sensibility to Romanticism*. Ed. Frederick W. Hilles and Harold Bloom. New York: Oxford University Press, 1965.
—*Poetry and Repression*. New Haven: Yale University Press, 1976.
—*Shakespeare: The Invention of the Human*. New York: Riverhead Books, 1998.
Bornstein, George. *Transformations of Romanticism in Yeats, Eliot and Stevens*. Chicago: The University of Chicago Press, 1976.

Boyers, Robert. *Lionel Trilling: Negative Capability and the Wisdom of Avoidance.* Columbia: University of Missouri Press, 1977.

Bradley, A. C. *Oxford Lectures on Poetry.* London: Macmillan, 1965.

Bridges, Robert. *Collected Essays, Papers, &c of Robert Bridges.* Vol.4. London: Oxford University Press, 1929.

Bromwich, David. *Hazlitt: The Mind of a Critic.* 1983. New Haven: Yale University Press, 1999.

Bush, Douglas. *John Keats.* New York: Collier Books, 1967.

—'Keats and His Ideas'. *The Major English Romantic Poets.* Ed. Clarence D. Thorpe, Carlos Baker and Bennett Weaver. Carbondale: Southern Illinois University Press, 1957.

Coetzee, J. M. *Elizabeth Costello: Eight Lessons.* London: Secker & Warburg, 2003.

Coleridge, Samuel Taylor. *Shakespearean Criticism.* 2 Vols. Ed. Thomas Middleton Raysor. London: J. M. Dent, 1960.

Colvin, Sidney. *Keats.* London: Macmillan, 1887.

Davies, R. T. 'Keats and Hazlitt'. *Keats–Shelley Memorial Bulletin* 1957: 1–8.

de Man, Paul. 'Introduction to the Poetry of John Keats (1966)'. *Critical Writings 1953–1978.* Ed. Lindsay Waters. Minneapolis: University of Minnesota Press, 1989.

Eliot, T. S. *The Complete Poems and Plays.* New York: Harcourt, 1930.

—*The Letters of T. S. Eliot.* Vol. I. Ed. Valerie Eliot. London: Faber and Faber, 1988.

—*On Poetry and Poets.* London: Faber and Faber, 1957.

—*The Sacred Wood.* London: Methuen, 1920.

—*Selected Essays.* London: Faber and Faber, 1951.

—*Selected Prose of T. S. Eliot.* Ed. Frank Kermode. London: Faber and Faber, 1975.

—*To Criticize the Critic and Other Writings.* London: Faber and Faber, 1965.

—*The Use of Poetry and the Use of Criticism.* London: Faber and Faber, 1933.

Ellmann, Maud. *The Poetics of Impersonality: T. S. Eliot and Ezra Pound.* Brighton, Sussex: The Harvester Press, 1987.

Ellmann, Richard. *The Identity of Yeats.* London: Faber and Faber, 1964.

—*Yeats: the Man and the Masks.* New York: Norton, 1978.

— and Charles Feidelson, Jr., eds. *The Modern Tradition: Backgrounds of Modern Literature.* Oxford: Oxford University Press, 1965.

Engell, James. *The Creative Imagination: Enlightenment to Romanticism.* Cambridge, MA: Harvard University Press, 1981.

Faulkner, William. *Essays, Speeches & Public Letters.* Ed. James B. Meriwether. New York: Modern Library, 2004.

Finneran, Richard J., ed. *Critical Essays on W. B. Yeats.* Boston: G. K. Hall, 1986.

Finney, Claudee Lee. *The Evolution of Keats's Poetry.* 2 Vols. New York: Russell & Russell, 1936.

Fitzgerald, F. Scott. *The Crack-Up.* Penguin, 1965.

Frye, Northrop. *T. S. Eliot.* Edinburgh: Oliver and Boyd, 1963.

Gardner, Helen. *T. S. Eliot and the English Poetic Tradition.* Nottingham: The University of Nottingham, 1965.

Garrod, H. W. *Keats.* Oxford: Oxford University Press, 1926.

Ginsberg, Allen. 'Negative Capability: Kerouac's Buddhist Ethic'. *Tricycle: The Buddhist Review* Fall 1992: www.tricycle.com/issues/tricycle/2_1/ancestors/991-1.html.

Gittings, Robert. *John Keats.* London: Heinemann, 1968.

—*John Keats: The Living Year.* Cambridge, MA: Harvard University Press, 1954.

Goldberg, M. A. *The Poetics of Romanticism.* Yellow Springs, Ohio: The Antioch Press, 1969.

Goldberg, S. L. *An Essay on* King Lear. Cambridge: Cambridge University Press, 1974.

Greenblatt, Stephen, ed. *The Norton Anthology of English Literature.* Vol. 2. 8th edn. New York: Norton, 2006.

Habib, M. A. R. *The Early T. S. Eliot and Western Philosophy.* Cambridge: Cambridge University Press, 1999.

Haines, Simon. *Shelley's Poetry: The Divided Self.* New York: St. Martin's, 1997.

Harris, Laurie Lanzen and Mark W. Scott, eds. *Shakespearean Criticism.* Vol. I, II. Detroit: Gale, 1983.

Harrison, G. B. and Robert F. McDonnell, eds. King Lear: *Text, Sources, Criticism.* New York: Harcourt, 1962.

Hay, Eloise Knapp. *T. S. Eliot's Negative Way.* Cambridge, MA: Harvard University Press, 1982.

Hazlitt, William. *The Complete Works of William Hazlitt.* 21 Vols. Ed. P. P. Howe. London: J. M. Dent, 1930.

Henn, T. R. *The Lonely Tower.* London: Methuen, 1950.

Hilton, Timothy. *Keats and His World.* London: Thames and Hudson, 1971.

Hirst, Wolf Z. *John Keats.* Boston: Twayne, 1981.

Homans, Margaret. 'Keats Reading Women: Women Reading Keats'. *Studies in Romanticism* 29 (1990): 341–70.

Howe, P. P. *The Life of William Hazlitt.* Penguin, 1949.

Hume, David. *Essays: Moral, Political, and Literary.* Ed. Eugene F. Miller. Indianapolis: Liberty Fund, 1985.

Hutcheson, Francis. *An Inquiry into the Original of Our Ideas of Beauty and Virtue in Two Treatises.* Ed. Wolfgang Leidhold. Indianapolis: Liberty Fund, 2004.

James, D. G. 'Keats and *King Lear*'. *Shakespeare Survey* 13 (1966): 58–68.

Jay, Gregory S. *T. S. Eliot and the Poetics of Literary History.* Baton Rouge and London: Louisiana State University Press, 1983.

Jeffares, A. Norman. *W. B. Yeats: A New Biography.* New York: Farrar, 1988.

The John Keats Memorial Volume. London: John Lane, 1921.

Johnson, Samuel. *Johnson on Shakespeare.* Ed. Walter Raleigh. London: Oxford University Press, 1908.

—*Lives of the English Poets.* Vol. 1. London: Oxford University Press, 1906.

Jones, James Land. *Adam's Dream: Mythic Consciousness in Keats and Yeats.* Athens: The University of Georgia Press, 1975.

Kant, Immanuel. *Critique of the Power of Judgment.* Trans. Paul Guyer and Eric Matthews. Ed. Paul Guyer. Cambridge: Cambridge University Press, 2000.

Keats, John. *The Complete Works of John Keats.* Vol.4. Ed. H. B. Forman. Glasgow: Gowars & Gray, 1900–1901.

—*John Keats (The Oxford Authors).* Ed. Elizabeth Cook. Oxford: Oxford University Press, 1990.

—*The Letters of John Keats.* Ed. M. B. Forman. Oxford: Oxford University Press, 1931.

—*The Letters of John Keats, 1814–1821.* 2 Vols. Ed. Hyder Edward Rollins. Cambridge, MA: Harvard University Press, 1958.

—'Mr. Kean'. *John Keats: The Complete Poems.* Ed. John Barnard. Penguin, 1988.

—*The Poems of John Keats.* Ed. Miriam Allott. London: Longman, 1970.

—*The Poems of John Keats.* Ed. Jack Stillinger. Cambridge, MA: The Belknap Press of Harvard University Press, 1978.

Kermode, Frank, ed. *Four Centuries of Shakespearian Criticism.* New York: Avon Books, 1965.

—ed. King Lear: *A Casebook.* London: Macmillan, 1969.

Kinnaird, John. 'Hazlitt, Keats, and the Poetics of Intersubjectivity'. *Criticism: A Quarterly for Literature and the Arts* 19 (1977): 1–16.

—*William Hazlitt: Critic of Power.* New York: Columbia University Press, 1978.

Kinnell, Galway. 'Walt Whitman and Negative Capability'. *Virginia Quarterly Review* Spring 2005: http://www.vqronline.org/articles/2005/spring/kinnell-walt-whitman.

Knapp, Steven. *Literary Interest: The Limits of Anti-formalism.* Cambridge, MA: Harvard University Press, 1993.

Kucich, Greg. 'John Keats'. *Literature of the Romantic Period: A Bibliographic Guide.* Ed. Michael O'Neill. Oxford: Clarendon Press, 1998.

—'Keats and English Poetry'. *The Cambridge Companion to Keats.* Ed. Susan J. Wolfson. Cambridge: Cambridge University Press, 2001.

Lamb, Charles. *The Complete Works and Letters of Charles Lamb.* New York: The Modern Library, 1935.

Langbaum, Robert. *The Poetry of Experience.* London: Chatto & Windus, 1972.

Lau, Beth. 'Jane Austen and John Keats: Negative Capability, Romance and Reality'. *Keats–Shelley Journal* 55 (2006): 81–110.

—*Keats's Reading of the Romantic Poets.* Ann Arbor: The University of Michigan Press, 1991.

Lee, Brian. *Theory and Personality: The Significance of T. S. Eliot's Criticism.* London: The Athlone Press, 1979.

Leech, Clifford. 'The Capability of Shakespeare'. *Shakespeare Quarterly* 11:2 (Spring 1960): 123-36.

Lobb, Edward. *T. S. Eliot and the Romantic Critical Tradition.* London: Routledge, 1981.

Lovejoy, Arthur O. *Essays in the History of Ideas.* 1948. Westport, CT: Greenwood Press, 1978.

—*The Great Chain of Being.* Cambridge, MA: Harvard University Press, 1936.

Lowell, Amy. *John Keats.* 2 Vols. London: Jonathan Cape, 1924.

Lyndall, Gordon. *Eliot's Early Years.* Oxford: Oxford University Press, 1977.

—*Eliot's New Life.* New York: Farrar, 1988.

Matthews, G. M., ed. *Keats: The Critical Heritage.* London: Routledge, 1971.

Matthiessen, F. O. *The Achievement of T. S. Eliot.* New York: Oxford University Press, 1958.

Mellor, Anne K. *Romanticism and Gender.* New York: Routledge, 1993.

Menand, Louis. *Discovering Modernism: T. S. Eliot and His Context.* New York: Oxford University Press, 1987.

Milnes, R. M. *The Life and Letters of John Keats.* 1867. Everyman Library, 1927.

Moody, A. David. *Thomas Stearns Eliot: Poet.* Cambridge: Cambridge University Press, 1994.

Motion, Andrew. *Keats.* London: Faber & Faber, 1997.

Muir, Kenneth, ed. 'Introduction'. *The Arden King Lear.* London: Methuen, 1972.

—ed. *John Keats: A Reassessment.* Liverpool: Liverpool University Press, 1958.

Murphy, Patrick D. 'Eliot's Polemic with Keats in *The Waste Land*'. *Papers on Language and Literature* 24:1 (Winter 1988): 91–3.

Murry, J. Middleton. *Keats and Shakespeare.* London: Oxford University Press, 1925.

—'Keats's Thought: A Discovery of Truth'. *The Major English Romantic Poets.* Ed. Clarence D. Thorpe, Carlos Baker and Bennett Weaver. Carbondale: Southern Illinois University Press, 1957.

Natarajan, Uttara. *Hazlitt and the Reach of Sense.* Oxford: Clarendon Press, 1998.

—'Power and Capability: Hazlitt, Keats and the Discrimination of Poetic Self'. *Romanticism: The Journal of Romantic Culture and Criticism* 2:1 (1996): 54–67.

'Negative Capability'. BBC. http://www.bbc.co.uk/dna/h2g2/A813962.

'Negative Capability'. *Encyclopaedia Britannica.* http://www.britannica.com.

'Negative Capability'. Everything. http://www.everything2.com/index.pl?node_id=124.

'Negative Capability'. *Harpers.* http://harpers.org/negativecapability.html.

'Negative Capability'. Jung Circle. http://www.jungcircle.com/muse/maureen.html.

'Negative Capability'. *Psychoanalysis Encyclopedia.* http://soc.enotes.com/psychoanalysis-encyclopedia.

'Negative Capability'. *Wikipedia.* http://en.wikipedia.org/wiki/Negative_Capability.

Norris, Kathleen. 'Exile, Homeland, and Negative Capability'. *The New Religious Humanists.* Ed. Gregory Wolfe. New York: Free Press, 1997.

Park, Roy. *Hazlitt and the Spirit of the Age.* Oxford: Clarendon Press, 1971.

Parker, David. *Ethics, Theory, and the Novel.* Cambridge: Cambridge University Press, 1994.

Preminger, Alex and T. V. F. Brogan, eds. *The New Princeton Encyclopedia of Poetry and Poetics.* Princeton: Princeton University Press, 1993.

Reisner, Gavriel (Ben-Ephraim). *The Death-Ego and the Vital Self.* Madison: Fairleigh Dickinson University Press, 2003.

Ricks, Christopher. *Keats and Embarrassment.* Oxford: Clarendon Press, 1974.

Ridley, M. R. *Keats' Craftsmanship.* 1933. London: Methuen, 1963.

Roe, Nicholas, ed. *Keats and History.* Cambridge: Cambridge University Press, 1995.

Rollins, Hyder Edward, ed. *The Keats Circle.* 2 Vols. Cambridge, MA: Harvard University Press, 1965.

Rosenbaum, Barbara, ed. *Index of English Literary Manuscripts.* Vol. IV. London: Mansell, 1990.

Rossetti, William Michael. *Life of John Keats.* London: Walter Scott, 1887.

Ryan, Robert M. and Ronald A. Sharp, eds. *The Persistence of Poetry: Bicentennial Essays on Keats.* Amherst: University of Massachusetts Press, 1998.

Rzepka, Charles J. 'Keats: Watcher and Witness'. *The Self as Mind: Vision and Identity in Wordsworth, Coleridge, Keats.* Cambridge, MA: Harvard University Press, 1986.

Sallé, Jean-Claude. 'Negative Capability'. *A Handbook to English Romanticism.* Ed. Jean Raimond and J. R. Watson. New York: St. Martin's Press, 1992.

Schanzer, Ernest. '"Sailing to Byzantium", Keats and Andersen'. *English Studies* 41 (1960): 376–80.

Shaaber, M. A. 'Shakespeare Criticism: Dryden to Bradley'. *A New Companion to Shakespeare Studies*. Ed. Kenneth Muir and S. Schoenbaum. Cambridge: Cambridge University Press, 1976.

Shaftesbury, Anthony. *Characteristics of Men, Manners, Opinions, Times*. 2 Vols. Ed. Philip Ayres. Oxford: Clarendon Press, 1999.

Shakespeare, William. *Mr William Shakspeares Comedies, Histories, and Tragedies*. London, 1623; rpt. 1808. The London Metropolitan Archives.

—*The Norton Shakespeare*. Ed. Stephen Greenblatt. New York: Norton, 1997.

—*The Poetical Works*. London, 1806. The London Metropolitan Archives.

Siebers, Tobin. *The Ethics of Criticism*. Ithaca: Cornell University Press, 1988.

Simmons, Dan. 'Skinwalkers and Shapeshifters: Wabash and the Nurturing of "Negative Capability"'. http://www.wabash.edu/Magazine/1998/Spring/features/end.htm.

Simpson, John, ed. *Oxford English Dictionary*. Oxford: Oxford University Press, 2007. http://www.oed.com.

Slote, Bernice. *Keats and the Dramatic Principle*. Lincoln: University of Nebraska Press, 1958.

Smidt, Kristian. *Poetry and Belief in the Work of T. S. Eliot*. London: Routledge, 1949.

Smith, Adam. *The Theory of Moral Sentiments*. Ed. D. D. Raphael and A. L. Macfie. Oxford: Clarendon Press, 1976.

Smith, D. Nichol, ed. *Shakespeare Criticism: A Selection*. Oxford: Oxford University Press, 1954.

Smith, Grover. *T. S. Eliot's Poetry and Plays: A Study in Sources and Meaning*. Chicago: The University of Chicago Press, 1956.

Spanos, William V. 'Charles Olson and Negative Capability'. *Contemporary Literature* 21.1 (Winter 1980): 38–80.

Sperry, Stuart M. *Keats the Poet*. Princeton: Princeton University Press, 1973.

Spurgeon, Caroline. *Keats's Shakespeare: A Descriptive Study Based on New Material*. London: Oxford University Press, 1928.

Stillinger, Jack. *The Hoodwinking of Madeline and Other Essays on Keats's Poems*. Urbana, Chicago, London: University of Illinois Press, 1971.

—'John Keats'. *The English Romantic Poets: A Review of Research and Criticism*. 4th edn. Ed. Frank Jordan. New York: MLA, 1985.

Swaminathan, S. R. 'Keats and Benjamin West's *King Lear*'. *Keats–Shelley Journal* 18 (1969): 15–16.

Tatum, John. '"Negative Capability": A Successful Indicator of Second Language Learner Aptitude'. *Asian EFL Journal* January 2005: http://www.asian-efl-journal.com/pta_jan_04_jt.php.

Thorpe, Clarence D. 'Keats and Hazlitt: A Record of Personal Relationship and Critical Estimate'. *PMLA* 62:2 (June 1947): 487–502.

— and David Perkins. 'Keats'. *The English Romantic Poets: A Review of Research and Criticism*. 3rd edn. Ed. Frank Jordan. New York: MLA, 1972.

Trilling, Lionel. 'Introduction'. *The Selected Letters of John Keats*. Garden City, NY: Doubleday, 1951. Rpt. 'The Poet as Hero: Keats in His Letters'. *The Opposing Self*. Garden City, NY: Doubleday, 1951.

—*Sincerity and Authenticity*. London: Oxford University Press, 1972.

Vendler, Helen. *The Odes of John Keats*. Cambridge, MA: The Belknap Press of Harvard University Press, 1983.

Waldoff, Leon. *Keats and the Silent Work of Imagination*. Urbana: University of Illinois Press, 1985.

Ward, Aileen. *John Keats: The Making of the Poet*. London: Secker & Warburg. 1963.

Wardle, Ralph M. *Hazlitt*. Lincoln: University of Nebraska Press, 1971.

Wellek, René. *A History of Modern Criticism: 1750–1950, the Romantic Age*. New Haven: Yale University Press, 1955.

White, R. S. *Keats as a Reader of Shakespeare*. London: The Athlone Press, 1987.

Wigod, Jacob D. 'Negative Capability and Wise Passiveness'. *PMLA* 67 (1952): 383–90.

Willey, Basil. *Nineteenth Century Studies: Coleridge to Matthew Arnold*. London: Chatto & Windus, 1961.

Williams, Porter, Jr. 'Keats' "On Sitting Down to Read *King Lear* Once Again", 11', *The Explicator* 29 (Nov. 1970): 26.

Woolf, Virginia. 'William Hazlitt'. *The Second Common Reader*. New York: Harcourt, 1932.

Yeats, W. B. *Autobiographies*. London: Macmillan, 1961.

—*The Collected Poems of W. B. Yeats*. Ed. Richard J. Finneran. New York: Scribner, 1996.

—*Essays and Introductions*. London: Macmillan, 1961.

—'Introduction'. *The Oxford Book of Modern Verse*. London: Oxford University Press, 1936.

—*The Letters of W. B. Yeats*. Ed. Allan Wade. London: Rupert Hart-Davis, 1954.

—*Memoirs*. London: Macmillan, 1972.

—*Mythologies*. London: Macmillan, 1962.

—*Uncollected Prose by W. B. Yeats*. Ed. John P. Frayne. London: Macmillan, 1970.

—*A Vision*. London: Macmillan, 1962.

Index

Printed in Great Britain
by Amazon